"Col. Pipes" viewing his property known as "Pipesville," situated on Mission street, in the city of San Francisco, California; mounted on one of Chickering's Grand Pianos, and suggesting to a distinguished Celestial, named Hyson Bohea, Esq., that it would suit him as a residence to a T (ea). The whole photographed by the immortal "Fredericks," of Broadway, N. Y., from the original drawing taken on the spot.

"DRIFTING ABOUT,"

OR WHAT

"JEEMS PIPES OF PIPESVILLE"

SAW–AND–DID.

AN AUTOBIOGRAPHY

BY

STEPHEN C. MASSETT.

WITH MANY COMIC ILLUSTRATIONS BY MULLEN.

NEW YORK:

Carleton, Publisher, 413 Broadway,

M DCCC LXIII.

R. CRAIGHEAD,
Printer, Stereotyper, and Electrotyper,
Carton Building,
81, 83, and 85 Centre Street.

TO

JAMES T. BRADY, ESQ.,

THIS VOLUME IS DEDICATED

AS A

SLIGHT TOKEN OF AFFECTIONATE REGARD,

BY THE AUTHOR.

NEW YORK, February, 1868.

CONTENTS.

DRIFTING ABOUT.

INTRODUCTION.

Beginning! That's the difficulty. In what form can I weave together the incidents of travel and adventure, the experiences and vicissitudes of my life for the last sixteen years?

Take a seat, my kind reader! Taste that wine. It's cheering and cheerful, isn't it? Light a cigar—or you—Miss or Madame—sip a little tea or coffee, imagine yourself, pray, in a position of entire repose, and listen while I recite what has happened to me "by field and by flood." I'll try not to bore you. The chapters shall be short—and we can pause when you choose.

I would like, above all things, to interest and amuse you. I will try to give advice worth nothing to those who may hereafter travel over the same lands I have journeyed through. I am told that the Spaniards have a proverb to the effect, that no man has accomplished anything who has not *begotten a son, built a house, or written a book.* Despite my numerous and persistent efforts to become a respectable married man, there is no such thing as filial affection for me, but I *can* boast of a noble, gorgeous, and architectural triumph, which is expressed in the musical word "*Pipesville.*" You will find out all about that achievement if you keep me company. And now I proceed to gratify some one who exclaims, "Oh that mine enemy would write a book." It will have some marked peculiarities—it will not have particular 'style'—because I know nothing about 'style,' except getting over several in my native country! There will be little of cohesion, and nothing of vanity in the composition. What I jot down may make some laugh, others weep, a few praise, many censure, but no one will be injured by hearing what I have to say.

I shall not rely much on fancy, I am going to deal with facts, turn up or trump up what may—funny or precocious, laughable or lugubrious, pithy or puffy, grave or gay.

Persons more than things, shall engage my attention.

Reader!—I mean to give you "chat," bald, disjointed chat—it may be, or chatter as some may complain. So put yourself at rest, hearken, be good-natured, let me shake your hand, exclaim "God bless you"—and then begin—

Now Then—

I.

MY FIRST VOYAGE.

In the summer of 1837, I, then a small-sized boy, could have been seen wending my way to the St. Katherine's Dock in the good old City of London, to take a look at the ship (which happens to be a bark by the way) in which I had taken passage for New York. She was an old West Indiaman, and had for years been employed in the Sugar trade. Her name was the "Hampton," and the Captain's, David Balderston. Her cabin windows projected, in the style of an old man-o'-war's-man, she had a high poop deck, large portholes, and resembled more an old tub than anything else I know of. I shall not endeavor to draw upon the sensibilities of the reader by endeavoring to depict the grief at parting with relations and friends; or by describing the singular sensations I experienced in driving, for the last time as I thought, through the crowded thoroughfares of my native city in a "Hansom" to the dock gates. The utter uncertainty of the future, as I had no fixed object in view upon landing in America, only rendered my leaving the old homestead the more exciting; but the picture, even after a lapse of twenty-three years, is still present with me, so much so, that I shall for a moment transfer to paper the little scene in the parlor of our home, for the pleasures of memory are sometimes painfully sweet! —when, for the last time in this life, I heard the voice of affectionate counsel of a father and a sister. The "God bless you, my dear boy," of our only surviving parent (my beloved mother having died two years before), as the tears coursed down his wrinkled face, is still ringing in my ears, and as he placed in my hand a little memento of affection, and with trembling voice said, "may the Lord preserve you, and keep you unto his heavenly kingdom," it seemed as though we should never meet again; and it was with difficulty that I could control my feelings. I shall never forget the look of my sister—long since departed, nor her last words; they will live in my memory for ever. The grave has closed over all save *three* who were present at that farewell gathering, yet still I cling with undying tenacity and affectionate remembrance to this last scene of my youthful home; and can but hope that we may be in another world reunited.

The peculiar hurry and scurry on board a New York and London Packet Ship in olden times, is so happily hit off by one whose name I have forgotten, that I am tempted to transcribe it from some manuscript notes I have by me.

The seamen as usual lighten their labor with song and chorus, and the one they sang on our old ship was peculiarly musical, the chorus of "Old Sally Brown" being given by the whole crew with great emphasis. I took my seat on the upper deck, and listened.

"Heave away there forward."

"Ay, ay, Sir."

[*Sailors.*] "Sally Brown, oh my dear Sally,
Oh Sally Brown. [*Chorus.*]
Sally Brown of Bubble Alley,
Oh Sally Brown."

"Avast heaving there, send all aft to clear the boat."

"Ay, ay, Sir, where are we to stow these casks, Mr. Fisher?"

"Stow them, Heaven knows, get them in at all events."

[*Woman's voice.*] "Captain H., Captain H., there's my Piano still on deck, it will be quite spoiled, indeed it will!"

"Don't be alarmed, Ma'am, don't be alarmed, as soon as we're under weigh, we'll hoist the cow up and get the Piano down."

"What, under the cow?"

"No, Ma'am, but the cow's under the hatchway."

"Now then, my lads, forward to the windlass."

"I went to town to get some toddy,
Oh Sally Brown,
'Twasn't fit for any body
Oh Sally Brown!"

"Out there and clear away the jib!"

"Ay, ay, Sir."

"Mr. Fisher, how much cable is there out?"

"Plenty yct, Sir,"—"Heave away, my lads."

"Sally is a bright Mullattar,
Oh Sally Brown,
Pretty girl, but can't get at her,
Oh Sally———"

"Avast heaving, send the Man up to whip the ladies in."

"Dear me, I had no idea they did such horrible things aboard ship!"

"Now, Miss, only set down, and don't be afraid, and you'll be in, in no time. Whip away, my lads, handsomely, steady her with the guy!"

"Oh dear, oh dear!" [*woman.*]

"There, Miss, now you're safely *landed!*"

[*Woman.*] "*Landed* am I, I thought I was shipped!"

"Very good indeed—very good, Miss, you'll make an excellent sailor!"

"I should make a better sailor's wife, I guess, Captain."

"Excellent, allow me to hand you aft—you'll excuse me. Forward now, my men, heave away!"

"Seven years I courted Sally,
Oh Sally Brown,
Seven more of Shilly Shally,
Oh Sally Brown.
She won't wed——"

"Avast heaving—up there and loose the topsails, stretch along the topsail sheets; upon my soul—half these children will be killed, whose child are you?"

[*Child.*] "I—d—on't—know."

"Go, and find out, there's a dear!"

"Let fall—sheet home—belay starboard sheet—clap on the larboard—belay all that. Now then, Mr. Fisher."

"Ay, ay, Sir—heave away, my lads."

"She won't wed a Yankee Sailor,
Oh Sally Brown."

"Heave away, my men—heave and in sight. Hurrah, my lads."

"Sally Brown—oh, my dear Sally,
Oh Sally Brown;
Sally Brown of Bubble Alley,
Oh Sally Brown;
Sally was a cross old Granny,
Oh————"

"Heave and fall—jib halyards. Hoist away!"

[*Woman.*] "Oh dear, oh dear. The clumsy brute has half killed the girl."

"Don't cry, my dear."

"Pick up the child, Tom, and shove it out of the way."

[*Tom.*] "Where shall I put her?"

"Oh, any where just now, put her into the Turkey Coop—"

"Starboard—"

"I say, clap on some of you he chaps or else get out of the way."

[*Woman.*] "Sailor, please mind my bandbox."

"Starboard."

"Starboard it is—steady—so—."

Thus with the trifling matter of maiming half-a-dozen children; upsetting two or three women; smashing the lids of a few trunks; and crushing some bandboxes as flat as a muffin, the ship proceeded on her voyage.

Oh! the tediousness of this first voyage! for it will scarcely be believed that we were 95 *days* in reaching New York; a succession of calms, head-winds, strong gales, and indeed every variety of wind and weather was ours. I think it was about the end of August that we entered the harbor of Manhattan—the day a lovely one, and I recollect distinctly being struck by the brightness of the atmosphere, the gaiety and beauty of the craft, with their milk-white sails, that covered the bay; the lovely verdure and bright green foliage of the shore on each side, and the general bustle, lightness, jollity, and go-a-head-atives that pervaded everything, and everybody. And even when the "Pilot" jumped on board and put a "New York Herald" (a small, single sheet in those days!) in the Captain's hand, I felt that I could know him in five minutes, and that *without* an introduction.

II.

A PEARL STREET BOARDING-HOUSE IN 1837.

We landed, if I remember right, at Jersey City, and I and my brother Jack crossed over in a steam tug, with our traps, to the foot of Coenties slip, from thence to a "Boarding House" in Pearl street. Well do I remember the first dinner in our temporary American home. Two long dining tables, covered with a white cloth—that only wanted two or three bodies on them to make the resemblance very vivid to a dissecting room—half a dozen great big white jugs full of cold water, and each one of the boarders with a big corn cob in his mouth. The meats tasted as though they had been all cooked at the same time, and the gravy, seemingly a decoction of oil and dripping, was ladled out of a large bowl, and would have certainly done more justice to the operations of a cart-wheel than to the organs of mastication. The repast wound up with a series of slices of flat pies in round cans, containing brown apples smashed, the "crust" of the institution being all dough, and highly flavored with brown paper and hot tin.

We sat down to dinner at one o'clock, and at a quarter past not a soul was to be seen!

III.

MY FIRST SAUNTER UP BROADWAY.

THE heat was intense (it was the month of August) as I strolled up, for the first time, this celebrated thoroughfare.

In those days the trees, with their bright green leaves and waving branches, were very much more common, making this fashionable promenade picturesque and elegant. The limit of my walk was "White street," whither I was bound to find the whereabouts of my eldest brother. As I turned from Wall street into Broadway, I stood for a moment to look at Old Trinity, and read some of the inscriptions on the tombstones. Broadway was full of life, gaiety, and sunshine. "Kip and Brown's" and "Brower's" stages, some with "four in hand," were rattling up and down—the fare then twelve-and-a-half cents. I recollect distinctly the "pump" opposite the City Hospital, where the "Gingerbread man" used to wash his mouth, the Washington Hotel (where A. T. Stewart's store now stands), and where I first met my esteemed friend Dr. Carnochan and many others.

The Park Theatre (then the crack house of amusement) was pointed out to me—the City Hall, decidedly the most imposing looking edifice I had yet seen, with the bright green foliage of the trees—the Masonic Hall, where Fanny Wright used to lecture—the Café de Mille Colonnes of old

Palmo, and the large store of Venables & Co. near Chambers street.

IV.

SCENE ON A CANAL BOAT.

In the latter end of August I took passage in the steamer "Swallow," Captain McLean, for Albany. The scenery of the magnificent Hudson has been so frequently described by tourists, journalists, and others, that it would be idle for me to attempt to give my earliest or present impréssions. Never having, at that time, seen a river bigger than the Thames, I was of course astounded and delighted at its magnitude, and charmed by the variety, richness, and grandeur of its scenery.

Upon our arrival at Albany I took passage in one of the "Canal Boats" (my stock of money being rather limited) for the "Queen City of the Lakes." We were about eight days in making the "voyage," which was certainly, to me, a very novel affair; the method of making up the "cots" for sleeping purposes being particularly amusing. It was something in the following style. After "supper" was over, three rows of portable cots, attached to each other by ropes swung against the two sides of the boat, resembling more the slats in a baker's oven than a resting-place for the body, and then the passengers, by dint of sundry gymnastic feats, managed to crawl into their holes. The heated and close air soon became insufferable; so I determined to roll myself up in a blanket and lie on the deck. But just as I had made up my mind to leave my place of baking, the cot above me, containing a big fat man weighing certainly over three hundred-weight, gave way, falling upon me, and smashing me almost to a jelly. I gave a yell which aroused all the sleepers; at the same moment the "skipper," who was steering, called out "Bridge," too late, however, (the night being dark) to save the head of a poor "Paddy from Cork," who, ignorant of the approaching arch, was by the concussion sent clean overboard, and, but for the shallowness of the stream, would have been instantly drowned. His cries of

"Blood and murther!" and such like delicate exclamations, with the crash in the cabin, the shrieks of men, women, and children, rendered the place a perfect pandemonium. The relief I experienced when on the "eighth day out" the glittering cupolas of the city of Buffalo greeted me, it would be difficult to describe.

V.

I BECOME A LAW STUDENT.

I HAD been in Buffalo about a month, when I entered the office of Mr. Thomas Jefferson Nevins, 200 Main street, exactly opposite the Farmers' Hotel, then (and I believe now) kept by Philip Dorsheimer, the present State Treasurer.

I think about the third day of my initiation into the mysteries of "Coke upon Littleton," I was directed to serve a paper upon some one in the office of Fillmore, Hall, and Haven, and there and then met a young student, named C———, about whom I shall have something to say hereafter.

I used to go by the name of the "red-faced little Englishman;" and I remember Mr. Fillmore speaking very kindly to me, asking me sundry questions as to the time of my being in America, and whether I intended becoming a lawyer, and was assiduous in my studies, &c.

I do not think, at that time, he ever dreamed of being "President of the United States."

My duties were not very arduous, consisting chiefly of filling in several blank notices, in which the name "T. R. Boors" was constantly occurring, the only suit (excepting one I bought) the office could boast of for many months; reading occasionally a line or so of "Blackstone's Commentaries," varied with half a page of "Kent," or a speech of "Charles Phillips."

At intervals I began to study Shakespeare, and it ended in my learning Richard III. by heart, portions of Othello, and a scene or so from Macbeth.

About this time "Ben Rathbun" burst up, and Buffalo

was in a great state of excitement thereat. A paper called the "Buffalonian" was started by a Mr. Arlington, its editor and proprietor, who was imprisoned in the Buffalo Jail for libel. This gentleman afterwards came to New York, and is now lecturing on Catholicism.

Brown, Buckland, and Co. were celebrated bankers in those days, and were decidedly the most notable men about town. They had a private box at the theatre, and drove a first-rate team on the macadamized road. Brown died years ago, and John Buckland married the beautiful Miss Kate Horn.

VI.

THE EAGLE STREET THEATRE.

THE first play I saw in America was in this city; it was Richard the Third, and Mr. Charles H. Eaton was the hero of the night. The names of the managers were Dean and McKenny, but a Mr. Thompson (an Englishman) had something to do with the internal arrangements, and to him it was that I was indebted for an occasional "order." The first opera I ever saw was Cinderella, with Edwin as the Prince, and Miss Melton (sister of Charles Walcot) as the Princess. Among the performers was a Miss Powell, a beautiful English girl, who afterwards became Mrs. Charles Walcot.

Here I first saw the play of the Lady of Lyons, with Ellen Tree as Pauline, and Mr. Fredericks as Claude. Mr. Fredericks is, I believe, at present in the city, and Miss Ellen Tree, as all the world knows, has long since been Mrs. Charles Kean (whom I had the pleasure of meeting at a party in London in 1858, just twenty years afterwards!).

It is useless to deny the fact, that I became seized with a desire to "go upon the stage;" and the great amount of time I had upon my hands gave me opportunities for studying, thus fanning the flame which I fancied would burst forth and electrify everybody. A lot of young students started a Thespian Society, and our first performance took place on the Kremlin Block. The play was (of course)

Richard; I enacting the "crooked-backed tyrant," and my friend C——, the student, Richmond. Lady Anne was played by a Mr. O——, and the Queen by another limb of the law. I got along pretty well until the last scene with Richmond; but as with the words, "My soul and body on the action both," we struck the usual attitude to commence the fight, my sword, being made of wood covered with tin, snapped in two pieces, one end taking effect on the eye of the leader of the "orchestra," a small-sized boy, who immediately dropped his instrument (a broken-keyed melodeon), and ran out of the building crying. This mishap, of course, killed the scene, and the words, "Perdition catch my arm," &c., were entirely lost in a whirlwind of laughter and shouting. The comical termination of the play rather damped my theatrical ardor; and when it became known to our employers that we belonged to an association of the kind, our fun was at an end, and our acting days and nights numbered.

Probably one of the most exciting incidents of the year 1838 that occurred in Buffalo was the burning of the steamer Caroline and the occupation of Navy Island by the citizen soldiery. The city wore a very military aspect, the English were denounced, and the Buffalonians were ripe for a fight with John Bull.

A mass meeting was held at the Theatre, when the Canadian patriot (?), William Lyon Mackenzie, addressed the meeting, together with Mr. Seth C. Hawley, one of the then leading men of the bar, whose remark of "Be sure you're right, then go ahead," brought down from the sympathizers a storm of applause. The streets were eternally filled with the paradings of military companies, "City Guards" were formed, drums and fifes and bands of music were heard from morning to night, and the excitement lasted for days.

A great sensation was also created here by the announcement in the daily papers of the arrival at New York of the steamship Sirius, and a few days after of the British Queen, in which came passengers Madame Vestris and Mr. Charles Mathews.

During my sojourn in Buffalo, I made a brief trip to the Falls of Niagara, and of course was delighted therewith.

They have been described so graphically and minutely, from time immemorial, that I shall not attempt it; but this I confess: my first impression was certainly one of disappointment. I had imagined the fall of water much higher than I found it, fully expecting to see it come down from the clouds, or somewhere in that vicinity.

VII.

DRIFTING.

THINKING the chances very slim of my ever becoming distinguished at the bar, and not being able to penetrate at all into the mysteries of Coke, Kent, Blackstone, or "any other man," I left the handling of law books, foolscap, and red tape, for the counting-house of a "forwarding merchant" on the Dock, by name, Mr. A. H. Scoville; a delightful person, by the way, who treated me most kindly, and, as far as his means would permit, liberally.

The store was very long and my duties very short. My "boss" was supposed to sell flour on commission, and I think, when I arrived to take charge of the "books" and keep the cash, there were just four barrels at one end of the store, which was about 100 feet deep. This struck me as being rather a light stock; but I had an accompanying sensation of consolation that my duties as "bookkeeper" would be proportionably easy. My inward feeling of horror at the idea of "opening a set of books" (excepting Scott's, Bulwer's, or Cooper's novels), can be imagined by the reader, when I inform him that when running *up* a column of figures, the result was always entirely different from the running *down;* and that as to what should go to the "Dr." and what should go to the "Cr." side of the "Cash" or "Day" Book, I was in a state of blissful ignorance. My "boss" was an extremely pleasant, kind-hearted man, and came to my relief like a good fellow, when the momentous time arrived for me to make the first (and I believe the last) entry. I happened to write a good hand, and this was half the battle, and my employer was only too happy to relieve the monotony of the day, usually passed in "whittling," walking the dock, or chewing tobacco, by doing the "cyphering" portion of the books. Business did not "look up," and my boss and his solitary clerk looked "down." My brother had written from New York that he had a situation as *assistant* bookkeeper, collector, &c., in a large carpet warehouse. I packed up my "duds," bade good-bye to many kind friends in Buffalo, and landed, in the summer of '39, once again in Gotham, and immediately made for the store of Thomas L. Chester, 203 Broadway.

Here I went duly to work as out-door clerk, and occasionally salesman. I was here about a year and a half, during which time a few singular incidents occurred. I will mention one or two.

I was living for a short time at the Broadway Hotel, 112 Broadway, kept by Cotter & Leveret, and being extremely fond of music, and having a pretty good voice, was introduced to and "patronized" by several musical celebrities. At this hotel I first met Mr. Giubelei, the then celebrated basso of the Park Theatre, who, with his wife, and Miss Poole, were singing then in opera, together with Mrs. Martyn (née Miss Inverarity) and Mr. Martyn, and Mr. Manvers (the latter now in England).

Many pleasant walks had I with the "pretty little Miss Poole" on the Battery, winding up with a cozy little *goûter* at the Hotel Française, near Peter Harmony's, on Broadway. Mr. Giubelei frequently gave me "orders," and once or twice I was admitted behind the scenes. I was delighted; and Theatre Alley, with the "stage-door" entrance, had many more charms for me than a lounge on the Fifth Avenue has to-day.

At a concert at the City Hotel, given by Mr. Charles E. Horn, I had the pleasure of being introduced by him to the author of "Woodman, spare that tree," General George P. Morris. Upon the occasion referred to, Mrs. C. E. Horn sang, for the first time in New York, the "Northern Refrain," or "Through the streets of New York city," a little chimneysweep's carol, written by General Morris. The song was a great success, being enthusiastically encored, and, when published, met with an extraordinary sale. In those days I was very young, and proportionably modest, and was very much taken by the "General's" kind and genial manner in shaking hands with me; little dreaming then that *I* should ever in public sing his songs, or be criticized by him in his Journal. I shall take the liberty of referring again to this genial and delightful song writer.

In this year the opera of Amilie, or the Love Test, was produced at the National Theatre in Leonard street, under the management of the veteran James W. Wallack, of this city. There was a dress rehearsal one Saturday night, and I had a card of admission. The vocalists engaged had recently arrived from England. Their names were Miss Jane Shirreff, Mr. Wilson, and Mr. and Mrs. Edward Seguin.

The stage was lighted up, chairs were placed for the "principals," and when the time came for the aria, "My boyhood's home," on walked Mr. Seguin, in his rough pea jacket, as if just from sea, and with his magnificent voice charmed every one present by the rendering of this popular melody. The opera was a great success, and ran for many consecutive nights, and the "trio," particularly "Ned Seguin," were for a long time the pets of the public.

About this time, also, Mr. Washington Coster, (who then resided at 61 White street, his sleeping apartment being now used as the publication office of "Porter's Spirit," and his once upon a time gorgeous parlor now the shop of a German tailor,) recently returned from Paris, created quite a sensation among the beau monde, by the introduction in Broadway of an open style of "Landau," in which he, his beautiful wife, and lovely children, used to ride. He was quite a remarkable-looking man, with long flaxen hair, falling over his shoulders, mounted by a broad-rimmed, oval-shaped black hat. Dandy Marx was also one of the notables, as was also George L. Pride, whom the Herald, in one of its sketchy, descriptive articles, dubbed the "Pride of the Road." These gentlemen, and their establishments, were all lithographed by a Mr. Baker, of Wall street, (now the efficient Fire Marshal,) and the caricatures created a great commotion, and caused much amusement about town.

My first legitimate theatrical sensation was at the National Theatre, in 1839, when I was entranced and delighted with the representations of Mr. Edwin Forrest in Richelieu and King Lear; and at the present writing, though twenty years have intervened, the impressions of my youth remain.

I have recently seen this distinguished actor, in the characters above referred to, at Niblo's Garden, under the management of Mr. William Wheatley; and although, on the one hand, as my ancient friend Mrs. Malaprop observed, "Comparisons are odorous," and, on the other, I have no intention of being invidious or personal, I conceive the genius of this great actor, in these impersonations, towers so immeasurably above the efforts of all others I have seen, that it is simply ridiculous to place them in the same category.

In those days the Battery was the fashionable promenade, and in the summer months, from four to six and seven, the lower part of Broadway was filled with beautiful and gaily-dressed women and handsome men, wending their way to the Bowling Green, to enjoy the cooling breezes and shady walks of the dear old Battery. I know that I caught the "fever," and upon the slightest provocation, in the shape of a request to go and collect a bill, or do any "out-door" business, I would find time to pay my respects to this favorite locality. Besides, I fear I must briefly inform thee, my patient reader, that about these days a pair of hazel eyes had made fearful havoc with my young and tender heart and affections, and it was in daily expectation of receiving a pleasant smile or nod from my inamorata that I hurried my way thitherward. Twenty years ago! how changed the scene! Then the nicely-gravelled walks, (the centre one was my favorite,) the shady branches of the trees waved on high their "plumes of green"—though the "worms" that hung from them were *rayther* annoying —the bright waters of the bay, with a fleet of craft of every name and size floating on its bosom, and Castle Garden, with its bath-houses and refreshment saloons, all, all, crowd upon my memory with the most vivid and delightful recollections and associations. Now a dreary and desolate waste, is this once upon a time fashionable resort, and a Depôt for Emigrants reigns where the Baths of Dr. Rabineau invited the swimmers, or the dulcet tones of Jenny Lind were first heard.

The fashionable music stores and lounges for musical people, at the date I am writing, were Atwill's Music Saloon, at the sign of the Golden Lyre, 201 Broadway; Millett's, Broadway (Mr. Millet still remaining in the same store); Firth and Hall, Franklin square; and Davis and Horn, of Broadway.

The first establishment, being next door to my place of business, I quickly became acquainted with its proprietor, Mr. Joseph F. Atwill, (now and for a long time past a resident of California,) and many a delightful hour was passed by me there, and I was thus brought into immediate connexion, if not intimacy, with numbers of musical people.

Among the celebrities that in the year 1840 flashed for a while upon the musical horizon, and who were daily to be seen at Joe Atwill's, were Braham, Joseph Philip Knight, (the author of "She wore a wreath of roses,") Signor De Begnis, Henry Russell, Mrs. Edward Loder, Mrs. Sutton, (an American prima donna,) Madame Dolores de Goñi (guitarist), and Mr. Henry C. Watson, a young English musician and composer, who has since made his mark as one of the very best critics of this city, and who was the arbiter of matters musical in the old times of the Albion, the Evening Signal, and the New World.

Here very often was to be seen a handsome, rosy-cheeked, dark-haired, sailor-looking fellow, who used to delight me by the off-hand and brilliant manner of his "touch" at the piano, and it was not long before we "froze" to each other, he being pleased with my singing, I with his playing, and there are many alive now who will remember the kind-hearted, jolly, and good-natured "Jack Poole," with a tear of regret; for he was lost in the steamer Erie, with three hundred others, which was burnt on the lake of that name about this period. John Poole was distinctly a musical genius; for without the slightest knowledge of the art, or acknowledging any method, he would rattle off the most brilliant and original compositions, consisting principally of waltzes, polkas, &c., and went so far as to publish a set, called the Amaranth Waltzes, which became quite the rage, dedicated to Miss Mary Jones, a great belle at that time. My friend Colonel Jim Burnham (afterwards City Marshal) will remember the pleasant evening we had with poor John Poole at a family gathering in the "old homestead" on the Bloomingdale road.

The Tabernacle, in Broadway, and the Apollo Rooms, were the fashionable places where concerts were given.

On the first night of the veteran Braham's appearance in America, it rained in torrents; but, in spite of wind and weather, the Tabernacle was crowded to overflowing. He was assisted by Mrs. Edward Loder, as the principal lady vocalist, who chose this occasion to present herself for the suffrages of the New York public. Mrs. Loder's classical method and sweet voice were greatly appreciated by the audience; and for many years she was one of the leading features of the concerts given in this city; certainly, no sacred concert seemed complete without the appearance of this lady. I remember a remark that Braham made, upon her observing to him that she thought he appeared "a little nervous," and that she was surprised that he, who for more than half a century had appeared before audiences in every part of the world, should exhibit any agitation upon a first appearance in America:—"Ah, my dear madam, it is appearing before a *nation* for the first time." Braham sang with all his former fire and vigor, and his debut was highly successful. He sang "Martin Luther's Hymn," with trumpet accompaniment of the celebrated John T. Norton, and "Comfort ye, my people," from the Messiah. The tickets were one dollar each, and the Tabernacle crowded to suffocation.

At the Park Theatre, in this year, Power, the Irish actor, was in all his glory; filling the house nightly, and delighting everybody. It was in 1840 that he left New York in the ill-fated steamship President; and I well remember seeing him in Wall street, whither I had gone to collect an account at the Banking-house of Prime, Ward, and King, then the great guns in the banking line; and Power, with his hat a little cocked on the side of his head, and a closely buttoned coat with fur collar, was chatting with John Povey on the corner of William street. Curiosity led me to the steamer, and I saw poor Power go up the plank, shaking hands with many friends who had come to bid him good-bye. I particularly noticed a very melancholy expression in his face, and I believe he remarked to an intimate acquaintance that, when it came to the point of starting, he did not care to leave, or words to that effect. It will be remembered that the steamer returned after an absence of a day or so, some accident having occurred to the machinery, and left again never to be seen or heard of more! Power had with him in cash, $50,000, the results of his engagements in America, and I believe it was his intention to pass the remainder of his days in retirement.

VIII.

A FULL AND TRUE ACCOUNT OF MY FIRST AND LAST DEPOSIT IN A SAVINGS BANK.

IN this year, I "opened," I think they call it, an account at the Chambers street Savings Bank. By dint of extraordinary exertion, and depriving myself of many luxuries, I had managed to save up some $16 in hard cash. Now, I had been informed when quite a small boy, that if I only commenced to save my coppers and deposit them in bank, by the time I was one-and-twenty those coppers would, by some wonderful system of "hocus pocus," amount to a small fortune. The famous motto, "take care of the pence, and the pounds will take care of themselves," had not only been stuck up in every nook and corner of our house, and written in large text hand in my copy-books, but seemed—so strongly was it engraven on my memory—to have been sandwiched with every piece of bread and butter I had taken, from my school-boy days and upwards.

It was, therefore, that on a bright summer afternoon, about the hour of two, I wended my way from Chester's carpet store, 203 Broadway (now the gorgeous head-quarters of Hegeman & Co., the druggists, the house with which my old friend Harry King has been so long connected), to the Chambers street Savings Bank, with a roll of dirty one dollar bank-notes in one hand, and a lot of carpet bills for collection in the other.

I arrived at the portals of the institution, trembling from head to foot with the frightful responsibility of my position, and with shaky fingers, counting over and over again, the greasy pieces of paper, taking my place among files of chambermaids, cooks, waiters, carmen, mechanics, young and old, fat and thin, clean and dirty.

I think it was about four o'clock before my time came.

Arrived at the hole and looking through some wire grating, I beheld an elderly gentleman with a very bald head, seated on a very high stool, having on the top of his very red nose a pair of the largest kind of spectacles.

I managed to get off the fact, that I wished to open an account there, to which he replied, in a very gruff and disagreeable voice,—

"Well, sir! what's the amount?" To which I hesitatingly replied, "$16 sir."

Gruntingly, "$16? that all?" (Here an audible titter from two or three of the clerks, and instantly caught up by the whole row of depositors, made me so nervous that I nearly fainted, and I'd have given all the world if I'd been *out*side instead of *in!*)

In a book about the size of a Chinese trunk, with a couple of brass clasps, as big as the hinges of St. Paul's church door, the fatal entry was made; and in another book, of not *quite* so large dimensions, another entry was made, and the *last* book handed to me with the request that I would *always bring* it when making any future deposits!

This I faithfully promised to do. These proceedings seemed to take an age.

How I made my way out of the bank I know not—but, upon gaining the street, I felt my penniless situation, and bitterly regretted the step I had taken. I awoke in the morning feeling certain the bank would break. When sent out to collect a bill of carpeting, I invariably walked down Chambers street to see if the Institution had not closed; and every alarm of fire set me in a high fever.

This suspense took away my appetite. I must feign sickness or a death in the family, or a journey westward, or something—but the money I must have—though I felt perfectly ashamed to go in, and get it——

What *would* the man in the spectacles say? what would he do? why he would wither me with a look! but get it out I must; and in I went, wondering all the time what excuse I should give him.

The money had been in the bank I think forty-eight hours—perhaps a little more perhaps a little less—and after wasting a quire of paper in trying to get out what the simple, or the compound interest, or both would be, at—I didn't know how much per cent. per annum—I found myself at the dreaded hole with the wire round it.

To the interrogatory, "What is it, Sir?"

I feebly replied that I had a little "account to settle" with him!

Now whether the old cock thought I was going to punch him in the eye or throw something at him through the little hole, I know not, but he involuntarily drew back, saying,

"I don't understand you, Sir!"

"Well, Sir," said I, "the fact is, Sir, I deposited some money here the other day (all this time the people were crowding and pressing in, the heat was intense, and I in a perfect vapor bath of excitement), and in consequence of a large death in our small family, Sir, I have to go to sea."

"See what, Sir? I don't comprehend you, Sir!"

"No, no, Sir! I mean a sea voyage, Sir. I want the money for an outfit, Sir; to pay my passage to Rhode Island, Sir; where the ship is, Sir."

Oh Lor! I was nearly fainting, but I then intended to "stick it out."

With a look of perfect contempt at me over his specks, that haunted me for years afterwards, he fumbled over the leaves of his big book with the clasps, came to the unfortunate letter "M," and with pointed finger at the wretched item (I saw from the top my name in large letters occupying the two entire sheets), gave a "click" with the pen, went to the drawer, and counting out the sixteen dollars, added, with a sneer, that there was just *one cent interest due me!*

Then, with a look of intense disgust at me and my red face, he very impertinently, I thought, suggested, that the *next time* I made a deposit in a banking house I should have *something* to put in it!

IX.

MORE FUNNY SCENES.

WHEN my outdoor duties were over, it was the wish of my employer that I should, as he called it, "lay hold of" the customers, particularly if we were short of salesmen, or if they were engaged. Now I must premise that my knowledge of the different varieties of carpet was about as clear and lucid as my arithmetical, and accordingly I was all the while making mistakes in the different qualities.

One of these occasions I distinctly remember. A lady alighted from her carriage, and there being at the time no one in the store, I, of course, did the bidding of my "boss," and laid hold of her, that is to say, I asked her the style of carpet she wished to look at. "Super ingrain," said she. "Step this way if you please, Mum," said I; upon which I asked Michael, the porter, to show the lady a "roll" of, what I supposed, the latest pattern of "ingrain." The lady was delighted, the pattern was charming, and she ordered sixty yards, the price being eight shillings and sixpence a yard. I immediately rushed to the order-book, feeling quite proud that I had actually made a sale, and feeling also an inward conviction that my salary would be instantly raised. The carpet was cut off, and actually in the cart, when, to my horror and astonishment, the "Col," as we called the head of the house, caught a glimpse of the departing drugget, and calling out to the carman to bring it back, exclaimed, "Why, who the devil's been selling 'Super Royal Wilton' for 'Ingrain?' Is that you, Sir?" said he, addressing me. I remarked, "that I was directed to 'lay hold of' the customers, and in doing so had committed the unpardonable sin of selling a three dollar and fifty cents a yard carpet for one that would cost only eight shillings and sixpence!"

It was in vain for me to plead ignorance of the different varieties or qualities. I was looked upon, and called "a stupid ass," and fell several degrees lower in the estimation of everybody.

I recollect upon another occasion, a man came in to look at one of Hare & Son's oil cloths; this was to me perfectly distressing, for I *never could* get "the hang" of the difference between a "square" and a "running" yard, and many a sheet of paper have I wasted in endeavoring to understand the mystery.

He selected the cloth, and wished to know (giving me the length and breadth of his entry) how many running or square yards it would require, and how much the square or the running yard was! I was nervous to a degree and perspiring from head to foot, my moist fingers bedaubing the paper with blotches of ink, and upon the inquiry of my employer as to what I made it, I found the paper covered with caricatures and all sorts of "figures" but the right ones. My brother came to my relief and I incontinently "sloped."

Whether it was in this year or not I do not remember, but somewhere about this time my head was felt by the celebrated Mr. Coombe, and he told me that I had *not* the bump of "calculation," that I might possibly know that 2 and 2 made 4, but I could never, by any possible chance, learn the multiplication table.

The only article in the store that I felt at all easy in offering for sale was "binding;" this being only sixpence a yard I could manage to get through my thick head the price of any *moderate* number of yards. My success was really great in "getting off" this valuable article.

One warm day in summer, I was standing alone in the store, when in walked a little man very seedily dressed, with a very unsteady gait, a glassy look of the eye, and compressed lips. He caught hold of the railing that surrounded the desk, and looking me straight in the eye, said, "Do—you—know—who—I am—young—man?" I replied, "that I had not the honor." "N—o—r didshe—never—she—me—afore?" "No sir," I said. "Well—shir—my names—Booth—and I wish—look at sucarpits." "With pleasure, sir." I was about to explain the different styles, when, to my surprise, he abruptly turned round, and growled out that he'd see me —— first, slammed the door and left.

There are a good many who will remember "Jim Grant," the Ann street barber. I was first taken there by a countryman of mine, shortly after my arrival from England, it being the best place, I was informed, to have my hair cut, in the city. Mr. J. G. Bennett was among his regular patrons, and I believe for years enjoyed the luxury of one of "Jimmy's" best shaves. Well, it was in this identical shop that I met a gentleman one evening, to whom I had been previously introduced, who, as will shortly appear, had a great deal to do in changing the whole current of my life, and directing my young thoughts to matters not at all allied to my duties as clerk in a carpet store. Turning to me he said, "I heard you sing 'My Boyhood's Home' devilish well the other evening—you've got a capital voice and ought to make (excuse the joke) *capital* out of it! Why don't you go on the stage?"

My first impression was, that my friend was poking fun at me, or perhaps I had not heard distinctly, and he had asked me to ride up in a stage. The reply I made, I forget, but it ended in our strolling up Broadway together, going in to John Anderson's cigar shop next the hospital, and getting one shilling's worth of cigars, handed us by the pretty Mary Rogers, who so suddenly disappeared and was supposed to have been murdered in Hoboken. John has made a fortune, and can be daily seen at his wholesale factory, on the corner of Cedar street and Broadway. Well, my friend A—— having expressed a wish to introduce me to Mr. Latham, the manager of the Charleston Theatre, we dropped in upon him at his residence at the "Halleck House," on the corner of Reade and Broadway. We found him at home, and at his request I sang him one or two songs—"The Lads of the Village" and "Oh! would I were a boy again." He remarked that I had a voice that would realize for me some day a fortune, and that he would be most happy to have me accompany him to Charleston—that he would instruct me in music, and indeed do any and everything to forward my interest, and bring me out successfully. This was the first time that I had at all realized the force of my friend A.'s remark in the Barber's shop, that I should "go on the stage." The idea haunted me; I felt that I never was intended for a business man; figures and accounts were a dead letter to me; of music I was passionately fond, had a quick ear, a retentive memory, and everybody said, a first-rate voice. About this time the carpet trade being a little slack, I obtained through the kindness of an old and esteemed friend, a situation in the office of W. C. Pickersgill & Co., in Wall street, at a salary of $500 a year; but what my actual position or duties were, I never could ascertain, nor did I fully appreciate the awful hornets' nest I had voluntarily got into, in the shape of arithmetical troubles, until I had passed my first week in that dread counting-room.

My friend, Col. L. (the book-keeper), was a very facetious person, and knew full well when he offered me the "berth," not only that I had a horror of figures, but was actually ignorant of the method of keeping the simplest accounts; and to this day, I believe he thought it a good joke, and inwardly enjoyed the nervous state of excitement and agony of mind I was constantly in, when engaged in some (to me) abstruse calculation, and which I tried in vain to conceal. He had distinctly told me, that my duties would be very simple, and that I was looked upon as his assistant, and when any difficulty presented itself in the shape of a "calculation," he could assist me, and, in fact, "put me through."

After the first two or three days, I began to gain a little confidence—and so certain did I feel my footing to be, although my "footing up" was always so shaky in the establishment, and so easy my affairs prospectively seemed in money matters, that I immediately rushed to Reynolds's outfitting shop in Broadway near Cedar, and ordered a dozen shirts, and sundry other necessaries, to replenish my scanty wardrobe.

I have informed the reader before, that I wrote a pretty good hand; accordingly I had a lot of accounts to enter in a large book, letters to copy, etc., my caligraphic powers being universally admired from the principal (my friend the "Col." calling his particular attention thereto) to the office boy. I was not destined long to enjoy the dignities of my position as junior clerk in the house of W. C. P. & Co., for whether from an intuitive knowledge of my deficiencies, or from noticing, upon one occasion, my agitated state in going up and down a column of figures for almost half a day, and the result never being the same *twice* I say, the cause I know not, but certain it is, that while trying to add up a column, he put a piece of paper on my book, which, as I glanced at it askance, I felt in a moment was a death-knell to my hopes, prospects, and position, as assistant book-keeper, in that highly influential, wealthy, and aristocratic banking-house. My boss wished to test my arithmetical powers, and had given me some such problem as the following:—

"I wish to buy a draft on London, through a house in Philadelphia at Pa, or Ma (I forget which), at 3¾ per cent. for £198, 6, 4¾, which amount give me in American money, and calculate the compound interest at 7 per cent. per annum, payable quarterly in advance."

I have never known the sensation of sea-sickness, and very rarely felt sick at the stomach; but for the moment, I thought I should have fallen off the stool, I became faint, the perspiration started from my forehead in rows of beads, and dripped from the ends of my fingers, and if the executioner had stood by me, with a rope around my neck, I am sure my anguish would not have been more intense. There stood Mr. Pick, looking at his unfortunate "Newman Noggs," my eyes became filmy, my head dizzy, and I looked in vain for a consoling glance or word of assistance from the head book-keeper. Mr. Pick left me to make the "calculation;" in vain I tried—my paper was covered with figures—I went over to the Exchange Reading-Room to get a look at the Philadelphia Inquirer, and other journals, vainly supposing I might get some information, at any rate, in their money articles, upon the subject. I got at the interest tables—made sundry gesticulations to the "Col." to do it for me, but he, the last plank to which I clung, slipped from under me, and in my hour of tribulation—was—" nowhar." My time was up, and oh! horror—from the inner-room, the sanctum sanctorum, the place where no sound louder than a whisper was ever heard, where no one hardly dared to enter, but privileged persons, and where the high railings of mahogany, covered with green silk, kept entirely hidden from the vulgar gaze the distinguished individual who was to decide my fate, and in whose presence I felt a degree of mental agony and nervous excitement never experienced before or since;—from this chamber of terrors, issued the words, in a sort of sympathizing and conciliatory tone: "Mr. Massett, will you step in this way if you please?" My time had come at last, and I felt a melancholy relief, I thought he couldn't do much more than discharge me, and my poor brain had been so bothered with the infernal figures that I rather preferred to leave than otherwise. "The head of the house of W. C. P. & Co. suggested that he thought I was not sufficiently advanced in the mysteries of book-keeping and accounts to be of any very great assistance to their firm, and that, though I could remain until I had found another 'berth,' he thought it necessary to engage a more experienced accountant."

I left the presence—my first feeling being one of uncertainty as to how I was going to pay for my dozen shirts, and sundry other articles that I had prospectively bought—and I wended my way to my boarding-house, kept by Mrs. Waterbury (mother to the distinguished Nelson J.), No. 4 Dey street, in a very melancholy state of mind.

In a day or two after these events, I met again my friend A——, who informed me that, on the following Saturday, the schooner Signet, Captain Knudson, would sail for Charleston, and he advised me very strongly to go in her.

X.

COMIC SCENES AT THE CHARLESTON (S. C.) THEATRE.

Somewhere in the month of November, 1841, I arrived in Charleston, S. C., and proceeded at once to the residence of Mr. Latham, the manager, at the Victoria Hotel, in King street. I was emphatically a stranger in a strange land; he, at that time, being the only person I had ever even spoken to in that city. The business of the theatre had been very bad, and he had not the sweetest temper imaginable, and the consequence was that I was not greeted by him in the most affectionate or agreeable manner.

The promise he had made me in New York was, that I was to be by him well instructed and informed in matters musical, and referring to the stage, before I made my first appearance, in speaking, attitudinizing, and all that sort of thing; in fact, I was to look upon myself as his pupil, and that he would be in no hurry to bring me out, wishing me to feel, before that momentous time arrived, perfectly composed and at ease in my new occupation.

The reader can then judge of my surprise, when upon the third day of my arrival, upon strolling leisurely into the "Green Room," Mr. Latham said to me, "What two songs will you sing to-morrow night, sir?"

I was astonished and frightened, and suggested that I was not prepared to make my appearance so soon, reminding him of his promise in New York of instruction, to which he replied, in the most heartless manner, "Oh, I can't afford to be paying idle people, or wait till it suits their convenience. I thought you had a hundred songs at your tongue's end." I felt it would be useless to argue—useless to back out. I had made my bed, and meant to lie in it. I mentioned two. "The Light of other Days," and "Oh! Would I were a Boy again." "Where are your parts, sir?" said Mr. Latham. "My what, sir?" said I; for I really did not know his meaning. "Why (with a fearful expletive) your orchestral parts. You can't sing without orchestral parts, sir—where are they?" I quietly said I never had any, and of that fact he must have been aware! With another oath, he took the songs, and in a short time returned with the "band parts," he being a capital musician, and I, for the first time, at rehearsal, sang the songs to an orchestral accompaniment. They went well, and all congratulated me upon my maiden effort.

The night of my "*first appearance upon any stage*" was to me a momentous occurrence; and though my duties upon that occasion were very simple, the state of mental prostration under which I labored during the whole of that day, I shall never forget. I could eat nothing—I could drink nothing; and as the hour approached for proceeding to the theatre, I felt more like a convict going to execution than anything else. The performances commenced with (as the bills said) the "Heir at Law," after which a "Concert," in which Mr. Stephens (myself) would make his first appearance as a vocalist. I was not needed before nine o'clock, yet I thought it necessary to be "on hand" by seven. The entrance to the stage-door was up a long, dirty alley, which in rainy weather was ankle deep in mud and water, with all sorts of chunks of wood and stray bricks lying about loose; but who ever heard of a stage entrance to be in any other condition? Well, up this gloomy lane

I stumbled, and felt for the gloomier door, which, opening rather against its inclination, hindered by a big leaden weight attached to a long rope, closed with a bang that made me jump about a foot.

A dismal light revealed to my wondering eyes, very dimly though, the pathway, and likewise articles of every name, size, color, and style, with which this subterranean abode seemingly was filled.

There were broken chairs, stools, and tables, rusty helmets, swords, guns, pikes, banners, flags, thrones, sceptres, palaces, castles, streets, gardens, fountains, flower-pots, ships, thunder and lightning, clocks, bells, rain, hail, fishes, goblets, bottles, sky, sea, land, forests, torches, coffins, scaffolds, pokers, gravel walks made of canvas, rail-roads, boots, shoes, traps, paint, paste, paper, loaves of bread made of wood, balls, kettles, tea cups, coffee pots, cups and saucers, broken china, tin plates, shot, sheet iron, masks, bricks, mortar, spiders, rats, mice, flies, dust and dirt!

At last I found myself in the "greenroom," where those not wanted on the stage are supposed to wait until they are "called for."

I knew no one—spoke to no one, and tried very hard to "keep cool." It was the month of December, and though very near Christmas, the night was uncomfortably warm.

The comedy over, I was informed by Mr. L. that it was almost time for me to go on.

I suppose he *saw* the perturbed state of my mind, and taking me to one of the side wings, said, "Now, just look upon the audience as so many cabbage heads,"—this I didn't think very complimentary—"and keep your eye upon the middle chandelier, and it'll be all right." Miss Melton and a Mr. Denison preceded me, and upon a signal from the manager, on I went, not having any distinct idea where I was, and my head going round like a tetotum. When I arrived at the theatre, two hours previous, my shirt collar stood up stiff, touching my ears, but had receded to parts unknown long before I faced the footlights. The orchestra commenced a few bars of symphony (sympathy rather), introducing the aria, "The Light of other Days," and knowing the song well, I was easy on the score of properly commencing. I "got through" the first verse, and was applauded—through the second, and received a hearty "encore," and when with trembling legs and perspiring face I managed to gain the prompter's desk, I was immediately told to "Go on again;" Latham remarking, "I told you so." "See how they like you," &c. The song was repeated, as was also the next I sang; and when my task was ended, I made for my lodgings as quickly as possible, and felt that certainly *one* of the great events of my life had happened.

Singing a song upon the stage is one thing, speaking is another; and I was not destined long to enjoy this simple duty. The play of Rob Roy was put up in the little glass case in the green-room, and *I* was cast for McStuart; and though it was a week before the play was to be produced, my nervousness was great, and I flew to the room of the stage manager, Mr. Henry Tuthill (now, I believe, the proprietor of the Royal Hotel, in Dublin), who was extremely kind to me, and looked upon me as a sort of protegé, begging him to let me have, as quickly as possible, the book from which I could write out my part. Forty lines, I believe, is a "length," in theatrical parlance; and though there cannot be over a quarter of that number devoted to the important part of McStuart, I was at work at it for six days and nights, lying in bed, with candles on each side of me, vainly endeavoring to get it into my head.

Every rehearsal frightened me to death, and at the last, a sort of "dress" one, I couldn't remember a line, my nervousness being so great, that I had (notwithstanding the bullying of my tyrannical manager) to read it from the book.

The night arrived, and I had been carefully and indeed gorgeously attired for the dread occasion by my kind friend and patron, Harry T——; and when I retired to the green-room, to look at myself in a very dirty and not very large glass, I thought I resembled more one of the bagpipe men that I had often seen in the streets of London than anything else. I wore a large sword, which kept perpetually getting between my legs and tripping me up, and my naked legs, exposed for the first time to the gaze of the public, seemed to shrink from the ordeal; and though I was generally considered to be pretty straight on the pins, there appeared a feeling of sympathy between my knees, for they kept up a continual though slight communication with each other in the shape of knockings, all very well and friendly when I was by myself, but which (it seemed to me, having a quick eye for the ludicrous) from the front would look highly ridiculous.

At length the fatal time arrived, and we were, in theatrical parlance, "discovered," and *I* had to speak *the first words.* Never shall I forget them. They were these:—"Well, well; I can drink my quart of usquebaugh or brandy with any man; but we have work just now, and I had better look to it." Like all stage novices, I spoke in a low key, as if addressing some one in ordinary conversation in a room, and was gently (?) reminded of my defect by my sweet-mouthed manager (who was the Major Galbraith of the evening) with a fearful oath, "———! why don't you speak out, you ———?" which had the effect of frightening the remaining part entirely out of my head, and I (in a stage whisper) quickly replied, "he could speak the rest himself," for I knew nothing, and it was only when Mr. Bailie Nicol Jarvie came after me with a red-hot (stage) poker (which was precisely as lurid and glaring at the end of the performance as it was when first handled by the infuriated Scotchman), that the words of my part came to me, "Faugh, man, the next time you fight, fight like a man, and not like a wild Indian. My bonnie pladdie smells like a singed sheep's head."

How the rest of the play went on, I have forgotten, excepting that when I should have appeared at the "O. P." or "P. O." side with a company of soldiers to prevent Rob Roy from running off the stage and bumping his head against a brick wall, I—was snug in bed, with the inward conviction that I had not only made a great judy of myself, but that another of the "momentous crises" of my life had been passed.

About three weeks after this occurrence, the Seguin troupe were announced, the opening opera being Sonnambula, in which I figured as one of the male peasants, my duties being simply to come on and go off with one of the female ditto, joining in the chorus loud or soft as the case might be.

Fra Diavolo was underlined, and *I* was cast for Matteo, the innkeeper. Now this greatly perplexed me, for I found out that, though it seemed at first a very easy and subordinate part, it was, musically considered, most important, and as only two days were devoted to "getting it up," I politely but resolutely declined doing it; Mr. Seguin telling the manager that it was too much to expect a novice like myself, in so short a time, to learn the concerted music. The part was accordingly "read" by a Mr. Byrne. I found out that the promises made me by Manager Latham of instruction, dramatic and musical, amounted to nothing, and that I had no one to look up to or to depend upon but myself; and I accordingly acted as philosophically as possible, endeavoring to perform the parts allotted to me to the best of my ability.

About this time, a tragedian, by the name of Butler, made his appearance, his opening play being the Avenger. I was cast for Conradin (the part played by the pretty Mrs. Powell at the Park Theatre).

The play was first read in the green-room, and my friend Tuthill told me I had a beautiful part, and could make a hit in it if I was careful. It was certainly the longest I had yet studied.

In one of the scenes I had to make love (for the first time) to one of the ladies of the play (I think it was Miss Charlotte Barnes, now Mrs. G. Comer), and at rehearsal was told by the stage manager to kneel on my left knee, or the one nearest the audience; but at the proper time and place, I was so agitated and nervous, that I bent one and then the other, to the great annoyance of the lady and the laughter of the audience.

The plot of the play I know nothing of; all I remember is, that the lady and her mother were friends of the Austrians, and that I (being the valet of the Avenger) addressing the younger of the two females, had to say:—"I heard you this moment own yourselves friends of the Austrians, and that name alone, but breathed in this place, would call the walls down on you. 'Tis the Avenger's house!"

With this announcement, both ladies gave a loud shriek, when I, taking the hand of the youngest, replied—

"I'll quickly find occasion to release you hence."

The old lady—

"Oh! with what can we reward you?"

I replied—

"'Tis my reward to serve this bright perfection; to gaze e'en thus a moment on her looks; and if I merit guerdon beyond this, let me, but on my bended (here I kept bobbing up and down) knee, press this hand once to my lips, with a devotion as pure and holy as that you breathe in worship at your saint's shrine!" Oh lord! oh lord!

I managed to get this off so well that I received a round of applause, which so frightened me that I forgot my part, and remained speechless on both knees, kissing the lady's hand, she saying—

"Ask not for more"—I thought of Oliver Twist, and wished myself at the devil.

"Do get up," whispered the lady. "I can't," said I. "Do go, you're keeping the stage waiting." "But I must go," called out the prompter. "I wish I could," thought I. "Go off the stage, sir," cried out Mr. Butler, who wanted to come on. I, still kneeling, and perspiring from head to foot, at last caught the words, "But I must go, for Walden will be here; and if but once suspected, you are lost!" I received a general bullying when I got off the stage, and became more and more disgusted with lengthy parts.

The play of the Lady of Lyons was performed one night to a *six dollar* house—cash. I was one of the three distinguished officers who come on in the fifth act and talk about the gallant Col. Morier. I wore a cap, blue frock coat, red sash, and carried a sword, so that I resembled one of our N. Y. policemen. Upon the present occasion I had what they called, "doubled;" that is played two parts having in the earlier part of the drama enacted "Gaspard;" the consequence was that I got the parts all mixed up, and began talking of—

"Blows to a French citizen" to the utter confusion of my brother officers, who, in a sotto voce tone, suggested that I should "clear out," which advice I instantly took—marching off, as if on the most important business. I wasn't visible again that night.

The play of Hamlet afforded me the opportunity of appearing in the arduous rôle of "Gueldencrantz," or

"Rozenstern," I forget which, for they are both much about the same.

I remember the "business" was somewhat particular, and I was requested to be on the "*right*" *side of Hamlet* (knowing the Tragedian pretty well I thought this would be an easy matter). This of course I didn't do and the whole scene went wrong, and when "Hamlet," after inviting me to play an air on the flute, and my respectfully replying—

"My Lord, I cannot"—

Threw away the instrument—whether purposely or not I couldn't find out, as it caught me on one of my legs and I "hollered" right out, and rushed off the stage the audience roaring with laughter.

Upon another occasion, I was cast for the part of the "Duke of Buckingham" in Henry the Sixth. I think my turn comes after "Hotspur's" celebrated speech, commencing,—"My liege, I did deny no prisoners" (this part, I may mention, was very effectively rendered by the celebrated scenepainter, Mr. Henry Isherwood); well, the language I found very difficult, so much so, that I had taken the precaution to write it out in a bold hand and stick it inside of my hat, and was in the act of reading it, when King Henry the Sixth seeing what I was doing, said to me with an oath:—"Haven't you had plenty of time to learn your part, Sir, without reading it here?" which rebuke had the effect, not only of rendering the Duke speechless, but causing an audible "titter" among the lords and ladies of the "Court."

The play of London Assurance was produced with great splendor. The cast, if I remember right, was as follows:—Sir Harcourt, Mr. Harry Tuthill; Dazzle, Mr. Charles Howard; Meddle, Mr. Latham; Lady Gay Spanker, Miss Melton; Charles Conolly, Mr. Byrne; Pert, Mr. Henry; Dolly Spanker, Mr. Henry, and "Cool" myself.

I was told I acted in this very well, and, the play happening to run for several nights, I felt quite easy in it.

Mr. Hackett was announced as Falstaff and I was cast for Pistol, in the Merry Wives of Windsor, carrying a sword that was twice as big as I was, and dressed in the most ungainly suit imaginable. My crowning triumph, however, was reserved for the occasion of Miss Charlotte Barnes's Benefit, when she asked me to play the part of "Paris" in Romeo and Juliet. I was attired by my good-natured patron, Harry T., most gorgeously, and having very little to do in the earlier portions of the tragedy, felt composed and tolerably at my ease. At rehearsal in the fencing scene, knowing little or nothing of the mysteries of that gentlemanly art, I suggested to Mr. Romeo (C. Howard), that he should let me off quickly and easily, giving me one or two "stage" digs in the side and letting me drop.

This he agreed to do. At length the time arrived when in front of the pasteboard tomb of the "Capulets" he makes for his rival, Paris. We both struck an attitude, I requesting him to stab me quickly; I fell, supposed to be dead, and as I lay, the carpenter (as I found out afterwards), in one of the flies above me, let some water drop in my eyes causing me to move my head. This made the audience laugh; down came more water—drip, drip, drip—my head moving to the other side—audience convulsed. Poor

Howard could not imagine the cause, and, looking at his legs, thought there might (as he afterwards said) be a hole in his tights. "What's the matter?" he cried; nobody could tell, and the curtain came down amid the boisterous laughter of the audience. After it was over I explained what I supposed to be the cause, and the carpenter received a severe reprimand from the manager and I a good blowing up from Mr. Romeo.

During my residence in Charleston, happening to fall in love with a large pair of dark eyes, I gave vent to my feelings in the words and music of a song—my maiden effort, which I believe "still lives," and enjoys a fair share of public favor.

The song is called "When the Moon on the Lake is beaming," and the following are the words:—

When the Moon on the lake is beaming,
And the night is calm and still,
And the stars in their bright light gleaming,
Shine forth on some distant hill—
Wilt thou come, love, come?
Oh, come with me,
And I'll give thee a happy home,
Where a true heart waits for thee!

When the vesper bells are ringing
Their evening melody,
Our maidens sweet are singing
Their simple minstrelsy—
Wilt thou come, love, come?
Oh, come with me,
And I'll give thee a happy home,
Where a true heart waits for thee!

Upon my arrival in New York, I took the song to Mr. William Dubois in Broadway, who gave me the magnificent sum of five dollars, cash, for it, and fifty copies, which were distributed among my friends. The song has gone through several editions, and is now published by William Hall & Sons, Broadway.

A circumstance occurred one night after the performances were all over, as I was returning home, that again changed the current of my life.

I was accosted by a gentleman, who, with extended hand and pleasant voice, said—

"I think, sir, your name is M——, is it not? for I believe I made a voyage from England with a brother of yours, in the 'Vibilea' some years ago?"

I replied that I was delighted to have had the pleasure of meeting him, and accepted his kind invitation to dine with him on the following day.

This resulted in my being introduced to Col. Keith and my being once again installed at the desk, and for several months I was one of the clerks in the Secretary of State's office, in the old iron building near Broad street, in the Palmetto city.

I may mention here that though my stipulated salary with Harry Latham was six dollars a week, board included, all I received from the treasurer for my magnificent performances during my entire theatrical career in Charleston, was *two dollars and a half!*

The intense heat and a slight touch of yellow fever, determined me to take passage to New York, in the ship Catharine, Captain Berry.

Here I was one night, at a party at Dr. Levitt's, the dentist (who then lived on the corner of Warren street and Broadway), introduced to Mr. William Mitchell, then the manager of the Olympic Theatre, which was located where the City Assembly Rooms now are.

XI.

THE OLD OLYMPIC.

Some delightful evenings were passed in the doctor's pleasant rooms, and he being very musical and at the same time theatrically inclined, was constantly entertaining at his hospitable apartments members of the profession, musicians, artists, editors, etc. Horncastle, Mitchell, Bengough, Geo. Loder, Henry Watson, and others were among his frequent visitors.

The opera of "Amilie," George Loder suggested, should be brought out at the little Olympic, and he told Mitchell that I was the proper person to personate the Count.

I at first could not entertain the idea at all, my career at Charleston upon the stage having been anything but pleasant; I intended to return, if possible, to some private employment.

In this I did not succeed, and accordingly, at the urgent solicitation of many, I accepted the offer of Mr. Manager Mitchell, who christened me Mr. Raymond. Accordingly, on October 2d, 1842, the first night of "Amilie" was announced at the Olympic.

The cast was as follows:

AMILIE, ... *Mrs. Timm.*
JOS. SPECKBACKER, ... *Miss Mary Taylor.*
GEN. COUNT VAN DER TIEMER, . *Mr. Raymond.*

Mr. Ben Baker, now attached to Laura Keene's Theatre, was the efficient prompter, and I may here add that he not only "rang up" the *first curtain* upon the occasion of the opening night, but he rang down the last.

If I *had* gone through the ordeal of a first appearance—as I unquestionably had at Charleston—it went for nothing; the to me terrible fact of appearing in New York city, where, I felt, almost everybody knew me, I never properly realized until the fatal day arrived.

We had many rehearsals; and as to the music, I felt unconcerned. My "make up" was quite attractive. A blue frock coat, lined with white satin, was faultlessly made by Pearson, the tailor, the foraging cap by Mealio, the hatter (still to be found on the corner of Canal street and Broadway), my patent-leathers (how they *did* hurt my feet) by a distinguished Dutchman, and my red trowsers, with gold lace, by the aforesaid tailor; the whole surmounted by a pair of gorgeous epaulets, lent to me by my friend Captain McArdle.

My manager found me at Windust's, in Park Row, about half-past two, eating minced veal, I having heard that chopped meat was the right thing to "do" on this thrilling occasion—thus preventing the possibility of anything "sticking" in my throat; a something I fully expected would happen on the stage.

As the hour drew near I experienced for the *second* time the fearful sensation of making a *first* appearance. The night I remember well—it was damp, misty, and foggy—and as I approached the front of the theatre a crowd besieged the doors, the pit entrance being completely blocked up by market boys, butcher boys, newsboys, big boys, small boys, of every age, shape, and size.

The stage entrance was through a cellar-way in Broadway, the narrow and gloomy passage slightly illuminated by one or two jets of gas, which "Tom the Gasman" (quite a character in those days, and one of the "institutions") had a few moments before lighted.

The dressing-room appointed for me was about the size of an old-fashioned shower-bath, having just room enough for me to stand up and sit down in, and the perfume I encountered as I opened the rickety door, with its rusty iron latch, was highly suggestive of the sick-ward in a hospital, or a half-cleaned pigstye.

The wooden walls were covered with caricatures in chalk, old playbills, and from long tenpenny nails hung remnants of tights, old hats, waistcoats, etc.; upon the half dusted bench upon which my stage traps were supposed to be placed was a paper of rouge, a pink saucer, some India ink, and a broken looking-glass.

In my excitement I had forgotten, as I was informed, a very essential article. I had been instructed in the art of "making up" my face, that is, the method of putting on the rouge with a *hare's foot*—this latter thing I had lost sight of. I accordingly told the dresser, a good natured darkey, to go as quickly as he could to the market near Grand street, and get me a defunct rabbit, and to cut off his fore or hind leg and bring it to me immediately.

I could not help smiling as he produced the leg of the animal, that had been chopped off, and threw the remaining portion on the dressing-table. I commenced bedaubing my face with the red powder, and (not being able in those days to sport any real hair) with the India ink I painted a moustache on my upper lip.

Taking a farewell look in the glass I proceeded to the

"Greenroom," awaiting the dread word of the "call boy," "Count wanted."

The house was packed to suffocation, and everyone seemed on the tiptoe of excitement. It was the first attempt to produce a legitimate and entire opera at this little bandbox of a theatre, which, up to this time, had been celebrated for its burlesques, funny farces, and, indeed, turning everything into ridicule.

The overture was finished, capitally played by the compact little orchestra, and when I mention among those composing its members such names as John A. Kyle, George Loder, George Bristow, Henry C. Timm, and Aupick, the reader can well understand its excellence.

The curtain was rung up, and the opening chorus, with the song of Amilie, was admirably given and vociferously cheered.

I believe I was supposed to be a general in the Austrian army, returned after many years' absence to the scenes of my youth.

The stage was cleared, a canvas inn erected, with a paper window and a swinging sign, upon which Mr. Bengough had painted: "The only Inn on the Horse-road to Durich."

I was pretty cool, though I felt I had a fearful ordeal to go through; the "wings" on each side of the stage were crowded with the various performers, ballet-girls, supernumeraries, and a few privileged persons who had the entrée behind the scenes, and Mitchell, who was to give me the word, when to "come on."

A few bars of symphony, introducing the song of "My Boyhood's Home," was the cue for me to appear—and on I walked, looking stiff, feeling stiff, and acting "stiffer."

My red trowsers, thank Providence, hid the shakiness of my legs, and, as my fright did not particularly affect my voice, and I knew the song perfectly, I got through it so as to be encored; and I imagined as I sat down at the table, and took up an empty tin can that was (supposed to be) full of wine, I was a veritable soldier, and had returned to "my native heath," after a series of hardships and mishaps.

The opera was a great success, and Miss Mary Taylor, Miss Singleton, and Mrs. Timm, were enthusiastically received; indeed, the opera ran some thirty consecutive nights, and the boxes of the Olympic were nightly filled with the élite of the city. Many funny scenes occurred during the brief period of my stay as a member of the Olympic Company, and I shall content myself, by jotting down from my memory, one or two incidents that may amuse the reader.

Upon one occasion my red trowsers, in which I played the Count, had been borrowed by one of the lady members of the company who happened to be a very large woman, and having to be emphatically "let out" in a region not necessary to mention, were entirely spoiled for me. The opera being suddenly "put up," and I forgetting that I had loaned my pants, was at the last moment constrained to borrow a pair of thin *white ones*, very badly made; the night was intensely cold, and I was shivering, added to all this, my nether appendages were so tight a fit, that every motion of my legs could be easily seen—it was useless for me to try to stand still—my teeth chattered, my legs shook; how I got through the music I know not; but I do know, that after that night I never allowed any woman to "let out" or "take in" my trowsers.

Charles Dickens came to see one of his pieces performed one evening; a private box having been set apart for himself and wife, by Mr. Mitchell. All eyes were turned to the box, and little attention seemed to be given by the actors or the audience to the performances. He dropped into the Green-room during the performance, and was for some minutes chatting with Mr. Mitchell in his dressing-room.

XII.

ALL ABOUT A CALF'S HEAD.

An incident occurred on the night of my benefit, which at the time created a little excitement; the "Sunday papers," I remember, being particularly eloquent upon the subject, each giving a very graphic, and (of course) different version of the affair.

Now, it must be remembered, that that part of the house known as the "pit" was usually occupied by a crowd of butcher-boys, market, and newsboys, whose great delight consisted, upon the occasion of any one's benefit, in throwing upon the stage some friendly recognition of their appreciation of the efforts of their favorite—these delicate attentions consisted, in part, of articles from the green-grocer's, the tallow-chandler's, or the butcher's, such as wreaths of onions, large-sized carrots, with turnips to match, a string of tallow-candles, and occasional "red-herring," and in one instance an immense cod-fish.

It was reserved for me, however, to have the finishing touch put to my theatrical career, in the shape of a delicate souvenir from a friendly butcher-boy, who, if he ever happens to read these lines, will remember the awful consternation, and the shrieks of laughter, the audience was thrown into by the appearance on the stage of his considerate and friendly memento.

I had selected the first act of the Sonnambula for my benefit, introducing the well-known air, "As I view now."

Mary Taylor was the Amina, and Mr. Charles Walcot the Elvino, who sang the music charmingly.

I was got up regardless of expense, had just crossed the bridge at the back of the stage, and was walking down the middle thereof, the villagers standing bowing on each side of me, when, just as I commenced the words, "As I view now!"—whack came down a "calf's head," white as milk, beautifully clean-shaved, tied with blue ribbons, and a fine large lemon in its mouth!

I stepped back aghast, but perfectly resigned; the utmost

confusion prevailed, some ladies laughing, others crying. Mitchell (who had been in the orchestra, watching the progress of the opera) jumped into the pit, and endeavored to lay hold of the "disturber of the peace." Officers were flying about, and the whole house in a perfect uproar. Walcot kindly suggested to me to "keep cool," and he would "pick it up." I stood till I thought I must look very foolish, and walking up to the "dead head," took hold of the blue silk with which it was bandaged, when, to my horror, it again dropped; this disconcerted me, and I stepped back to await the result of the disturbance.

Elvino, at this moment, took compassion upon me, and carried the "head" off, and presented it to the call-boy, who had some first-rate soup made of it, of which we all partook on the following day—not an act of soup-ererogation, but in grateful remembrance of the liberal donor.

I was "called out," as was the usual custom, at the end of the performance, but had left for home long before that time.

Mr. Mitchell appeared before the curtain, stating, in a sharp and even indignant manner, to the audience, that, "Mr. Raymond had retired for the night, but had requested him (Mr. Mitchell) to present his compliments to the gentleman who had thrown him *his likeness*."

At this the audience collapsed in an extraordinary state of ironical laughter, and Mitchell, perceiving the ambiguity of his remark, left the stage in high dudgeon, the boys in the pit following with hoots of laughter.

It may be well here to remark, that the audience usually attending the Olympic was composed of two classes: the boxes containing the first people in the city—as frequently the body of the first tier would be occupied by a party of ladies and gentlemen made up for the occasion—while the pit possessed the usual characteristics of the galleries in a London theatre, and was always composed of the same materials, the butcher-boys usually predominating.

Mitchell had so used his audience to jokes and double entendre, that they were always looking out for such things; he frequently having confidential conversations with the pit, in regard to their conduct, during the progress of the play; so that the manager and the pittites, and the audience generally, felt on terms of quite friendly intercourse at all times.

It will thus be seen, when Mitchell made this mistake, that the pit took advantage of it, and returned his attempt at rebuke with shouts of laughter.

When this was reported in the papers, I thought it somewhat equivocal, and to this day I cannot find out whether he intended the compliment for me or my unknown friend.

XIII.

YANKEE HILL.

During my stay at the Olympic, I had been introduced to Mr. George H. Hill, commonly known as Yankee Hill. Upon the close of the season, he suggested to me the propriety of accompanying him on a lecturing and musical tour through the Eastern States, commencing in Boston, and he offered me $10 a week and my travelling expenses.

We had rare fun together, and passed through many funny scenes. He announced me in the bills as "Mr. Raymond, the celebrated London Vocalist."

He gave his first entertainment à la Dr. Valentine at the Melodeon, I assisting by singing two or three ballads.

Signor De Begnis, quite a celebrity in those days, gave a concert, and with Mr. Hill's permission I sang *for the first time* in public my own song, "*When the Moon on the Lake.*"

Yankee Hill was an inveterate joker, and very fond of playing his tricks upon strangers. Upon the steamer in which we had taken passage for Boston, we noticed several clergymen, going, I believe, to some religious convention. Hill picking out one of the most sanctimonious-looking, said to me, "What do you bet I don't go and ask that man for a pinch of snuff, and 'how his mother is?'" I replied, I didn't think he could do it and keep his face straight. With this, I went to the other side of the boat, so that I could see and not be noticed, when Hill, putting on a very lóng face and throwing his head back, came softly behind the reverend gentleman, giving a tremendous sneeze that made him jump several feet; Hill remarking that he hoped he had not alarmed him, but the fact was he had a very bad cold, and his only remedy was a pinch of snuff, and he had left his box at home; following it up with the promised question, "Could you give me a pinch?" The clergyman replied, that he thought it a sin to use tobacco in any shape; that he had religiously obeyed the injunctions of his father and mother,—when Hill, interrupting him, said, "Wasn't your mother from Plymouth, and her name—Benson?" (This was a favorite name of his.) "No, sir; my mother, who, thank God, is still living, resides in Vermeount, and she is a Snodgrass, sir!" "A—what—grass, sir?" says Hill. "I am, as you see, a little *deef*, owing to this infernal—I beg pardon—troublesome cold; but I had an aunt Snodgrass, sir, on my mother's side, and I *did* think I saw a *re*-semblance; *was* your mother's name Mary?"—(Hill always insisted that was a safe question.)—"It *were*, sir," replied the clergyman; when to my horror, and to the explosion of half a dozen bystanders into a perfect tornado of laughter, Hill followed it up with the most imperturbable gravity—"and *how is your mother?*" his face assuming an inquiring and sympathetic expression. I could stand it no longer, and asked him not to repeat the joke on anyone else.

It soon became known that Yankee Hill was on board, and everybody was on his guard, fearing to come in contact with him.

We gave entertainments together at Portland, Augusta, Belfast, and other towns in Maine, generally in the dining-rooms of the different taverns at which we stopped.

In the town of Augusta, where we stayed some two or three days, and where I was much interested in passing several hours in the Insane Asylum, not as an inmate, but as a visitor. At Augusta we were advertised—or rather it was "Yankee Hill's Budget of Fun and Comic Olio"—to give a "show" on Saturday night; tickets twenty-five cents.

The hall was the eating-room of the hotel, a screen with a sheet thrown over it separating us from the view of the audience. We had been out fishing in the earlier part of the day and were both dreadfully burnt, so much so, that we had been advised by our landlady to "grease" our faces before the concert came off.

Supper being over, and the hour of commencing near, Hill suggested to me to go and "play 'em in." I replied, that I knew no pieces, other than a few accompaniments to my songs, and I was not a piano-forte player (we had discharged our accompanyist long before for want of funds and business). "Oh, no matter," said Hill, "go and give him a chord or so, thump on it, run up and down the keys, anything to make a noise, and directly you see anybody come in, cut behind that sheet, and I'll walk in as if I was one of the audience."

I did as directed, and the result was one old woman appeared and a small boy. She stood at the door several minutes insisting that she couldn't give over twelve and a half cents for her son. I then left for the screen, and having made a hole with my penknife in the sheet, counted, by the time Mr. Hill made his appearance on the stand, just a dozen persons including the servants of the house, the proprietor and proprietress. The proceeds of the night amounted to thirty-seven and a half cents.

Hill commenced by saying, "Ladies and Gentlemen (Hill very red in the face, and nearly bursting with suppressed laughter, and I behind the sheet joining in), I presume it is—owing to the excessive—cold—no—heat—of the day—that—that—there are so many—I mean—few—here to-night;—but the fact is—it is almost impossible to—er—go through a laborious entertainment like mine, when the audience is so sparse, and therefore, I'll give you one or two imitations, and Mr. Raymond will sing you one or two songs, and as it's Saturday night, we'll conclude the whole with PRAYER!" I burst out laughing, the screen fell down, Hill couldn't keep his face, and the audience joined in too; the consequence was, that a song from me, and a Yankee story from Hill, completed the night's performance, and the thirty-seven and a half cents were invested in some toddies before we retired for the night.

It was during a brief stay in Portland that I met a young man who informed me he was very shortly going to Italy, upon a visit to some relations; but for the sake of the voyage, he intended to take passage in a vessel which in a few days would sail for Malta and Smyrna, and he wished me very much to try and arrange my affairs so as to make the trip with him.

I was always very fond of the sea, and the idea of making a summer voyage along the classic shores of the Mediterranean was too great a temptation to be lightly thought of, so I accordingly husbanded my resources, and bent all my energies to the accomplishment of my wishes.

XIV.

SUMMER TRIP UP THE MEDITERRANEAN.

It was somewhere about the end of July, in the year 1843, that I found myself on the deck of the barque "George Henry," Captain Michael Watson, bound for Malta and Smyrna.

Prior to leaving I had promisedmy friend, William T. Porter, Esq., then the Editor of "The Spirit of the Times," whom I accidentally met at the "Tremont House," at a quiet little "sit down," in company with Captain Ryrie, Henry Russell the vocalist, John Olmstead, Jack Smith, Major Whitcomb, and the "Deacon," that I would scribble an occasional letter for his journal.

I had been christened by the Editor of the "Spirit" during my "Olympic" campaign "Col. Pipes," one evening during a session of the "Barclay Street Guards," at a locality known in those days as "Franks," and I thought it a good name to perpetuate, accordingly my communications were signed "Jeems Pipes," a few of which I have preserved, and will now, with the reader's permission, herewith introduce—

SOME "NOTES OF A VOYAGER," DURING A TRIP UP THE MEDITERRANEAN IN THE SUMMER OF 1843.

After a delightful run of twenty days, we saw the land of Spain, about six o'clock on the morning of the 18th of

August, and shortly after came in sight of Cape Trafalgar. We had a splendid view of the City of Tangiers on the Moorish side, and the Island of Tarifa with its Lighthouse on the Spanish side. I noticed several Feluccas; these boats sail remarkably well, I am told. They have at Tarifa a celebrated "Gipsey Inn," about which there are many extraordinary legends.

Feluccas laden with hides for Cadiz stop here in order to perform quarantine. The island is charmingly situated, and is only fifteen miles from Gibraltar.

We arrived in the Bay about one o'clock, and at three the Rock was in sight.

The finest view you get is from the east side, where it rises perfectly straight out of the water. On the extreme point of the rock, there seemed to be, as I viewed it through the glass, an observatory or something of the kind. We had a fine sight of the Road, and a fleet of vessels anchored there.

Hoisted the Ensign and Signal and passed the Rock, with fine strong breezes, and clear weather, our beautiful barque going a good ten knots an hour, and lay our course for Malta.

The weather at this season of the year, on the Mediterranean, is magnificent. I had often *read* of the beauty of the sunsets, but must confess I knew little of their grandeur until I had for myself gazed with wonder and delight upon them. One evening in particular I shall never forget. The day had been lovely, not too warm, and a clear blue Italian sky had stretched above us since morning. At about six the whole western sky assumed a deep salmon color, from which the sun, like a ball of fire, glared out, gradually but almost imperceptibly approaching nearer and nearer the water's edge—a long, long range of clouds of fleecy whiteness, appearing in the distance like some happy land far away, spread itself a short space above the horizon.

The sun while slowly descending gilded the tops of these clouds, giving them the appearance of long roads covered with golden sand. Then it just touched the edge of the water sending forth a stream of yellow light upon the bosom of the ocean—lower, lower, lower, until just for an instant it looks like a star on the horizon, and is gone!

For a few minutes the sky seems as brilliant as ever, when gradually the dazzling colors die away, leaving a faint glow upon the clouds, but now so fairy-like and beautiful, marking where glory once had been. Never shall I forget this sunset.

On the 1st of September came in sight of the Island of Galeta. As we neared the Island of Goza, I could see several old ruins, monasteries, etc., and some one or two small towns. The Island seemed barren—all rock, nothing green to relieve the eye. Commona is the next Island, next came Malta. Some two miles from this place; we were beset by about twenty boats, filled with the most extraordinary looking fellows, jabbering away in the funniest manner possible. "Cap*teen*, Cap*teen*, twelve dollare, only twelve dollare—twenty boats goot one's—small vessels pay twelve dollare cap*teen!*" It seems they wished to pilot us in, all vessels entering the Port of Malta have to be towed in by these boats. They are *something* in the shape of a canoe, and are propelled by some four or five men, who stand and paddle precisely as an Indian would. Captain Watson, who had been to Malta frequently, and knew well the imposing nature of these "d—d scoundrels," as he called them, said, "No, no, I'll give you six dollars and no more." "Oh," cried the foremost man, "Cap*teen*, I'll tell you, give nine dollare—all pay dat!" Away they kept yelling out, following our vessel, until one of them cried, "Well, well, this time six dollare." "Hoist away," sang out the Captain, and in a few minutes we soon hauled up into the harbor.

We had to undergo the miseries of a fine day's quarantine—so we hoisted the yellow flag, to prevent any boats coming near us, with the exception of the "Spenditors." All shore boats are kept off, and the office boats on service, and the pilot boats always keep on the weather side, at the regular distance.

Immediately after our ship came to anchor, all the letters and papers, brought by her, were sent to the Lazaretto for fumigation, and then forwarded to the Post-office for delivery. All the ship's boats wear a yellow flag in the bow, and they are not permitted to go to any part of the harbor, except to the Parlatory at the Quarantine Office and at the Lazaretto, or to the watering-place, after due permission—and to these places only during office hours when the flag is flying.

The boats are always attended by a health guardian, and on no pretence are they allowed to go alongside other vessels in quarantine. They do not allow even sails to be used in boats. We soon saw one of the Spendit or boats making for our barque, bringing all kinds of provisions—grapes and every variety of fruit. In this harbor I had a good view of the town. There were several men-of-war lying here. H.M. Frigate Belvidera, H.M. Brig Savage, and Frigate Tyne, also the Queen, a 120-gun ship, (having the flag of Vice-Admiral Sir E. Rich. Owen, K.C.B.,) also several French men-of-war steamers. The Maltese seem to be a kind of mixture of the Chinese and Indian in their appearance,—their complexion is of a copper-color, and their language, as I heard them bawling from the quays, seems to be the most horrid jargon imaginable. The American Consul, Mr. Andrews, paid us a visit, and informed us that we should obtain pratique the following day. The next morning at about six o'clock, I went in the ship's boat on shore, and met the Editor of the "Mediterranean Gazette," a gentleman to whom I was introduced by our Captain. We went first to the Casino, and thence to his house in the Strada Reale, where we breakfasted.

We then hired a *caleche*, and drove first to the church of St. John's. There is nothing at all striking in the exterior of this building. It appears built (I write from recollection) of a yellow kind of stone, but the interior is magnificent. The church is not very large, but is splendidly ornamented.

Then there are a great many interesting associations connected with it. Here have reposed for many hundred years the bones of haughty knights and cardinals of high order. I was shown by a man with shaved head, black surplice, beads and cross to boot, all over the cathedral, and visited all the chapels. In one he pointed out to me a magnificent silver gate, saved from the hands of the French by being painted black, they, thinking it a wooden railing, passed it by; thus leaving the most valuable relic behind. We next went into the vaults beneath to see the tombs, our guide preceding us with a torch down many a well-worn step, until we reached the iron door leading to the abode of the dead. In his right hand was a bunch of large rusty keys, and upon applying one to the huge door, it opened with a harsh grating noise. The atmosphere was damp in the extreme. It was a long and rather low arched vault, on each side of which were several marble tombs, carved most beautifully, with the bodies of the knights in armor, cut out in marble, with hands, as in the act of praying, resting on the breast; also cardinals full-robed, chiselled out most exquisitely. At the further end of the vault there was an altar with some long old iron candlesticks and black marble steps, all dark with age, at which perhaps the very knights here entombed had often knelt in prayer. A small dark-colored ivory crucifix hung from the wall, before which our guide bowed very reverently. There is to me something awfully imposing in the Catholic form of religion, and I lingered, looking at this relic of by-gone days, until beckoned by my friend to proceed into the cathedral. High mass was being performed. The altar is very grand, and is adorned with golden candlesticks and magnificent paintings. The interior of this church is very spacious and of great architectural beauty.

On one side of the altar is a throne for the Bishop, and on the opposite, one for the Governor of Malta, with the royal arms over it. The pavement is richly emblazoned with the armorial bearings of the knights in mosaic, most beautifully blended, and under the arms are engraved long Latin inscriptions. The walls are completely studded with tablets, busts, banners, &c., and are carved in the most elaborate manner to the roof, pencilled with gold and the richest colors imaginable. From the body of the cathedral, on each side, are different chapels belonging to the different saints, all equally beautiful. I stayed for hours admiring the many memorials here left of the Knights of St. John and their companions.

I passed several old confessionals, where priests were occupied with many a fair penitent. Service is carried on all day; and every day in the week, in and out walk all sorts of people, rich and poor, noble and ignoble.

Dotted about here and there, I saw many an old friar, with shaved head, save a rim round his forehead, with eyes and hands upraised, *appearing* at least excessively devotional. So delighted was I with this place, that I visited it several times during my stay. From hence we went to the Floriana Gardens.

XV.

MALTA.

THE Floriana Gardens are situated near the Regina Piazza, and are very beautiful.

Long grounds walled in with stone, having at each end flights of steps with high iron gates. Almost every thing here is artificial, as very little grows in Malta, the island being rocky and barren; but plants of every description, flowers of various kinds, and trees of every name and height fill the air with all sorts of delicious odors.

Then there are long well-laid-out walks, shady groves, playful fountains, and warbling birds.

These gardens are frequented by numbers of persons; but all beggars, and the lower orders of the female Maltese, are excluded.

Methinks 't would be a sweet place to breathe a tale of love into the ear of some fair one; for I find that here, as well as in Venice, "they do let heaven see the pranks they dare not show their husbands." The streets of Malta are crowded with a pale set of the most persecuting beggars, whose supplications for "Carita" are annoying in the extreme. Sometimes they will even lay hold of your coat, and follow you till you throw them a few coppers.

The boats, which are very numerous, deserve particular attention. I had a better opportunity of seeing these on shore than I had from the vessel. They are very commodious, and are kept beautifully clean by the natives. The one I took was a perfect little palace, painted with the gayest colors—a large eye adorning each side of the stern—being provided with a white awning and a beautiful set of curtains. The hire is very moderate—the boatman charging me two-pence English for my ride.

Towards evening I went into a saloon, No. 62 Strada Reale, where was a grand "Cosmorama," comprising some of the most beautiful and interesting views taken from nature that I had ever witnessed; a portion being views of Malta, then a grand panoramic view of Constantinople, taken from the Russian Ambassador's Palace, a very beautiful view of the Frozen Sea, and the grand chains of the Caucasus Mountains.

They were painted by a Signor Diamanti, and were superb. The price of admission was only an English shilling. I and my friend then took a caleche, and had a delightful ride from Valetta to the celebrated bay, where the apostle Paul is supposed to have been shipwrecked. I returned about eight, when I took boat and crossed over to Slema, a kind of watering-place, where the wealthier portion of the Maltese usually spend their summer months. There was to be a grand display of fire-works, it being the anniversary of some saint or other, and the company assembled was numerous, but the fire-works were execrable, and would have been hissed in any decent town in America. In Slema reside the Austrian, French, Russian, American, and other consuls, the Admiral of the Port, etc. It is beautifully situated on the sea shore, the Mediterranean washing its banks. The weather at this time of the year is lovely, rainy very seldom—bright blue-skies, and warm sun. The scene on Saturday evening was a novel one, at least for me. Here then were hundreds of men, women and children jabbering away in different languages, and at the top of their voices; some admiring the fire-works, some yelling and hooting, others singing; then the band of the "Queen" just heard above the riot, ladies innumerable walking to and fro, dressed in white, with black silk hoods covering their heads and shoulders, resting on the arm of some baffy fellow, or quietly seated on a projecting piece of rock, watching the gay scene. Then, a turbaned Turk, with long beard and pipe in mouth, would pass me. Then some funny looking fellow, dressed in black cloth, quaker-cut clothes, black silk stockings, low shoes, and three-cornered hats—these I took to be some church worthies. Spaniards, Italians, Turks, Greeks, Maltese, passed and repassed. We had the moon high above us· the pale and placid moon, while the myriad stars, that were twinkling their silver eyes, as if in wonder at the scene beneath them, were reflected in the clear water as in a mirror. It was a heavenly night! The bright blue Mediterranean lay calm and still as an infant slumbering; and Malta in the distance, with its many turrets, towers and fortresses, formed altogether a most lovely picture. I was wandering along alone, and had progressed sufficiently far to be rid of the noise of the people, when I saw in the distance the figure of a woman standing in front of a very recherché looking villa. As I approached she slightly drew back, I turned round, she was still looking. I doffed my chapeau, retraced my steps—spoke to her, and to my no small delight and astonishment, she returned answer in English, with a very slight Spanish accent. I now had a good opportunity of looking at her more particularly. She was about the middle height, and though her features were good, her eyes black and piercing, and her hair also dark, she was not *exactly* handsome. There were certain traces of care and anxiety about the face, giving it a melancholy sadness of expression. She was symmetrically formed, and had the prettiest foot and ankle imaginable. It was not difficult to get her consent to walk, and we strolled therefore to the sea shore, and having, after some trouble, found a very quiet little nook, where we might remain free from intruders, we sat down, the waters of the Mediterranean rippling at our feet. The place of our choice had evidently been appropriated by some Sicilian fishermen to purposes of use, in keeping their nets, tackle, etc. In the distance, we could see numbers of little feluccas, looking like birds on the water; it was as light as day, and the sea sparkled like diamonds in the moonlight. Well, it was not long ere I found out the history of my pretty brunette. She had been married at the early age of fourteen to a man some thirty years older than herself, for whom she had never entertained the slightest affection, and also at the wish of an old father, who had been in the army, whose sole reason for insisting on the union was the immense wealth of the Spanish suitor. Her mother had died in giving her birth, and she was therefore at an early age left to the complete control and care of her father. She was a native of Goza, the sister island of Malta, and from her occasional intercourse with some of her father's friends had acquired a knowledge of the English language. Her remaining parent had long since died, and she had therefore no one left to her but her husband, whose harsh and cruel treatment embittered every hour of her existence. It was painful in the extreme to witness the deep-rooted sorrow of this poor girl, and the comparative resignation with which she tried to bear up under her troubles. She had every luxury in life—wanted for nothing, but there were no kindred spirits with whom her youthful heart could sympathize. Love was congealed within her bosom, and it appeared to her very strange that anybody could enter into the spirit of her thoughts, or endeavor to relieve her mind from its present gloom. She had ever since her marriage been kept so strictly, that, with one or two exceptions, she had never seen a human face but her husband's, or the domestics of the house. Her husband traded between the two islands, and had left early that morning, or this very unlooked for and somewhat romantic meeting would not have taken place. Fancying the lateness of the hour might excite suspicion in some of the inmates of her dwelling, I proposed returning: she then asked me if I would accept the hospitality of her household, as I had told her the vessel in which I intended to sail for Smyrna would leave the following morning, and prevent me paying her another visit. I thanked her, and gladly availed myself of her kind offer, and we both strolled in the direction of her dwelling. The night was still, not the slightest wind stirring, and no sound to be heard save our own feet crushing the tiny shell of the beach as we walked along—then those lines of Lord Byron came vividly to me—

> "There is a dangerous stillness in that hour,
> A stillness which leaves room for the full soul
> To open all itself, without the power
> Of calling wholly back its self-control.
> The silver light, which, hallowing tree and bower,
> Sheds beauty and deep softness, o'er the whole,
> Breathes also to the heart, and o'er it throws
> A loving languor, which is not repose."

In time we reached the Villa; some Greek servants quickly

brought me some coffee and a pipe, which having enjoyed very much, I was shown to my chamber by my interesting hostess. The room appointed for me was fitted up in the most chaste and beautiful style imaginable; in the corner opposite the door was a *divan* covered with a rich colored silk, about two feet from the floor, over which hung the lightest network, to prevent any annoyance from insects, etc. The floor was inlaid with woods of different color, and every variety of figure, and was as bright as the most polished mahogany. The windows opened into a kind of Aviary of the most elegant trellis work; where birds of every variety of plumage were quietly roosting. Numbers of beautiful flowers adorned the lower parts of the windows, filling the room with delicious fragrance.

"HUBBY"

The scene from the window was lovely indeed; the bright moon creeping through the thin lattice-work, danced in a thousand fantastic forms on the curiously carved walls; occasionally through the open lattice, I could hear the gentle splash of the muffled oar of a Gondolier, bringing upon the night breeze to my grateful ears the warbling of sweet voices as it passed along—while as far as the eye could reach stretched out before me the bright blue waters. I took a whiff or two more at my pipe, and feeling somewhat drowsy, sought my novel couch, and it was not long ere I was rambling in the land of dreams.

I had not been asleep, I should think, more than an hour, when I was suddenly awakened by a loud knocking proceeding from the lower part of the house. I immediately jumped up, and, taking with me an *unloaded* pistol that I found in the room, quietly opened the door and listened. Louder and louder the knocking continued—bells were ringing in every direction—still all seemed quiet up stairs. I crept to the top of the staircase, and could from my position *see* everything without being *seen.*

Two men servants were trying, as well as they could with their eyes only half open, to unbar the door, in which they ultimately succeeded, when suddenly they were knocked down by a tall brawny savage-looking Italian, who with eyes flashing fire, cried out, "Perchè Diavolo mi faceste aspettare tanto prima d'aprire," when the foremost of the men replied "Dormivamo si profondamente, che non udimmo il vostro picchiare, se non quando vennimo svegliati dal campanello di madama." The Italian seemed a little more composed upon receiving the reply, and directing one of them to unsaddle his horse, he gave to the other a small packet, at the same time pointing up stairs in the direction of the lady's chamber. I remained unobserved in my covert, until the man had descended, when it being somewhat dark, and not having properly noted my own door, I unfortunately pounced in upon my lady, startling her greatly. Of course I was greatly embarrassed, and was bowing myself out in the best manner I could, when she motioned me to sit down, placing her finger to her mouth for me to observe silence. This room exceeded by far in beauty and elegance the one I had lately occupied; every ornament seemed either of silver or gold: delicious odors emanated from pastile burners of the most curious workmanship, and in the further end of the apartment a very beautiful marble fountain, some three or four feet in height, sent forth a bewitching little Spanish melody. In about the middle of the apartment, on a small divan of the most gorgeous colors, reclined the fair occupant of the chamber. Her black hair hung in long flowing tresses over shoulders of the most perfect symmetry, her head being lightly bound with a thin band of gold, from the centre of which glistened a large diamond.

In her hand was the letter brought by the Italian, over which she seemed to be anxiously poring. She started up suddenly, saying, "he comes home early this morning!" The letter was from her husband, and had been brought by one of his servants; something unexpected had happened on the island, calling him immediately home.

I saw evidently my stay would now be short, and therefore with a sad, sad heart prepared to take my leave. Who could have gazed on such a being of light and loveliness as this—who had told me the secrets of her heart—without feeling a pang at parting? I knew full well that that day would *for ever* end the happy hours we had passed together—that thousands of miles of water would soon roll between us! I cannot remember what took place—but never in the course of my wanderings did I so bitterly regret the hour of parting. She watched at the gateway, till the windings of the cliff prevented me seeing her more.

I left the next day,—and in a few hours we were going a good ten knots in the "George Henry," bound for Smyrna, Asia Minor.

XVI.

SMYRNA.

On the 10th of September we set sail, though not with a fair wind, for Smyrna. The day was beautiful, and a few hours found us again, far out upon the sea. On the morning of the 16th, after some days' calm, a fine breeze sprang up, about six blowing a complete gale; we hauled in studding sails, furled mainsail and jib, reefed topsails, etc. Blew a gale all night, smashing all the porter, ale, wine, and brandy we had on board. About evening the peninsula of the Morea came in sight.

On the 20th we entered the Archipelago from the westward between Cerigo and the Main; we seemed perfectly surrounded by land, passed the islands of Santarin, Nauplio, Amargo, Inolo, Syphanto, Syra, etc.

Several of these we saw very plainly, and on the island of Thermia I could with the glass count something like fifty or sixty windmills!

We then passed the islands of Ipsara and Scio.

Ipsara is celebrated as the birth-place of the Greek admiral, Canaris, the commander of the Greek fireships. On the 25th we got through the straits between Ipsara and Scio, although the winds were baffling; when well through, a fine breeze caught us, carrying us up to Smyrna Bay, having our studding sails, and every sail set that would draw.

The first remarkable place in the last mentioned bay, which claimed my attention, was a promontory called the "Iron Head."

It is on these mountains, our Captain informed me, that the much sought for Sultana raisins are cultivated. When we got abreast of these, we shaped our course along the land—mountainous, and sprinkled with the most beautiful vineyards, villas, etc., belonging to the wealthier portions of the Turks,—for another range of mountains called the "Two Brothers," which appellation they have obtained from the fact of their having two very conspicuous mounds rising higher than the rest, and of precisely the same height.

When close under these I had the first view of the beautiful country about Smyrna.

Smyrna is a city of the first rank in the Turkish Empire, and is the capital of Asia Minor, and next to Constantinople, I believe, is the largest city in Turkey.

It is beautifully situated, along the margin of a large bay, under Mount Pagus; and is the grand emporium of Levantine commerce.

The population is estimated at about 150,000, consisting of a mixture of all nations; Turks, Greeks, Jews, Armenians, Persians, Arabs, Franks, etc. The approach to the town is beautiful with the numberless towering minarets—the white domes of the mosques, the sombre-looking groves of cypress-trees, etc.

But I found upon entering it, all its beauty vanished.

We immediately obtained a pratique, having a "clean bill of health" from Malta, and of course went on shore without any difficulty. The streets are dreadfully dirty and ill-paved; hardly worth the name of alleys, and so narrow, that it would not be very difficult to shake hands from opposite windows.

I went immediately to a hotel, kept by an Italian, named Salvo Zara, where I was introduced by the Captain to my future fellow-passenger, S——, with whom I dined and passed the rest of the day.

In the morning taking with me a guide—for it is quite impossible to find your way alone in Smyrna, the innumerable twists and twinings, alleys, courts, and curious windings, rendering it impracticable—we went through some of the bazaars, gazing with delight and astonishment on the multitudes of men and women, with every variety of dress and costume, that passed and repassed me; each seeming to speak in a different tongue. Here came donkeys with huge saddles—then long trains of camels with tinkling bells, carrying heavy loads of fruit.

The house at which Lord Byron resided during his brief sojourn here was shown me in the portion of the town known as the "Frank Quarter."

The camel and dromedary are names given to two varieties of the same animal. The principal and perhaps the only sensible difference by which these two races are distinguished consists in this: that the camel has two humps upon his back, whereas the dromedary has but one; the latter, also, is neither so large nor so strong as the camel. This is the usually received opinion; but, according to some, the difference between them is not that one has two humps on its back, and the other only one; it is like the difference between a heavy cart horse and a swift riding horse. The dromedary is much lighter, swifter, and quicker in its motions, but the Arabian camel and dromedary have both only one hump, though the camels of other regions are said to have two. Of the two varieties, the dromedary is by far the most numerous, the camel being scarcely found, except in Turkey and the countries of the Levant, while the other is found spread all over the deserts of Arabia, the southern parts of Africa, Persia, Tartary, and a great part of the Eastern

Indies. Thus, the one inhabits an immense tract of country; the other, in comparison, is confined to a province: the one inhabits the sultry countries of the torrid zone; the other delights in a warm, but not a burning climate. They seem formed for those countries where shrubs are plentiful and water scarce; where they can travel along the sandy desert without being impeded by rivers, and find food at expected distances.

The camel, I am told, travels several days without drinking. In the vast deserts, where the earth is everywhere dry and sandy, where there are neither birds, beasts, nor vegetables, where nothing is seen but heaps of stone, it travels, posting forwards sometimes, I am informed, at the rate of twelve miles within the hour, without requiring drink or pasture, and is often found to go six or seven days without any sustenance whatever. The feet of this animal seem to be formed for travelling on sand, and utterly unfit for moist or marshy places; the inhabitants, therefore, find a most useful assistant in this animal, where no other could subsist; and by its means cross the deserts with safety, which would be impossible by any other mode of conveyance. Well does it merit the appellation given to it, the "Desert Ship."

I could not help noticing the great beauty of the Greek women; but, generally speaking, their forms are bad, and their feet somewhat large. The style of cap they wear is pretty; it is covered with gold or silver lace, their hair being braided around it. The Armenian women are extremely beautiful and fair; they have their own quarter of the town, and wear also a costume of their own. I went to see them worship in one of their churches. The men and women were separated by bars—kneeling and praying, thumping their foreheads pretty frequently. The women, veiled in white, kissed the priest's hand—left the church—first putting on their shoes. I then took a stroll into the Jewish quarter of the town, and was struck with the handsome appearance of the men. Such magnificent heads! studies for an artist!—large, high foreheads—aquiline nose—piercing black eye—swarthy complexion and long grey beards. The other sects seem to hold them in derision, and heap upon them all kinds of oppression and contumely.

Some of the women are very beautiful; their dress is

extremely picturesque—a girdle of magnificent gold links twisted round the waist, a fillet of gold around the head, and thick bracelets on the wrists, all of the same material.

Having brought with me a letter of introduction, from a gentleman in Boston, to Mr. L——, an American merchant, who had resided many years in Smyrna, I called at his office to present it, upon which he very politely invited me to spend a few days with him at his country house in Boujah, a beautiful little village where the American and English merchants usually spend their summer months. At about six, Mr. L. and I started from our hotel. Two very comely-looking mules, with very capacious saddles, were now brought to the door. We mounted, followed by a little Greek boy, whose province it was to drive the animal onward, by applying, and pretty smartly, too, a thick stick to his back.

Away we jolted through innumerable small streets, alleys, carts, and gateways, the boy continually crying out, "*Duer! duer!*" which my friend told me, in Yankee meant, "*Go lang!*"

Having trotted pretty rapidly, we soon reached the Turkish burial-ground, about which I will make but the briefest mention.

Wending my way through intricate and curious alleyways, streets, and zigzag windings, I suddenly came upon the burial-place of the dead. I was struck with the solemn grandeur of the place. Thousands of majestic cypress trees waved around me; the ground was literally covered with white marble tombs of all shapes and sizes, curiously carved; the greater part having a turban cut in stone at the top. It was getting quite dark, and we had progressed sufficiently far to be rid of the noise in the city. Everything still as the hearts of those now lying beneath our feet.

I turned my mule's head towards the town to observe its appearance, when lighted up—it happened to be the time of the Ramazan, or feasting month, and in the evening all is hilarity and glee—hundreds of lights glistened brightly from the tops of the different minarets, looking like crowns of variegated lamps suspended in the air. So long as the sun is in the sky, the faithful abstain wholly from eating, drinking, and sleeping; but as soon as the sun goes down, all are cheerful, nay even boisterous. We rode along until we came in sight of the summit of an old castle, standing near the site of ancient Smyrna. These walls have remained something like 2200 years! The front of the fortress was just visible, and part of the tower. The rising moon just tipped its old walls with silver, rendering the view more imposing. We jogged along slowly up, as I thought, a steep hill, when upon coming to the top, my companion turned to me and said: "Now we are some 2000 feet above the level of the sea:" so it seems we had been trudging up a mountain.

We soon found ourselves nearing the little village of Boujah; two colored lamps shone brightly from among the trees in the distance which our mules seemed to understand, for they kept up a continual gallop until we came in sight of the village.

The road for about a quarter of a mile before you enter is pretty good. As soon as we got within a stone's throw of the place, we were beset by a multitude of Greek boys, wishing to take our mules. On each side of the road—a little wider than the streets of the city—were small shops occupied by Greeks. Different colored lamps lighted up each, and at the doors were seated groups of these handsome fellows smoking long pipes, the comeliest women the sun ever shone upon, occasionally bringing them their coffee in dapper little china cups with plated bowls.

We left our mules at a little hotel, kept by the Italian of whom I have before spoken, and at the suggestion of my friend L——, took a pedestrian trip over the mountains. The night was lovely, indeed; and the view of the town of Smyrna, lit up, as it was, by a thousand variegated lights, was magnificent.

The sky studded with stars, a few faint clouds, slightly tinged with the hues of evening, lingered on the horizon, like the last incense from some mighty altar. The air was still, and breathing the odor of the wild jessamines and myrtle which clothed the side of the mountain; all was richness, splendor, and repose.

As the breeze came freshly up the mountain, our eyes roved over the glorious scene; above, the silent and glittering stars; far below, the sweep of the ocean, on which were the sails of many nations; even the deep murmur of the waves came over our ears, mingled with the softer sounds of the pipe and tamborine, the music of the hamlets.

It was besides, as I said before, the night of the Ramazan; this, all the world knows, is the only thing wanting to make a Turkish summer evening the perfection of beauty. As I was standing, I heard the evening gun fire, and the whole famous exhibition rapidly followed. Mosque after mosque blazed out in light as if it were roofed with jewels. Towers, hitherto invisible, suddenly shot up, like fixed flames, of all shapes, heights, and colors, all was glittering, glowing, and magnificent. We then strolled in the direction of Mr. L——'s dwelling. The gate was quickly opened by a pretty Greek girl, and we entered the grounds. The house stands in about the centre of the garden, and is beautifully constructed; all the rooms on the lower floor—there being no second story—and on each side, are large and commodious wings for sleeping apartments.

Mr. L. soon appeared. I was then introduced to his lady, a charming-looking Greek woman, a native of Smyrna.

I never can forget the kindness, hospitality, and attention received at the hands of this excellent family; and it affords me infinite pleasure in being thus able to record their kind-heartedness and liberality. The next day I had another view of real Asiatic scenery. On the mountain elevation you have a most extended view of the distant islands, the beautiful harbor, and the ocean. Herds of camels were grazing quietly near me, attended by the handsomest looking shepherds imaginable.

XVII.

CONSTANTINOPLE.

Having received a polite invitation from Captain Paige, formerly of Augusta, Maine, who I believe was the first to run a steamship on the Turkish waters, I accompanied him in his snug little craft to the far-famed City of the Sultan. We came to anchor in the Golden Horn about midnight. To the left we had just passed the Seven Towers, peeping out above the dark walls; everything was still, no rattling of carriages, no move of any kind. Here then burst upon my view the far-famed city of the Sultan! The night was clear, and the silvery moon shone brightly in the heavens. Groves upon groves of cypress trees followed each other in quick succession; then the bold mountain scenery, surrounding it on the Turkish as well as on the Asiatic side, giving to it a grandeur indescribable. Hundreds of glittering minarets, towering, white and majestic, their spires tipped with silver, and domes of gigantic mosques rose up before me.

Then the seraglio and harem of the Sultan were pointed out to me, consisting of palaces, rather modern than otherwise, and a very large range of rooms, looking like the cells of a prison. The wall is yet remaining, and is three miles in extent. This denotes the limit of the ancient city of Byzantium, called so when occupied by the Romans, under Constantine the Great.

The Ramazan was still kept up, and the sight of this immense city on a moonlight night was very imposing.

Thousands of variegated lamps, in the form of stars, and different kinds of flowers, trembled in the air, and the cupolas of all the mosques, illuminated so magnificently, that they seemed to spring from an ocean of variegated fire.

My eyes drank in with enthusiasm the magic of the scene before me, and my dreams that night were as fairy-like and lovely as the wondrous scenes I had that day witnessed. The next morning I, with my friend Captain Paige, (the present Commander of the "Marmora" Steamship,) went on shore early; the beautiful bay was literally covered with caiques, darting like arrows every minute, filled with veiled women and men of all nations. They are long narrow wherries, covered in the most elegant manner, adorned with golden bronze; but are so lightly built as to be in constant danger of upsetting, when you have to sit down at the bottom and endeavor to preserve the necessary equilibrium, by inflexions of the body, either to the right or left, as may be requisite from the motion of the waves.

They have the most delicious divans, cushions, etc., on which to recline, and are rowed by Turks dressed in the whitest linen, fitting close to the skin, having full sleeves, full linen trowsers coming down to the knee, and on the head a red cloth scull-cap, with long flowing silk tassel.

It is estimated that there are over 90,000 of these fairy-like boats on the Bosphorus. The hire is very reasonable, on account of their great number; you go a considerable distance for one piastre, or about two cents.

We went first to Pera, and put up at the Hotel de l'Europe, kept by an Italian. It is an excellently conducted house, and I would advise all travellers to go there: it is also exclusively the dwelling of the Franks.

The Hotel is situated in a long avenue called the Corso of Pera, from the windows of the front room of which may be witnessed many extraordinary sights, whilst the view from the back presents one of the most magnificent panoramas in the world. Underneath, to the left, stretches out before you the beautiful harbor of Top-hana; to the right is Galeta, built, I believe, by the Genoese; still beyond, the Golden Horn, upon whose waters many hundreds of colossal ships, from all parts of the globe, are quietly resting. Passing them you will see numbers of little gilt caiques cutting through the waves like dolphins.

On the opposite shore lies Constantinople, with its pointed Seraglio Tower, its beautiful cupolas, and its thousands of slim minarets peering upwards in the air. Across the Bosphorus, in another quarter of the world, yet hardly ten minutes' trip, lies Scutari, with all its groves of cypresses. The mountain chains of Asia are seen in the distance, and the beautiful "Prince Islands," raising their heads from the bosom of the Sea of Marmora. Taking a walk through the bazaars, I saw a large crowd collected at the corner of one of the streets, and upon inquiring of my companion, found out that one of the celebrated "story tellers" of Constantinople was delighting his numerous auditory with the recital of some extraordinary legend or other.

The man was raised some feet above his listeners, and seated in the same manner a tailor would be on his bench. The story seemed, from the great attention paid the speaker, to be of a highly interesting nature, for at its conclusion the astonishment of the multitude seemed great indeed. My friend translated to me, as we stood and listened, the somewhat extraordinary legend of the old Turk.

It was nearly in the following words:—

"In the town of Rabdju there lived, some hundred years ago, a Greek fisherman, who had amassed a goodly fortune by constantly trading in the islands of the Archipelago and buying up the loveliest Circassian women for the harems of the Sultan; he, besides this, owned more caiques than any other trader in the province. He had been from his earliest youth passionately fond of music, and having resided the former part of his life in some of the Neapolitan cities, had acquired a considerable taste for the science, and on all occasions had been an eager listener when anything musical was going on. He bought himself a guitar, and to the study of his instrument he devoted all his leisure time. As he grew up, he became more and more attached to his favorite amusement, and having amassed a very snug fortune by his trafficking, he married, and retired to pass the remainder of his days in the quiet little town of Rabdju, near the Gulf of Lepanto.

"Here he had nothing to disturb him in his devotedness to his favorite pastime, and as his children grew up their ears became familiar with the different Italian airs he would be constantly playing to them. One air in particular seemed to charm him above all others, and when, as the sun sank in the rosy west, and soft twilight followed, the old Greek would wander forth with one or two of his children to some favorite spot, and draw forth from his old rusty-looking instrument the tones that pleased him so well in his boyhood, his eyes would fill with tears, and for a time he seemed lost in thought.

"The effect of the music seemed to enervate him so completely, that it was deemed advisable to keep the guitar from his sight.

"He lingered a few years, and died very suddenly at an advanced age, and at his death it was found that he had locked up or hidden all his treasure, consisting of gold, silver, and precious stones, in some place unknown to any of his wives or children.

"Great was the consternation, great was the disappointment and vexation of his household; he not having left enough to pay the actual expenses of his burial.

"At last the youngest boy bethought him of an experiment—he really believed he could awaken his dead father!

"Accordingly, he took down the old instrument that had been forgotten for so long a time, and with streaming eyes commenced to sing and play over the body the air which was the favorite of the old man when living. Hour after hour passed—still no sign of recognition. But the little fellow continued, until, at last, watching steadily, he fancied the slightest color possible tinged the cheek of the dead man!

"Was it imagination? No! The ghastly hue of death had left the face—the lips quivered—the eyelids opened—the eye glared boldly around, and tears flowed in streams down the old man's cheeks. Life had indeed returned; the object was obtained. The old man lived sufficiently long to tell the hiding-place of his wealth."

Thus ended the tale of the "story teller" of Constantinople. Having brought letters of introduction to an English gentleman, who had resided some thirty years in Stamboul, and who offered me every kindness and attention, I had opportunities of seeing a good deal of the city and its delightful environs, during the short time I proposed staying; and I found in his son a very kind and gentlemanly companion, who was by my side constantly, and with whom I made several delightful excursions.

Having expressed a great wish to make a trip to the "Sweet Waters," I, with my friend, hired a caique, and comfortably reclining in the bottom of the boat on a very agreeable divan, I watched the magnificent landscapes that on all sides surrounded me. It is situated on the shores of the Bosphorus, near an Asiatic castle, in a very beautiful meadow, through which the river meanders. The Sultan has a country residence here, to which he retires in the summer time. On arriving, the scene was novel, picturesque, and beautiful.

The meadows and hills shone in a fresh verdant dress, and through the tall cypresses glittered the Sultan's splendid kiosk. Here were hundreds of Turkish men and women seated together in picturesque groups upon the grassy carpet.

We had taken with us some provisions, intending to remain one or two days, should the wind or weather prove agreeable. We therefore unpacked our eatables, and having drunk a little sherbet, left our caique, leaving the men to take care of her till our return.

The beautiful scenery surrounding me on all sides, I shall never forget. After a long walk, we returned to our boat, intending to proceed still further up the Bosphorus.

Having received an invitation from the American Consul, to attend the celebration of the disinterment of the remains of Commodore Porter, the late American Minister at the Turkish Court, I went on board the steamship "Eni Dunia," chartered by the resident Americans for that purpose.

The Commodore had died some nine months previously, and the body had been kept in spirits, in a large stone coffin; a grave had been temporarily dug for its reception in his own garden, near his summer mansion at St. Stephano.

The U. S. brig "Truxton" had been sent by the Government expressly to carry the remains of the gallant Commodore to his native land, and now lay in the Bosphorus for that purpose.

The party assembled on board the steamer, was very numerous, comprising the foreign ministers of the different countries, the officers of H. B. M. ship "Devastation" and the U. S. brig "Truxton" with the Commander, Lieutenant Upsher, and the resident American and English merchants. We left Stamboul about 11 o'clock. It was glorious day, and after a two hours' trip, we anchored at St. Stephano.

This is a beautiful little island eighteen miles from Constantinople, occupied by Greek and American families, and also a few Turks.

We walked in the direction of the late Commodore's dwelling. The old mansion looked gloomy indeed, shaded as it was by tall dark cypress trees. The house had been closed some time, the portion of his family residing with him at the time of his death having left for Galeta.

We then proceeded to the place of interment. As we neared the vault, we could see the American flag half mast high, waving over the place, a more lovely spot (close to the beautiful sea of Marmora) could not have been chosen; flowers of all kinds were glowing near his grave; roses in full bloom were sending forth their odor, mingled with that of numberless wild plants. Presently came about twenty of the sailors of the Truxton, marching slowly along. Arrived at the grave, they waited for the word of the First Lieutenant; at the given signal the immense coffin was hoisted from its temporary abode; the Commodore's regulation hat was then placed upon it, over which was thrown the Flag of the Union.

The cortége marched in the following order: First, the Deputies of the principal Legations; second, a piquet from the Truxton; then a body of marines, preceded by the band playing the dead march, followed by the Protestant clergy; next came the coffin, carried by twenty American sailors; then the Ministers of Sardinia and Spain, the Chargé d'Affaires of Sweden, Naples, and Belgium supporting the pall; then came the relations of the deceased; after them the American, English, and Russian Officers, Merchants, etc.; the sailors of the Truxton bringing up the rear. When arrived at the stairs, the cortége went on board the steamer; a guard of honor was placed around the coffin, and we quitted the peaceful shores of St. Stephano, one of the sweetest spots in the world.

When we arrived opposite the Seraglio point, the Truxton fired a salute of seventeen guns, which was answered by the English frigate Devastation. At five we anchored near the Truxton, and the body was soon placed on board.

Thus finished this interesting ceremony, which was conducted throughout with the greatest decorum, and the utmost solemnity; all alike, from the highest officer to the meanest seamen, seemed deeply impressed with the spirit of the scene.

The next day I, with my friend Churchill, went to see the "Thousand and one columns." The entrance lay down flights of steps, some hundreds of which we had to descend ere we reached the bottom of the subterranean caverns. The place was damp in the extreme; thousands of miserable, pale-looking Turks were here spinning silk. In olden times this place was used to carry water to its inhabitants. We were shown through the place by one of the spinners for the small sum of five piastres, with which he seemed mightily pleased.

We then went to the Tomb of the late Sultan Mahmoud; but to attempt to give any idea of the magnificence of this place would be ridiculous; I will simply mention that the tomb *alone* cost $500,000.

I had several opportunities of seeing the present Sultan, but, wishing to get a nearer peep, I took a caique, that I might see him as he crossed from his palace on his way to the mosque. Every Friday he visits a different one, either in Constantinople or the suburbs. Not knowing to which one he would direct his steps on this occasion, I went to a coffee-house in the vicinity of the Porte, whence I could conveniently make my observations. All was animation around the Seraglio; black and white eunuchs, court officials, and the Turkish soldiers were all in motion; the latter formed a long chain from the gate of the Seraglio to the chosen mosque. At some distance from each other military bands were placed.

The Sultan soon appeared, mounted on a very handsome white Arabian horse. The young prince has rather a fine head, but his face is devoid of the slightest expression, somewhat of a pale cast, large dark eyes, aquiline nose, and a very slight mustache and imperial. He was dressed in a blue frock military cut coat, blue trowsers, with red stripe, black French leather boots, whereto small brass spurs were attached. By his side he had a costly scimetar, and the simple red *fez*, with a blue tassel, was on his head.

A long suite of pages and court domestics, among whom was recognised the never-failing pipe-bearer, etc., closed the procession. The Sultan seemed to greet the people very courteously.

I was invited in the evening to the house of my young friend, Churchill. His father (an Englishman by birth) having resided many years in the Turkish capital, and who had married a Greek lady, by whom he had several children, lived quite in the Greek style. His daughters sang and played delightfully, and I was not a little surprised to see on the piano an *English* copy of the far-famed song, "*Woodman, spare that Tree!*" which one of these Greek ladies sang to me! The popularity of this song is unprecedented. There were several other pieces of music I noticed published in New York—among them songs by Charles Horn, and a beautiful little ballad by H. C. Watson, entitled, "There's a spot of earth more dear." It seemed funny to hear these songs warbled forth, very sweetly too, by a bewitching Greek girl.

The carriages used by Turkish ladies, to pay distant visits (the men are all equestrians), afford a singular spectacle. Their vehicles are called, as with us, Kotschi (coaches) or aroba. The box is fixed firmly upon the axle, and, as well as the wheels, is variously painted, and richly gilt, and sometimes covered with red cloth. At the sides there are closed blinds, which sometimes open to let the curious Frank see that an interesting female reposes within upon comfortable pillows, and the thin veil will not unfrequently wave about, in order that she may do execution with her dark gazelle-like eyes. The entrance of the carriage is generally from behind, where a small gilt ladder hangs to facilitate the ascent and descent of its fair burden.

Two oxen or buffaloes draw the set-out, and are very strongly accoutred. On the brow of each hangs a square, yellow shining plate; between the horns there is a smaller one, with trio vari colored horse's tails, and frequently I have seen both the head and neck of the animals decorated with garlands of flowers. The coachman walks, guiding his steeds with a sharply pointed stick; and, by way of guard, several domestics, armed to the teeth, follow the carriage.

I was strolling in the afternoon through one of the graveyards in Pera, admiring the beauty and variety of the different tombs, when, in the distance, I saw a funeral procession. As it is probable that my readers might like to have a slight idea of the manner of burial adopted by the Turks, I will endeavor to describe what I witnessed:—

Four men carried the corpse, which was covered with a variously colored cloth upon a bier. Numbers of Turks, each with a branch of cypress in one hand, while in the other rested the inseparable pipe, followed. The Imam preceded, occasionally reciting sentences from the Koran. When they arrived at the grave, the covering was removed, and the body deposited quite *naked.* The Imam prayed; the assembly shouted; and the grave was filled with earth. The mourners stuck their branches of cypress around, and a belief prevails if but *one* of these keep green, the deceased has gone into the cheerful paradise promised by his prophet Mahomet to the faithful.

There is a sect here called the "Dervises," and the extraordinary style of their worship amused me highly. They practise every Tuesday and Friday at noon, from one to two o'clock, in a small chapel near the Russian palace, and any Frank is allowed a free admittance.

There is a round box in the middle of the room; they have also another circle surrounded by a balustrade. On the outside of this the populace repeat their prayer. In the inner circle the Dervises collect, clothed in a long dark woollen raiment. They wear also on their heads a high woollen cap, slightly resembling a sugar loaf. Their countenances are uniformly pale, but of a beautiful expression. A short sermon is preached by their priest, after which a melodious song from one of the Dervises is given, sometimes accompanied by flutes. They then move in couples round the circle, their heads bent to the ground, under the guidance of two leaders, whose heads are bound round with a white band, as a mark of dignity. They turn three or four times round, whilst the two leaders squat down in Turkish fashion, in that part of the chapel nearest to Mecca. Then begins their singular dance; casting away their robes they stand up in broad dark green garments, reaching to their knees. One of them immediately stepped forth with closed eyes, and spreading his arms out, turned upon his right knee with great rapidity; a second then performed the same evolution; then others, until the whole company were twirling around like a set of mad people. During this motion, the air spreading out their gowns, gave them the most ludicrous appearance imaginable. This lasted about ten minutes, when suddenly they stood still and firm, and cast themselves to the earth, their faces all being turned towards Mecca. One leader, during the ceremony, went round to see if the gentlemen all twisted upon the right heel! At last, they all kiss the hand of their leaders, and march quietly away.

It being the time of the Ramazan, I could not obtain admission to any of the mosques, but walked round the exterior of almost all of them. St. Sophia (the oldest mosque in Turkey) does not produce a very agreeable impression; a low wall surrounds the colossal temple, and incloses also an ante-court, decorated with flowers, fountains, and cypresses. The chief dome rises from a heap of pilasters, cupolas, and other ornaments. The dingy-looking appearance of the walls suits the character of this venerable building.

XVIII.

STREET SCENES.

Taking a walk through the Bazaars, I saw a crowd collected, and found that a poor fellow was about to expiate his life that day by the summary method of decapitation; and never having seen the "modus operandi" of the Turks in this particular, I accompanied the crowd; and as it may be interesting to some of my readers, I give them the benefit of my observations. When a man has been killed, his friends lodge a complaint against the murderer, who is, without loss of time, dragged to the Mehkemmay, or Court of Justice of the district or parish where the crime was perpetrated, and a report is immediately drawn up, stating the particulars of the complaint, on which document he is instantly sent to prison. His trial subsequently takes place before the Grand Vizier, and if it be proved that he designedly, and without sufficient provocation, committed the murder, he is forwarded, with the whole details of his case, to the Sheikh ul Islam, who gives a decree declaring that an individual convicted of such a crime is, by the sacred law, condemned to suffer death by decapitation. Should there be any extenuating circumstances, for which the friends of the culprit imagine that due allowance has not been made, they draw up a petition to the Sultan, demanding a new trial. The matter is then submitted to a supreme Council of Justice, and if he be again condemned, the heir or next akin of the deceased is questioned as to whether he demands Kussass or Deeyet.

Kussass is the law of retaliation—blood for blood. Deeyet is the price of blood, or pecuniary compensation in lieu of it. This is generally one thousand drachms of silver, or near 1500 dollars, which, being a large sum, the authorities may, in the event of its being accepted in lieu of the life of the culprit, fix suitable periods for the payment, the culprit remaining in prison until the whole amount is paid. It is seldom taken unless in cases where the deceased has left a young family. for whose support the money is required.

If the heir be an adult, he usually spurns the idea of receiving gold as the price of the blood of his father or brother, and consequently insists upon the forfeiture of his life.

All the needful preliminaries having been settled, and the murderer condemned, the Grand Vizier (or the Sultan, should he have been petitioned on the subject) signs an order for the execution of the criminal. This order is sent to the Governor of the district, who decrees it over to the chief executioner, to whom he gives his verbal instructions as to the time and place of execution. The executioner has a copy of the sentence drawn out in large legible characters. The time fixed being arrived, he takes with him the order for the execution, on which the jailor delivers his prisoner. The executioner is accompanied by several assistants, who knock off the chains of the culprit, tie his arms behind him, and then he is immediately marched forward, without being informed for what purpose.

The day was hot in the extreme, and I had already walked some distance, following the immense crowd collected.

The unhappy man, thus secured and surrounded, and hurried along to the place of execution, near, I was told, where the crime had been committed, and in a thoroughfare through which thousands were constantly passing, he looked the very picture of wretchedness and despair. I shall never forget the look he gave, when suddenly he was told to kneel down! and if previously he had any doubts as to his fate, they were now quickly removed. Resistance was in vain: all hope had fled, and the wretched man did as he was ordered. His eyes were then bound, and the executioner stood for some moments, having already unsheathed his sword, which was straight, long, very broad, and exceedingly sharp. He then assumed an attitude, clenched his teeth, and having made two or three flourishes with his horrid weapon, raised his arm so as to bring his hand to his own left ear, and with the edge, close to the hilt, struck a tremendous blow on the left side of the neck of his victim, just above the shoulders. The man made horrid butchery of his work, and the poor fellow's head was hanging by a portion of the muscle when the executioner seized his hair, and completed the cruel task as well as he could. The head of the culprit rolled in the dust, and no sound was heard save the gurgling of the blood!

The body was then laid on its back, the head being placed under the right arm; the copy of the sentence was pinned on the body, which was then left "as a warning to others."

A thief or a burglar is hanged. His trial and condemnation take place in due form, and the executioners lead him forth in the same way. My friend Churchill described to me the singular method the Turks have of hanging. On reaching the spot chosen for his death, a rope with a sliding knot is thrown over his neck, and drawn pretty closely, the other end is passed over a hook, beam, or very large nail. The signal being given, two or three of the executioner's assistants haul upon it, the executioner himself assisting by lifting the culprit off the ground. The proper height having been attained (and very little suffices), the executioner with a thick stick strikes the rope over the head to tighten it, and adjusts the knot in a suitable position. He then pins, as before, the sentence on the breast, and his task is complete. He departs, and a guard is left to prevent any one from interfering with the body.

The most shocking punishment is reserved for Haidoots, or highway robbers—viz. impalement; which operation always takes place on a cross-road, and is performed, as nearly as I can recollect, as follows:—

The packsaddle of a horse is placed on the ground, and rendered firm by being put against a tree, stone, or some other support. This species of saddle has, before and behind, cross bars, to which are attached the loads. The felon is put with his face downwards, and his neck secured on the fore cross bars. Already stripped of everything but his shirt, whilst he lies in this position the executioner makes a cut with his knife, and applies a strong styptic to prevent the flowing of blood. The stake, which may be eight or nine feet long, and is sharply pointed at the end, is then introduced, and beaten out with a heavy mallet, until it appears through the upper part of the body.

My informant told me that only a few years ago thirteen or fourteen of these robbers were impaled at Adrianople. He was an eye-witness of the scene, and in one case he told me the stick came out at the back of the neck, in another through the chest, in two or three through a shoulder, in one through the throat! and in one instance through the top of the head!! He told me, however, that every one of the victims had first been strangled, so that they did not suffer afterwards, though the punishment appears so dreadful. They were formerly set upon the stake alive, and I heard of a case in which a man was at night removed from his stake by his friends, and none of the vital parts having been touched, he lived many years afterwards, but never subsequently stood straight.

But executions in Turkey are now, I am told, quite rare, and it would seem so, for the one I witnessed created a greater sensation than it would have done in America.

I went with my friend on board several very beautiful steamboats belonging to the Turkish Government; one in particular, the "Monarch," Capt. Howes, is very large and elegant. She was built in Glasgow expressly for the Government, and is employed in carrying troops to the different islands. There are also many large Austrian and French steamers constantly running to and fro.

After strolling through the grave-yards at Scutari, I returned to the city about eight, and slept on board the "Eni Dunia" steamer.

The next day I proceeded with my friend to the "Slave Market." It consists of a quadrangular edifice, including a square area of nearly two hundred feet, and is surrounded with rooms. Long platforms raised from the ground are in front, and you ascend steps, making a kind of colonnade. We entered by a gate, built in a high dark wall, leading to the market of female slaves. Not far from the entrance stood some young negroes, about fifteen years of age, but scantily furnished with clothing. Some old Turks seemed occupied in closely inspecting the luxurious figures of these poor creatures, whom the slave-dealer seemed to be recommending very highly. The place was excessively dirty. The price usually given for a young Circassian is about 7000 piastres, or five hundred dollars, and for a black intended to do servant's work, about eighty dollars.

We then walked through some of the bazaars, very much larger and on a more magnificent scale than those of Smyrna. They consist of many very intricate passages, and I should have found it difficult, had I been alone, to have made my way out again. The booths of which the alleys are formed, are divided with great order, so that in each series, wares of only one kind are to be met with.

I was interested greatly in the beautiful magazines of arms and pipes—but the shawl bazaar surpasses in richness and elegance anything I had ever witnessed. Cloths of the most delicate texture dazzle the eye with the brilliancy of their colors. The Turks are very simple in their mode of bargaining, they ask but one price, and seem to say in the language of Shakspeare "If you will take it—so; if not, adieu, and for my love I pray you wrong me not." The Jews and Armenians compose a great portion of the population of Constantinople. It is easy to perceive the contempt in which the Jews are held by the Turks, exposed continually, as they are, to all sorts of ill treatment and harsh abuse, in which abuse they are joined sometimes by the Christians residing there.

I took passage the next day in the French man-of-war steamer Pericles for Smyrna. We arrived in the Dardanelles about noon, where we were detained some hours; had a view of Sestos and Abydos. At the latter place we stopped to take some Turks and their women on board. The women were all closely veiled; no part of the face being visible, except the tip of the nose. We soon passed the Hellespont, only a mile and a half in width.

This bay is, I believe, the narrowest part of the Dardanelles, and is commanded on each side with extensive forts, batteries, &c., for a very long distance, giving it a formidable and warlike appearance. The scenery of the shores, and the many incidents of fable and history associated with these places, give them peculiar enchantment.

We arrived at Smyrna the next day.

After a very delightful run, I found myself once again in the "City of Figs," and I thought if those at home, who were so fond of devouring this much-prized fruit, could have been with me to witness the process of packing, they would not eat them with quite so much relish.

Up a long and dirty alley-way on each side were seated on the bare ground numbers of the dirtiest and lowest order of Greeks, men, women, boys, and girls, some picking, others stamping and pressing, the freshly-picked fruit into the "drums." With their bare and dirty feet and dirtier hands, they squeeze the fruit into the boxes, moistening and assisting its packing with an occasional stream of saliva from their filthy mouths. The figs are piled up like so many tons of coals, and are shovelled about and handled with little or no regard to care or cleanliness. The packers remain from morning till night in this position, and appear never to tire in their work. But by the time the voyage is over, and the figs are displayed on the tables of the rich as a bonne bouche or dessert after dinner, covered with the nice crisp coating of sugar, the method of packing is not inquired into or cared for, and they slip down as smoothly as if just plucked from the tree.

The next day I took with me a guide, an Algerine Jew who I found spoke a little English, and, mounting our donkeys, proceeded to the ruins of the old castle I had passed on the previous day. We ascended the hill without much difficulty. Upon arriving at the entrance of the building, I perceived, seated on the ground, some half dozen savage-looking fellows, smoking long, dirty-looking pipes, while some were cooking an extraordinary kind of stuff in a queer-looking iron bowl. I went to my guide, wishing to know if it would be safe to pass, understanding from several in Smyrna that robbers very frequently secreted themselves in and about the place, knowing that it is sought after by all travellers.

My guide told me there was no occasion for any alarm, and asking me for a few cigars, offered a bundle to the foremost of the men, who seemed quite pleased with the present. I could not help looking at the handsome fellows who had excited my suspicion. They were all very much sunburnt, had large black eyes, and teeth of perfect whiteness; a long and queerly-cut moustache covered their lips, which, when their faces were not in repose, made them look doubly savage.

Their singular dress pleased me much—a jacket of red-green velvet, fitting close to the waist, with full sleeves, open all the way down; over this they wore a red fly jacket, thrown loosely over the shoulder; a thick shawl belt circled the waist, from which the hilts of a pair of old-fashioned pistols peeped out, with the silver-hilted handle of a large-sized dagger; full trowsers of white linen came to their knees, their legs being quite bare; jauntily put on their heads, was a cap of red cloth, having a long silk tassel hanging therefrom. A herd of rams was quietly grazing at the old castle entrance, guarded by a ferocious-looking dog, who, upon seeing me, began to bark and move uneasily, but upon getting a pretty smart kick from one of the men, he quietly lay down, leaving us to pass by without interruption.

We entered through an old archway. Immediately to the right I noticed a small stone building, with a doorway and two steps at its entrance. It was an unoccupied inclosure, and contained a small ruin of an altar, with some steps leading to it, resting against the wall. This place is believed to have been the site of one of the "seven churches" of Asia. The walls were completely covered, from top to bottom, with the initials or names of different *distinguished* travellers, who had wandered amid these ruins from all parts of the globe. Among them I noticed the euphonious one of "John Smith, Penobscot, Maine!" and several of his relations. Nothing but the bare walls of the castle are remaining. Under the ground are innumerable vaults, which in olden time supplied water to the inmates. There is, also, a subterranean passage cut through to the city, but it is now stopped up, some people having lost their lives in attempting to reach the city by it, in consequence of the impurity of the atmosphere. I carried away with me some pieces of the wall and pavement of the chapel, and after remaining the better part of the day in and about the ruins, I mounted my donkey and returned to the city.

Having received a polite invitation from Mr. L. to accompany himself and wife to the opera—it being the first night of the season—I soon found myself quietly seated in a private box, listening to a new opera by Donizetti.

The bills were headed thus—

Aviso Teatrale.
Programma.
De llo spettacolo con cue verra aperta la stagione.
Teatrale di quest anno la sero del 30 Ottobre 1843.
Roberto Devreux.
Opera in musica del maestro
Gaetano Donizetti.
le parole sonno del.

The overture was very beautiful, and was played by the band splendidly. The singers did full justice to this lovely opera. The primo tenore had a song in the second act—which is given in prison—of such touching sweetness, and with such exquisite feeling, that the whole audience was in tears. It was a treat indeed. The theatre is rather small, having a parquette, and a first and second tier of private boxes. The price of admission is ten piastres, and thirty for a *seat* in a private box. They perform three times a week.

On the following day, having heard a great deal of the Turkish baths, I resolved to try their virtues for myself.

I accordingly went to the best one I could find in the city. I first entered a room, by the walls of which the most splendid divans are placed for repose; this arrangement seemed quite suited to the sensual character of the orientals. Numerous bathers, entirely naked, with the exception of a thin apron round their waist, and heavy wooden sandals on their feet, with the domestic of the bath, equipped in the same manner, were standing round. We then went into a spacious saloon of moderate temperature: after having stayed a little time, we were led into another room, still hotter: here I felt very faint—as every one does the first time one of these baths is taken. I got over it soon, and presently found myself in the last and hottest yet. Perspiration ran down me in streams—after I had been in five minutes, the sensation was delicious.

The ceiling of this room was an arched cupola, furnished with a multitude of windows; the walls and floor were of the finest marble; a hot, damp atmosphere fills the entire saloon. This is produced by water being sprinkled upon a highly heated floor. One thinks it impossible to bear this excessive heat at first; but the Turks speedily accustom themselves thereto. In the centre is a square marble elevation, less hot than the floor itself. Upon this the bather sits, and the attendant, whose hands are covered with rough woollen gloves, rubs and kneads the whole body down to the toes with great agility. A tap on the neck is the signal that this part of the ceremony is over.

I was then conducted to a niche (several of which surround the saloon) supplied with urns, from which hot or cold water can be procured at pleasure. My attendant covered me with soaps of every variety of scent, until I resembled a huge pillar of blancmange. After calling out lustily to the fellow to pump on me, or I should lose my eyes—the soap having penetrated somewhat—and he not having the most distant idea about what I was talking, *I* seized the cock, when in my flurry I turned the *hot* water on my head and shoulders, instead of the cold. Here the Turk gave a shriek, reverberating through the whole building, and *I* a spring that left all past and future vaulters entirely in the shade. The poor fellow beckoned to me to come back; and having pumped on me for some time, rubbed me down, placed a turban of towels round my head, and a piece of flannel round my body, and, having first put on my wooden shoes, returned to the first-mentioned room, I reclined upon one of the beautiful divans, where coffee and a pipe were soon brought to me.

The exhaustion that now succeeds—the species of tranquillity of soul and body—exceeds everything in its sensual voluptuousness. Thus an hour or more is passed, until this exhaustion is succeeded by a new energy, and a freshly excited state.

In front of all the baths, as before the mosques, an immense quantity of slippers and boots are always to be found.

All the Turks leave their boots or shoes behind, that they may not soil the carpets or variegated Egyptian mats, which are usually spread on the mosques and other elegant apartments; they enter with merely their leather sandals, generally attached to the pantaloons.

There are several very good billiard rooms in the Frank quarter of the town, and some prettily fitted up cafés on the

"*Marina.*" This is a promenade for both sexes during the summer evenings, and is generally well filled.

The vessel in which I intended to sail for Boston being ready for sea, I prepared to take my leave of the many kind friends I had met with during my short sojourn in this delightful part of the world; and accordingly on the 31st of October we left the good city of Smyrna, in the barque "George Henry," Captain Michael Watson, bound for Boston, Mass. On the 4th of November we found ourselves in the Ionian Sea—saw the land of Greece for the last time—and, with a fair wind, we were soon in the Mediterranean.

On the 7th of the month I had a splendid view of Mount Etna, and distinctly saw the snow on its summit.

Without entering into the minute particulars of a long and very dangerous passage, I will simply state that on the 28th of December we sprung a leak, and several thousand drums of figs were thrown overboard to lighten the vessel. We, however, through the goodness of Providence, and the skilfulness of our Captain—than whom a better sailor or a better man never walked—reached Boston on the 4th of January.

The danger in which we had been involved immediately preceding our arrival enhanced doubly the joy of once again treading solid ground. Our vessel attracted a good deal of attention, on account of her weather-beaten appearance, and curiosity was on tiptoe to see those who had braved with her the perils of the sea. Many came to congratulate us on our safe arrival, and one, knowing the length of time we had been out of fresh meat, was considerate enough to bring with him a large quantity for all hands. I think nothing that I have since tasted, has had the peculiarly rich and indescribable flavor of *that* beefsteak.

We went in the ship's boat on shore—the cold was excessive—the snow thick upon the ground—and the trees covered with icicles! How different this from the sunny and luxurious clime so recently left behind! The remembrance drew from me a heartfelt sigh, though probably my chattering teeth and shivering limbs had something to do with it.

A cheerful fire, and well-known and friendly faces, however, soon began to exert its genial influence, and when I entered the old "Tremont House," and was so cordially greeted by its jolly host, I felt rejoiced in once again being safely housed in the land of my adoption.

XIX.

AT THE FOOT-LIGHTS IN BOSTON.

STROLLING along Washington street on a cold morning in January, I was accosted by Mr. James G. Maeder, the well known composer, who, welcoming me back, remarked that I was just the "boy" he wanted for his opera that he was about to produce in Boston. Now, at the moment I had not the slightest intention of again appearing in public —but the state of my finances (I having about five piastres in my pocket when I landed) was such, that I had to go to work at something immediately. Accordingly after a little reflection, I accepted my friend's offer, and tarried in the city of notions some two weeks, having made my bow to a Boston audience in the opera of the "Peri," I taking the part of "Razlecroft the Wizard," and I believe I may say with considerable success.

XX.

AT HOME.

ARRIVING in New York once again in the month of March, 1844, with very little money, and without any fixed purpose or intention, it was somewhat refreshing to be greeted very cordially one evening by a gentleman, to whom I had been introduced one night at the Olympic, with the request that I would dine with him, and accompany him afterwards to the Park Theatre.

Upon his inquiring as to what my intentions, pursuits, or occupation, were for the future, and finding my answers extremely vague and indefinite, he invited me to call at his office at the City Hall, on the following day—the County Clerk's, I believe, Mr. James Connor then officiating in that capacity.

Here, then, in a little dark room—a sort of "tank," I was once again ensconced, assisting my friend B. H. J. in recording, etc., generally winding up our day's labor, which ended at four, by adjourning to "Windust's" in Park Row, and having a good dinner.

It was in one of those cozy little "boxes" that I first had the pleasure of being introduced to Mr. James T. Brady, who, through all my ups and downs, vicissitudes and changes, has remained my steadfast, firm, and cherished friend. My slender income was slightly augmented, by a situation I obtained in the choir of St. Thomas's Church, I receiving $200 a year as the "basso" thereof. Austin Phillips was the organist, and the singers, Mrs. Edward Loder, Miss Mary Taylor, Mr. Henry C. Watson, and myself.

The summer of this year was passed delightfully, I having been appointed "Coxswain" of the boat "Halcyon," owned conjointly by Mr. Jarvis, Mr. Brady, Mr. Thompson, and Mr. Sam. Jarvis.

We would leave the foot of Christopher street at about six o'clock, and pull up to the "Abbey," then kept by Van Ransellier, who would provide for the hungry oarsmen a superb supper—returning home by the "light of the moon," and enjoying to our hearts' content the cool night breezes, and the magnificent scenery of the glorious Hudson.

My friend Mr. J—— had hinted to me the probability of my obtaining a situation in Mr. Brady's office, should he be appointed "Counsel to the Corporation,"—accordingly the reader can judge of my delight, upon seeing one morning in the journals of the day, that he was the gentleman selected for that office.

XXI.

OH! LAW!

It was then in the month of June, 1845, that I found myself, the appointed clerk to the "Counsel of the Corporation," seated at a snug little table, at No. 10 Wall street—the name of the firm was then "Brady and Maurice."

The four years that I remained in this office were certainly passed by me most delightfully—and in looking back through the vista of years, after my world-wide wanderings, and the variety of my pursuits,—I cling with the greatest tenacity to some interesting scenes and incidents that occurred during the four years of my legal apprenticeship.

XXII.

THINGS AT "BRADY AND MAURICE'S."

My station was near the door, and it was reserved for me to answer the inquiries of clients, and to inform them, or not, as to the whereabouts of the head of the firm.

Sometimes they presented a heterogeneous and motley group, and the odor on a warm summer's day was not of the most delicate flavor, but they certainly had the faculty of enduring longer " waits" than I had ever known in my theatrical career.

Now the " Governor," as I used to call him, was not *quite* so hard to find as now, but I must confess that there *was* a degree of irregularity about his " arrival" and "departure," that sometimes operated very sensibly upon the nerves of the anxious " clients," and rendered my duties very perplexing.

Occasionally some very (to me) amusing incidents took place.

One old man named Smith, who first attracted my attention by the extraordinary cut of his clothes, and hat, presented himself, in somewhat the following style, once every other day, for about four years; and to this day I never knew—*and I'm sure he didn't*—what he came for—or why he so patiently and silently waited for so many hours, in the vain expectation of being gladdened by a sight of Mr. B.

The door would slowly open, and by the time I had looked up, I saw nothing but the back of a man, that seemed all hat and coat, the tails almost touching his heels. His hat, which bore the marks of age very strongly, and looked as if it had been as often sat upon as worn on the head, was drawn far over the face, resting upon the end of a large and very red nose, that seemed constantly requiring the application of a very dirty spotted cotton pocket-handkerchief. The coat was closely buttoned to the throat, but hung very loosely on his figure, giving the impression that he had either fallen away very materially, or that it had belonged to his great-grandfather. The cuffs, which bore strong evidence of their being used when the handkerchief was in the laundry, entirely covered his hands; and his trowsers, which fitted his legs very tightly, and were of the oldest " cut," upon his taking a seat, retreated far up his legs, revealing a pair of very dirty socks, and a half-boot, that would have been a good companion for " Boss Richard's" in Chatham street.

Well, he would give a slight puff or two, if it was summer, or a shiver if it was winter, put his hat under the chair, and sit, and sit, and sit, saying nothing, looking at nobody, and apparently lost in thought, or endeavoring to get at the cause of his difficulty.

His case was one, that at the time I took a great interest in, partly from the fact of my utter ignorance of its merits, and partly from the fun we all had, whenever old Smith came to see the "Counsellor."

I was greatly interested in the case of a poor little Irishwoman, long before I was informed by Mr. B—— of the nature of her repeated visits; not only the neatness of her costume, the punctuality of her appearance, generally, upon the Saturday of each and every week of the year, but the persistency with which she seemed to cling to the desire of her heart, aroused my sympathies.

The snow would be thick on the ground, and the cold intense, still the door would quietly open, and with her pretty face glowing with cold, and the excitement of her long walk, and with a little courtesy, she would ask, "Is Mr. B—— in, sir, if you please?" and often in a hot day in August, would this faithful little woman trudge from her home in Williamsburgh, upon the same errand of love and affection.

It appears that her husband was serving out a term of years in the State Prison, but his case presenting some mitigating circumstances, the clemency of Governor Kent was invoked in his behalf, by her faithful adviser Mr. B——, the result being, that her husband was released, and the little woman's heart made glad.

I shall never forget the beautiful expression of the face of that poor but handsome Irishwoman, as she entered the office to thank, in her artless and sincere manner, Mr. B—— for his efforts in her behalf; and I envied him the pleasurable emotions of gratification, that must have been his, upon seeing her wildering delight, and hearing her heartfelt and honest ejaculations of thankfulness to the Almighty, and of blessings, that she so earnestly prayed might be showered on the head of her benefactor.

It was Christmas morning when she received the joyful news, and there were at least two hearts in old St. Patrick's

Cathedral that not only beat in unison, but whose humble offerings of gratitude and thankfulness, as they knelt together in the temple, must have been acceptable to Heaven. So many delightful associations, remembrances, and reminiscences are connected with my four years' sojourn here, that I find it difficult, vivid as the scenes sometimes appear to me, to bring some of the most prominent and interesting to the notice of the reader.

There were four in the office, exclusive of the principals, viz. P. B. S., J. B. S., J. D. B., and myself, and occasionally a boy. Our relative positions and stations were well understood, and I think I can say, we lived in perfect harmony, good-will, and peace with each other.

The heavy work of the office fell principally upon P. B. S., and when the reader is informed that upon Mr. Brady taking possession of the Counsel's chair there were over six hundred suits to be attended, he will see that the office was no sinecure.

Though I was still looked upon as a student of law, my investigations into the mysteries and intricacies of that delightful profession were not a wit more extensive than when my presence illumined the office of Mr. Nevins in Buffalo; indeed, if any thing I was more ignorant than ever. But with the pen (which Mr. Richelieu says is mightier than the sword), I was entirely at home, and often have "got through" one hundred and fifty folios in a day. Indeed I think I may say that the caligraphic efforts of this office excited the admiration of Mr. Mayor Mickle and the entire corporation. We had a carte blanche at Rich and Loutrell's, the stationers, where Albert H. Nicolay (now a successful auctioneer), with his blandest smile, would hand me the choicest articles of pens, ink, paper, silk tape, etc., etc., and about twice a year the bill, which was paid upon being carefully examined and audited, as all claims against the City usually are.

The monotony of the day, in the usual routine of the office business, was sometimes relieved by making some rough caricatures of ourselves and our clients, that for the time created a good deal of merriment; one in particular was hugely relished by all who understood the joke.

It appears a "motion" (I think they call it) had to be

made against Mr. Charles O'Conor, in "Chambers." Now I was given to understand, by Mr. Maurice, that this was a very simple matter, and that as all the other gentlemen in the office were engaged, and that he could not possibly leave, it fell upon me to "open the case."

The dread of a "first appearance on the stage" vanished into nothingness, in comparison with this fearful ordeal —that, too, against the great Mr. O'C.; and the more Mr. Maurice endeavored to explain the case to me, the more agitated, confused, and agonized were my feelings.

"You see," said he, "it is simply this. You must move for judgment on proof of the filing (or rasping, or something like it) of the *lis pendens*, (or suspenders, I forget which,) and urge the ground that no fraud was shown on the *execution* of the mortgage—(I wished that the man who did make it had been executed first)—and that the *onerous probandi* lay on the defendant, and he had utterly failed to effect a conviction on the mind of the referee." Something was said about the *animal quo*, or *quo animo*—perhaps both; but if it was the former, I saw *that* animal in the shape of a very extensive elephant before I had finished; for on arriving at the "Chambers," and whilst waiting for the motion, an impertinent officer pronounced the magical words, "Sit down," and motioned or rather thrust me into a chair near a hot stove, I thinking that by the time the side nearest the stove should be well cooked, I should be effectually roasted in front by O'Conor and the Court. A profuse perspiration burst out from every pore, and between the oven on the one hand, and the dread and uncertainty of the thing I was about to attempt on the other, I was thrown into a condition of mental and physical agony, which was seriously augmented by the Court asking Mr. O'Conor if "he had a motion to bring on!"

Mr. O'Conor replied, that he expected *some one* from Mr. Brady's office, who would move for the confirmation of a referee's report, which he then attended "to oppose." This was said with a glance at *me*, and a good deal of emphasis on the words *some one*. "On this hint" I attempted to speak, and in making an effort to rise, discovered, by the vast weight which appeared to be resting on my knees, that my avoirdupois had increased to about six tons within the previous five minutes.

I managed to "get off" the name of the case, for that was written very legibly on the outside of the bundle of papers that I held in my trembling hand; and I then began to feel my reason gradually giving way. At this critical juncture, P. B. S. came to my relief, and in a masterly manner "put the thing entirely through."

I had not the remotest idea then, neither have I now, what it was all about; and indeed this is the rule—without one single exception—in all the cases of a legal nature in which my valuable services have been required.

XXIII.

I START FOR CALIFORNIA.

I REMAINED in the office of B. and M. until the latter end of the year 1848, about which time the California fever raged high.

I, with numberless others, caught the complaint, and accordingly, in the month of January, 1849, I bid good-bye to my friends in New York, and started for Baltimore, from which port, on the 13th of the month, I, with about one hundred others, sailed in the schooner Sovereign, Captain Peterson, bound for Vera Cruz, intending to take the overland trip through Mexico to reach San Francisco.

Some three or four days out, however, great disagreement occurred among the passengers; and it ended in our inducing the captain to head his vessel for Chagres, taking our chances of finding a vessel at Panama to convey us to the golden land.

I shall quickly pass over the scenes and incidents of this dreary and dismal trip, relating only one or two of the most comical and tragic.

The Isthmus was not then, as now, crossed in four hours, but the transit took about a week. We rested for a while in the romantic village of Chagres, which consisted of a series of mud huts, dingy, dirty, and ugly natives, forlorn-looking and half-starved chickens, skeleton dogs, and a few stray and half-starved-looking mules. The heat was intense, and our prospects most gloomy.

After forty-eight hours' propelling, by naked native boatmen, in a sort of covered canoe, up the Chagres River, we landed at Gorgona, a town very similar to the one we had just left.

Here we pitched our tents—(we were six in company: Dr. D., C. L., T., A. D., S. F., and myself,)—and at night formed ourselves into a watch or guard, for mutual protection.

Now it must be understood by the reader, that I have *never in my life* but once fired off a pistol or a gun. On the occasion referred to, being on a Fourth of July excursion with a friend, we were firing at a target, which was fixed on a haystack, somewhere in New Jersey, when I, standing within five or six yards of the stack, actually missed it;—consequently, I felt a little nervous, upon being told, one night, that it was my turn to go on guard, and that I should have to remain on duty four hours, and carry a musket, pistol, and bowie-knife.

To make my agony more intense, we had been informed that one or two bears had recently been seen and heard in our immediate neighborhood; and that tigers and panthers, attracted by the smell of the cooking of the emigrants, prowled about at night quite near our camps; that thieves were common; and that unless, when the watchword was required, it was immediately responded to, the one on guard was *shot dead.*

As night came on, I began to feel the awful responsibility of my position. I had been fully instructed by one of our company in my duties; and provided by him with a musket loaded to the muzzle, (the lock of which I was afraid to look at, let alone touch it, for fear it should "go off,") a Colt's revolver, and a bowie-knife, used in the day-time for eating purposes.

The night was excessively dark, a very heavy dew was falling, and altogether, the gloom outside and inside the several tents seemed universal.

I relieved the guard at twelve o'clock at midnight, and

of course had to remain on duty until four. The knowledge of my utter ignorance of matters military, as also of the proper use of fire-arms, rendered my position very perplexing, and upon the slightest noise I found myself not only shaking from head to foot, but stammering out the "watch-word," feeling certain that at the proper time I should certainly forget it.

Two or three hours—they seemed months to me—had actually passed, and the morning began to dawn in the dim distance, when I distinctly saw a large dark object, moving slowly but steadily towards the tent, in front of which I stood.

I shook from head to foot, I knew not what to do. I tried to speak, and found that both the "watch-word," and my voice, had gone off together. I would have "hollered" right out, if I could; but that, though it might have aroused the sleepers, would, I fancied, have brought down upon me instant destruction. The object came nearer and nearer; I was certain it was a bear!—and I had actually summoned sufficient resolution and courage to point the *butt-end of my gun* at it, and probably in another moment would have shot myself, when my unknown tormentor, who on all fours, and covered up with a black piece of india-rubber cloth, made the resemblance so perfect to an animal, threw off the covering, and with a roar resembling a wild beast, caused me to drop all my fire-arms, and run for my life!

The Doctor (for it was he) considered it a first-rate joke, as did all the party.

I didn't "see it" exactly, as the man says in the play; but all I know is, that I have been more on my "guard" ever since.

The rest of my journey across the Isthmus was performed on the back of a mule.

Up to this period my donkey-riding had been strictly confined to a six-penn'orth, on the aforesaid animal—that is an hour's worth—on Hampstead Heath, or on the Sands at Margate. I soon found to my great annoyance and fear, that the Spanish mule, or at least the one with which I was furnished, was not quite so tractable or docile as your English donkey; for upon being hoisted upon the back of one of these ugly looking animals by my muchacho, he commenced balancing himself on his fore-legs, and giving a kind of he-hau! that had the desired effect of pitching me off over his head, much to the delight of everybody, excepting myself. Regaining my saddle, and finding it impossible to be transferred to a less vicious animal, I proceeded on my journey, endeavoring to keep up with one or two of our party.

To those of my readers who remember the "rainy season" on the Isthmus of Panama, in January, 1849, these reminiscences will be fully appreciated, but will be little understood by the tourist to the "diggings" at the present day, who is transported from the Atlantic to the Pacific in luxuriant cars, over a capital railroad, and in four hours' time!

Away I went, fording rivers, tumbling into holes, donkey's belly-band giving way, saddle sliding off, and I with it—donkey cuts and runs—I after him—up to my middle in water—night coming on—dread of the fever, find myself alone — narrow, stony, flinty, and rugged pathway — all sorts of animals my companions, lizards, monkeys, alligators, snakes innumerable—boy catches donkey, fixes saddle, I remount, again to be jolted, again to be thrown off—boy wallops donkey, donkey kicks. I this time, by the "united aid of mane and tail," keep my seat—jolt, jolt, jolt, bump, bump, bump—off the donkey starts at a gallop. I, a mass of jelly and perspiration, stick to him like bricks—donkey comes to a stand-still—I am delighted and breathe freer—rivers, bogs, holes, precipices, streams, hills, valleys, are by me and Rosinante bravely passed, and the old towers of Panama at last loom up in the distance.

Eight days after we left Chagres we found ourselves in Panama.

Completely fagged out, jaded and "used up," I gladly availed myself as soon as possible, of a lay-down, and a bath, at the "American Hotel."

This establishment was not exactly equal to the Metropolitan; but after the fearful privations I had hitherto endured, anything was acceptable.

Panama is the capital of New Granada, and one of the oldest cities in South America.

XXIV.

A STRANGE ADVENTURE AT THE ISLAND OF TOBOGO.

WE remained here about a week, during which time our party had managed to charter the English bark, "John Ritson," Captain Kennedy, recently arrived from Maryport, Cumberland, (England,) with a cargo of coal, for the use of the English steamers—to convey us to San Francisco.

We were some 250 passengers and crew; and left the harbor of Panama, in the beginning of February, 1849, first stopping at the Island of Tobogo for water.

Here a singular incident happened to me.

I had been rambling over one of the mountains in the vicinity of the island, and was greatly exhausted and fatigued with the heat and the trip, and with my companion, Dr. B——, had found out a native hut, which at the same time had the appearance of a place of refreshment. In we ventured, and we managed between us, with the aid of a little book of Spanish and English dialogues, to make known our wishes.

A thin and haggard-looking white woman was cooking some extraordinary dish in an earthen pot, and I noticed that she looked at me rather steadily. At last upon my companion calling me by name, she suddenly stepped up to me, and in a strong Scotch accent, said: "Ah! Sir, ken ye the name o' Dr. Massett?" At first I thought she was slightly deranged, but upon her continuing, "Ah, Sir, I ken him veery weel, there's sic a reseemblance to him as died in Carthagena, that I thought you were his brither!"

I started, and replied: "Do you refer to Dr. Samuel M——, who married the British Consul's daughter in Carthagena, Mr. W——, and died there in 1826?"

"I do indeed, sir," she said. "I nursed the gentleman in his last illness, and he died in my arms, sir!"

I need not say I was deeply interested and affected by this strange and extraordinary adventure.

Twenty-three years had passed away since the death of my eldest brother, who had fallen a victim to the ravages of yellow fever during his first year's residence in South America; and in the very fastnesses of a barren mountain, many miles distant from the main-land, am I recognised as his brother, by an old Scotch nurse, who was the first to give a member of his family the deeply interesting though painful particulars of his last moments.

The little hut was visited by me every day, and at parting I felt sad and sorrowful.

To attempt any adequate description of the horrors of the voyage on board the "John Ritson," would not only be utterly useless, but impossible.

The trip to Acapulco in Mexico, for instance, is usually made in five or six days from Panama, by the Steamships of the P. M. S. S. Company. We accomplished it in thirty.

The voyage from Acapulco to San Francisco is usually performed in seven to eight days. We were sixty-five days in reaching it.

The facts are briefly these. The vessel was vilely provisioned, and the captain, an ignorant and illiterate North Shields mariner, was anxious to make all he could "out of the dom Yankees" as he called us, and instead of laying in any extra provisions, he permitted his ship to go to sea in the worst possible condition, with musty flour, wormy bread, rotten meat, and filthy water.

Upon leaving Acapulco, the winds were very light, and we crept along at a snail's pace. When out some two or three days, entirely out of sight of land, and right in the tropics, we were becalmed, and remained *stationary for over four weeks.*

How the time passed I know not. The heat was perfectly fearful, so much so, that double awnings were spread over our heads, and added to this, it was announced by the ship's doctor, that there were one or two cases of malignant fever on board, and the utmost precaution was necessary to prevent its spreading amongst the passengers and crew.

A THIRTY DAYS' CALM ON THE PACIFIC.

OH! the horrors of those thirty days and thirty nights! The sea a sheet of glass; not a ripple on its surface, the scorching, burning, furnace-like, and enervating rays of the sun penetrating even the double thick awning of canvas, and rendering the deck too hot to walk on with slippered feet, not one single breath of air—all motionless and still—scant of provisions and water—and, as if to aggravate our miserable condition, it was on the sixth day announced, that the fever had broken out among the passengers, that it was infectious, and the greatest precaution must be used to prevent its progress.

The dark wing of the angel of death hovered over the doomed ship, and two that night left us for the "undiscovered country."

The scene was painfully impressive.

The heat was so great in the cabins, that all who could find room on the deck carried up their mattresses and bedding, passing the night thereon. On the upper deck, hammocks had been swung for those who were sick, and every attention it was possible to give them, they received. The two cases I refer to were briefly these.

A young man, not over twenty-three, had managed to get a passage on board the ship at Acapulco—he having taken the overland route through Mexico—and full of apparent health and vigor, with the highest hopes and expectations of success in the new El Dorado, had joined our ship's company.

It appears that he had been indulging freely in the fruits which the natives for a trifling sum offer for sale, and to allay his thirst, had drunk to excess of the arguad'ente—a very inferior sort of liquor that is sold here, and thus became the first victim.

From the first he was perfectly conscious of his approaching fate—and in the most pitiable and heartrending manner called by name upon his relatives in his far distant home. I never shall forget the look of intensity and despair as his full black eyes, streaming with tears, looked up into mine, and exclaimed, "Oh! God—am I never to see my dear mother again ?—do—do," turning to the doctor, "try and save me!" and almost immediately after he had spoken these words, his cheeks assumed the unmistakable death pallor, and without uttering another word, he lingered in a perfectly unconscious state until midnight, when he died.

The other was an old man seventy-eight years of age, who had actually joined our vessel at Acapulco, with all the implements, tools, and utensils for a life of toil in the diggings, and who with his servant had taken passage for the land of gold.

But death had marked him for one of his victims—and after an illness of two days, he expired.

Hammocks were slung on the upper decks, and in them rested the dying and the dead.

The moon was at its full. The doomed ship lay still upon the waters—the sails hung lazily against the mast—the heat was most oppressive—there seemed to be no air at all—the deck was strewed with passengers—some sleeping—some watching—some talking in subdued tones—others listlessly lounging over the bulwarks.

The night was beyond description beautiful—although our frightful circumstances made its very beauty a mockery. The intense heat of the midday sun had given place to the milder beamings of the silvery orb, and despite the oppressiveness of the atmosphere, there was a sense of some relief in the motionless ship, with its burden of the living and the dead. Suddenly a shrill scream rang through the ship, and all eyes were turned to the hammock where the old man lay. His eyes were wide open—his jaw had fallen—the death dew lay on his forehead, and as the moon fell full upon his face, it seemed to be lighted up with an unearthly brightness. "There's another gone," says the captain, "call the watch to sew him up, he must be thrown overboard immediately!"

There's no knowing who'll be the next!

The unseen messenger was quietly walking through the ship, and singling out his victims, and each seemed to look at his fellow with sympathy, suspicion, and even dread.

The burial service was hurried over, and heavy stones attached to the feet of the dead men—who had first been sewed up in thin blankets, and afterwards in some canvas.

They were placed upon a board in a slanting position, and at a given signal were tossed into the sea.

The little son of the old man, only some thirteen years of age, stood by the ratlins, sobbing bitterly, and imploring some one to take care of him. We all tried to comfort —to reassure him that he should be well looked after; when, oh horror! he burst out afresh with an exclamation that his father *was* not dead—that he had been thrown overboard too soon—and that he and his companion in death were swimming to the ship! All eyes were turned to the spot; and there in the bright moonlight could be seen the heads of the victims, turned apparently to their late abiding-place and imploring for aid and succor; and there for days, in sight of the ship's crew—aye, days—they remained; the heavy stones that had been attached to their feet had slipped away, and the bodies arose to the surface.

But I must draw a veil over this dismal—this soul-harrowing scene; and could I inspire the reader with a tithe of the ecstatic emotions of pleasure experienced by that distressed ship's company when the heart-stirring cry of "a breeze! a breeze!" was heard I should rejoice. As the gentle ripple on the water, at first a small black speck, appeared larger and larger, until tiny waves chased each other in multitudinous and miraculous succession—all sparkling and dancing in the bright silvery light, and playfully splashing against the sides of our big ship, which, feeling the freshening impulse, moved from her fathomless moorings, and fluttering her wings to the wind, sped onward once again in the direction of the Golden Land, I felt a thrill of indescribable pleasure, and gave vent to my feelings in tears of joy.

"Once more upon the waters," how we danced and skipped and pranced through the waves; for the breeze had freshened into a pretty stiff gale, and our ship, as if wishing to make up for lost time, sped onward with lightning swiftness.

Off Cape St. Lucas, the first sight we obtained of the land of California, the wind increased to almost a hurricane, and the contrast was indeed great to the lengthened calms we had so recently experienced.

XXV.

ARRIVAL AT SAN FRANCISCO.

On the ninety-eighth day of our departure from Panama we arrived at the entrance to the Golden Gate, and on the morning of the ninety-ninth day entered the long looked for city of San Francisco, a city of tents and wooden shanties, somewhat difficult to describe, as a description of its actual condition in '49 would seem fabulous, as compared with any subsequent account.

As a faithful chronicler of my individual fortunes and adventures, I will state, that my amount of capital upon reaching the New El Dorado was six dollars in Mexican coin; one of the causes of the fearful depletion in the stock financial being a propensity to indulge in the good things of this life on board the John Ritson. Thus, starvation almost stared me in the face, when it suddenly became known that one of our German steerage passengers had purchased several hams and boxes of red herrings in Acapulco; these, at the proper time, he ladled out to the tune of *one dollar* a slice and *fifty cents* for a herring.

Being, unfortunately for my pocket, very fond of both these edibles, I invested several dollars in this line, until I found my funds had dwindled down to the scanty amount above named.

The German lived on a biscuit a day; and by the time of our arrival had, I heard, possessed himself of one or two hundred dollars, with which he commenced operations, and in the short space of six months left with (what he considered) a fortune.

The first person I met, that I had known slightly when in Mr. Brady's office in New York, was Col. J. D. Stevenson, who very kindly greeted me on the morning of my arrival. The Colonel, who it will be remembered was in command of the California Regiment that left New York in 1846, asked me what my intentions were in coming to California; and finding, as usual, that I had no very definite object in my ramblings, suggested that I should come the next day to his office, saying, "You are just the young man for me. You, of course, understand drawing deeds, mortgages, &c.; in fact, the general routine of a lawyer's office. You've been in a good school, and I think we can get along very well together. I have just purchased a tract of land —am going to build a new city—a second New York, sir! I call it, sir, 'New York of the Pacific,' sir. I'll make you Alcalde, sir! Notary Public, sir! Mayor of the City, sir! Come and breakfast with me, sir, to-morrow."

"At what time, colonel?" I feebly remarked.

"At six o'clock, sir—always rise with the lark—nothing like getting up early, sir—business man, sir. Go to bed early—keep steady—don't drink, and your fortune's made in no time! As to pay, I give you $150 a month to commence with, and your board—that's two ounces ($32) a week!"

I could scarcely stand. I was afraid the Colonel had made a mistake, and meant $150 a year! (But I soon found out that everything went *by the month* in California.) The stories of the Arabian Nights, the exploits of Baron

Munchausen, faded into insignificance, compared with my exploits; and when the Colonel, asking me if I wanted any money, was informed that there was a debt owing to a person on board of some $260, that I was very anxious to cancel, replied, "Oh yes, sir; tell him to come to the office in the morning, and I'll *weigh him out the dust*," I knew not whether I stood on my head or my heels, so delirious was I with surprise and delight.

My companions (the Coopers), kind-hearted Marylanders, whose generous offers of friendship and consideration I shall never forget, and who, one and all, if they ever read these lines, will be good enough, at this late day, to accept my warmest thanks, congratulated me on my good fortune, and joined with me in a general "hooray!" at my streak of luck—I being the *first one* of our ship's company that had found employment.

The next day, bright and early, I found out the Colonel, and after breakfast went with him to the office, which stood in those days on Montgomery street, at about where Genella's crockery store now stands, and next door to Joe Bedleman's store.

XXVI.

COLONEL STEVENSON'S OFFICE.

It was a wooden shanty, with a door that opened with a rusty old latch, immediately behind which was a wooden bunk, that was occupied at that time by the bookkeeper of C. W. Ross, a Scotchman by the name of Crogan. The room had one window in it that looked on the bay, the water, at high tide, coming up to our door sill, so that frequently I have had to wade up to my middle to get into my crib!

The walls were adorned with large maps, most gorgeously got up by my fellow clerk, who happened to be a brother Englishman, named Rowe. The "desk" was a long deal board, relieved at intervals by two old tea cups (both full of ink), paper, pens; and by its side was a cupboard, with two or three nameless utensils filled with gold dust; three wooden stools, very shaky and rickety, and the fixtures and furniture are complete.

On the outside the people were informed that that was J. D. Stevenson's Land Office and Agency of Lots in "New York of the Pacific."

Immediately under this they were also informed that Stephen C. Massett was a Notary Public and Commissioner of Deeds.

The rush for lots in this magnificent embryo city was great.

It was something in this style:—Man, just from the mines, comes in, and wants to invest his surplus "gold-dust."

"Got any good lots, Col.?" Col. S—— rises, and with a long stick points to the map, offering a few remarks like these to the astonished and bewildered purchaser.

"You see, sir, these lots are what we call water lots, sir. I couldn't part with these under $1000 a lot, as from their position—*this being the head of navigation*, sir—that is a fixed fact, sir—they will command shortly a very high figure. Now these on F. street I have reserved for the 'public schools.' I am determined to have an institution of this kind properly cared for—and next to this, sir, I have placed these lots on A. M. and A. for the 'Court House,' 'City Hall,' and the 'Hall of Records and Mayor's or Alcalde's office,'" (pointing to me, and remarking that I had just arrived from New York to take charge of this highly responsible, lucrative, and dignified position!)

The excited miner, with visions of prospective wealth, in the rapid and astounding advance of real estate in this golden land, pulls out his buckskin bag, and away rattles the gold into the Chinese scales; he takes *two lots*, pays his $500 (they are $250 apiece). I make out the "deeds," record them immediately, in fact do everything that in such cases is usually done, made, and provided.

The man leaves his gold-dust, and takes his deed—neither one nor the other to be heard of afterwards. This, during my stay in this exalted sphere of action, was invariably the case—with one single and honorable exception—which I shall presently mention.

Vessels were arriving almost daily from the Eastern States, particularly from New York, luring hundreds and hundreds of gold-seekers—many having letters of recommendation to "Col. Stevenson," some from those who knew the Col. only by name, others from old friends in the East.

Letters of introduction are very frequently an inconvenience, both to the giver and receiver, and as a means of intercourse ought to be very sparingly indulged in; but when they come by the dozen a day—they were sometimes more and sometimes less, they really become a nuisance almost intolerable.

One morning in particular I shall not easily forget.

The office was completely filled with "new arrivals," all anxious for direction and advice, and all feeling that the "Col." ought to be delighted to see them, and bestow upon them his entire, and undivided attention.

"Could you inform us, Col., which of the mines is the best to start for? How much gold they are taking out—could you show us some—how much does it cost to get up there, etc. etc.," and a thousand such queries would be asked and expected to be replied to. If the Col. was busy he would refer them to me, when of course, from my personal observation and lengthened residence in the country, they questions were very satisfactorily answered.

"The Southern mines, I think, are turning out larger quantities than any other," I replied; this was a standing answer.

On the day in question a clerical-looking individual, with a wife and two children, presented himself to the "Col." with a letter of introduction. And the liberal offer of the Col. to present him *free gratis* with a lot of land (*provided he would build a house within thirty days!*) in the beautifully situated, and flourishing town of "New York of the Pacific," with the prospect of being the very first clergyman settled in that delightful locality; and the additional promise of the "Col.," that the particular church, ordered by himself, and which was then "coming round the Horn," should be under his entire guidance and direction, induced the unfortunate minister of the gospel to pack up his traps that afternoon, and with his wife and infant children, and to leave in an open boat for the scene of his future labors.

If the reader, some weeks afterwards (for it had taken them seven days in an open boat to get up there), had seen the forlorn-looking object that presented itself at the office, upon inquiry almost daily, if the "tabernacle" had arrived, he would indeed have pitied him.

Prior to their having been almost entirely eaten up by mosquitoes, his wife and children had died of chills and fever, while he, with his face covered with blotches and pimples, was shaking with the same complaint.

After muttering to himself—that it was "the Lord's doings, and marvellous in his eyes," he left the office, and was never seen or heard of afterwards!

[See page 107.]

Incidents most comic were occurring daily; but decidedly one of the "cutest" and smartest, in reference to the purchasing of lots in the new and flourishing town of "New York of the Pacific," and the subsequent repudiation thereof, was the following, which will be fully appreciated, if these lines ever fall beneath the eye of my old friend,

Dick E——, of Philadelphia, now of Leghorn; it being the only instance in the memory of mortal man of the slightest realization of any money once invested in this (supposed to be) wonderful and rapidly growing locality.

Captain Mahlon D. E——, then, was the commander of a small-sized schooner, that he proposed running on the San Joaquin and Suisun Bay Rivers. He had been successful in his mining operations, and had returned to the "Bay" with several large and small-sized buckskin bags filled with the "ore." Attracted by the wonderful reports of the "Colonel's" newly laid out city, and of the rapidity of its growth, as also of the immense amount of lots that were daily sold; of the positive certainty of their future advancement, these were sufficient inducements for the gallant captain to present himself at our office, and in the blandest manner ask to inspect the map of the Colonel's flourishing city. I turned round, and to my great surprise saw a handsomely dressed, good-looking fellow, with an immense shirt-collar on. This latter was a luxury rarely indulged in, and it therefore excited my attention, for washing be it known was then eight and nine dollars a dozen! Upon my pointing out five available lots—lots that would certainly double in value in two months—and as the purchaser promised to *build within thirty days* (the old dodge), the "Col." in consideration thereof put at the surprisingly low figure of $1000.

Well—I made out the deeds and pocketed my $25 for recording—*this* was clear profit—the captain left the "land-office" with his five deeds, revelling doubtless in visions of being prospectively a wealthy landowner. Two months came along—so did the captain—who had tried in vain to get within miles of the locality, having I think he said lost several boats in endeavoring to reach the shore—and after great exertion in finding the "ranch," was rendered stone-blind by the myriads of mosquitoes that infested the place—stung to the quick by the appearance of things in general, and the loss of his money in particular—he rushed for our office, offering to *return the lots* for $600—this the "Col." gladly (?) assented to—the deeds were cancelled, and the "captain" walked off—the first and the last man that was ever known to have even realized a *portion* of the money invested in this "scheme." Many laughable, many strange and serious, incidents and adventures, I passed through during these early days of my California experience—but writing as I am now doing entirely from memory, aided only by some printed matter, and a few stray items in manuscript that I have preserved, renders it somewhat difficult to transfer them to paper.

XXVII.

FIRST CONCERT GIVEN IN CALIFORNIA.

In the month of June, 1849, some of my New York friends advised me to give an entertainment—there being at this time no place of amusement of any sort open in San Francisco. It was my first essay to appear in a monologue performance, and as it was the first public entertainment of any sort or kind on the Pacific coast, I think it may be entitled to a brief space in these my "adventures." The "Annals of San Francisco" gives the following in relation thereto:

"On Monday evening, June 22d, 1849, a concert of vocal music was performed at the old school-room on the south-west corner of the plaza, and this may probably be regarded as first among the regular amusements of San Francisco. It was given, entirely unassisted, by Mr. Stephen C. Massett, at the suggestion of many of his New York friends. The little room was crowded to suffocation, the proceeds yielding the vocalist over five hundred dollars. The following is the programme, a curiosity well worthy of preservation, printed at the office of the 'Alta California,' then the only paper in the city. 'Front seats,' it will be observed, were reserved for ladies, of whom there were but *four* present. The piano used (we believe there was only *one* in the country) upon the occasion, was loaned by Mr. E. Harrison, the collector of the port, and sixteen dollars were paid for removing it from the custom-house to the school-room, situated on opposite sides of Portsmouth Square."

PROGRAMME.

PART I.

1. Song.—" When the Moon on the Lake." Words and Music by S. C. Massett.
2. Recitation.—Mr. Massett: The Frenchman, the Exquisite, and the Yankee in Richard III.
3. Song.—Mr. Massett: "My Boyhood's Home," from the Opera of *Amilie.*
4. An Imitation of Madame Anna Bishop, in her song of "*The Banks of Guadalquiver.*"
5. Song.—" When a child I roamed." Words and Music by S. C. Massett.
6. An Imitation of an elderly lady and German girl, who applied for the situation of soprano and alto singers in one of the churches in Massachusetts. S. C. Massett.

PART II.

1. Song.—Mr. Massett: "When time hath bereft thee," from Gustavus III.
2. Mr. Massett: "Loss of the Steamship President," by Epes Sargent.
3. Mr. Massett: " I'm sitting on the stile, Mary," by W. R. Dempster.
4. An Imitation of the N. Y. Razor Strop Man, John Smith.
5. Ballad.—" She wore a wreath of Roses." (Mr. Massett.) J. P. Knight.
6. Ballad.—" List while I sing." Composed by Stephen C. Massett.
7. Yankee Imitation.—"Deacon Jones and Seth Slope." S. C. Massett.
8. To conclude with the celebrated

"YANKEE TOWN MEETING;"

In which Mr. Massett will give imitations of seven different persons, who had assembled for the purpose of "suppressing the press."

Tickets $3 each, to be had at Dr. Robinson's, *Chemist* and *Druggist*, on the plaza; at the "Parker House," of Mr. Massett; at the office of Col. J. D. Stevenson, and at the door on the night of the performance.

N. B.—" Front seats reserved for ladies!"

XXVIII.

I AM MADE (LORD) MAYOR OF N. Y. OF THE PACIFIC.

In looking over some old papers recently, I found my "Commission" as "Alcalde," "Notary Public," and Commissioner of Deeds for New York of the Pacific. Here is a copy—

"Know all men by these Presents, that I Bennet Riley, Brevet Brigadier General, U. S. A., and Governor of California, by virtue of authority in me vested, do hereby appoint and confirm Stephen C. Massett as Alcalde in and for the 'City of New York of the Pacific' in the State of California, and also a 'Notary Public" and 'Commissioner of Deeds' for the same City and County, to date from the 1st day of July, 1849.

Given under my hand and seal at Monterey, Lower California, June 28, 1849.

B. Riley,
[Official.] *Bt. Brig. Gen. U. S. Army, and Governor of California.*

H. W. Halleck,
Bt. Capt., and Secretary of State."

This was the first, and in all probability will be the last position of the kind I shall ever occupy. Those unacquainted with the definition of the word "Alcalde," are respectfully informed that it means the chief magistrate of a city. Added to this the highly important and lucrative offices of "Notary Public" and "Commissioner of Deeds," were fairly thrust upon me!

I began to feel the weight of office—and of course in a proportionate degree my own importance!—and when a letter came to me (sent by some cruel wag!) directed the Hon. S. C. Massett, Alcalde, etc., I nearly fell off the stool.

I was even seriously thinking of sending to London to get a pattern of the Lord Mayor's gown—wig—sword and mace. I had fully intended to have had a "Lord Mayor's

6

show on the ninth of November"—had settled upon the plan of my house—and determined upon engaging a Lady Mayoress—but castles built on the air are one thing—and houses on N. Y. of the Pacific are quite another—and when the reader is informed that of all the houses—iron at that—which in the month of May, 1849, Col. Stevenson sent for from New York to come "round the horn" or rather "in a horn"—not one up to this present writing has arrived—and that those—I believe two in all—built by some unfortunate wight—sank to rise no more, carrying owners and all with them, a few hours after their erection; they will understand and duly appreciate the height of the position from which I have fallen, and my indifference at the time to obey the mandate of the Colonel, "to take up my bed, and walk" to the scene of my future labors.

The reader was informed that when I landed in this wonderful city, I was the fortunate possessor of six dollars in current coin. Five dollars of this vanished in a meal for "two," at the Excelsior Restaurant, immediately upon our arrival—and if you would like to know why I invested so large a proportion of my capital, I reply that the most ordinary meal cost two dollars—that eggs were a dollar a-piece—that coffee was fifty cents a cup, and therefore, under the circumstances, the meal for myself and companion (considering our hungry state) was not so enormous. It will hardly be believed at the present day, that such prices were asked, and readily paid by the "new comers;" but having, fortunately for my own veracity, (voracity I think I ought to say) a real Simon Pure bill of fare of one of the *then* principal eating-houses of San Francisco—I present it entire, if only to certify to the correctness of my assertion.

Bill of Fare.

WARD HOUSE, RUSSELL AND MEYERS, PROPRIETORS,

THURSDAY, DECEMBER 27, 1849.

Soup.

Ox-tail (per dish) $1 00

Fish.

Baked trout, white and anchovy sauce $1 00

Roast.

Beef (per plate) . .	$1 00	Mutton	$1 00
Lamb	$1 00	Pork (apple sauce) . .	$1 00

Boiled.

Leg of mutton, caper sauce	$1 25	Corned beef and cabbage .	$1 25
Ham (per plate) . .	$1 00	Pig's feet . . .	$1 75

Entrees.

Curried sausages . .	$1 00	Tenderloin, lamb, gr. pease	$1 25
Beef, stewed with onions	$1 25	Venison, port wine sauce	$1 50

Stewed kidney, sauce de champagne $1 25

Extras.

Fresh California eggs (each) $1 00

Game.

Curlew, roast or boiled to order $3 00

Vegetables.

Sweet potatoes, baked	50 cents.	Irish potatoes, (mashed)	50 cents.
Irish " boiled	50 "	Cabbage . . .	50 "
Squash . . .	50 "	Beans . . .	50 "

Pastry.

Bread pudding . .	75 cents.	Rum omelette . .	$2 00
Mince pie . . .	75 "	Jelly	$2 00
Apple pie . . .	75 "	Cheese	50
Brandy Peach . .	2 dollars.	Stewed prunes . .	75

Wines.

Champagne (per bottle) .	$5 00	Claret (per bottle) . .	$2 00
Half bottle . . .	$2 00	Cider " . .	$2 00
Pale sherry . . .	$3 00	Porter " . .	$2 00
Old madeira . . .	$4 00	Ale " . .	$2 00
Old port (pints) . .	$1 75	Brandy " . .	$2 00

Breakfast from half-past seven to eleven, A.M.
Dinner from half-past one to six, P.M.
Tea from half-past six to twelve, P.M.

So endeth the bill of fare—and I will bet such another is not to be seen for the next hundred years.

The restaurant was always filled, and nobody went away without paying, though it is evident from a casual inspection of the above precious document, that an ordinary dinner for a gentleman of respectable appetite would have cost about ten dollars! I have heard it remarked that there was about this time extraordinary dissipation to be every day witnessed in and about the streets of San Francisco. The causes that led to it are not, however, generally known—the above bill may throw a little light upon the subject. What a temptation was offered to a man of slender means to procure a bottle of brandy at a dollar, and becoming intensely drunk thereon—to forget his hunger and purity together! Many a man could not afford to eat dinner in those days, and there can be no doubt that many unfortunates took to drinking brandy to calm the pangs of hunger, which they could not allay in a legitimate manner.

I was introduced by Col. Stevenson upon one occasion to Mr. Samuel Brannan, now one of, if not the most wealthy, citizens of that state, and at his suggestion, and promise that I should act as "auctioneer" on the contemplated sale of his large stock of goods at the "embarcadero," I left the Bay for its sister city, Sacramento.

In those days, the river bearing that name was navigated by "schooners," open boats, etc., no luxuriant steamers at that early period were to be seen. So packing up my "duds," and engaging a passage in the schooner, "Water Witch," for $25, I left "Clarke's Point" for a new scene of labor.

Arriving at Sacramento City in about six days (it is now done in ten hours) tired out and miserable, I sought the comforts of a "bath," and a "lay down."

The bath was accomplished by a "ducking" at even-tide in the river, after which I shouldered my trunk with a dozen others, having been directed to a "lodging-house" called the "City Hotel," which was then nearly completed, and as I think it might interest the present generation in general, and the keepers of taverns in particular, to see the style of accommodation, I propose to give a sketch of the interior of my sleeping apartment.

Here it is. I think mine was the corner "bunk," and if the reader will kindly look at the expression of my face, he or she will discover that I was not exactly lying upon a bed of roses.

The heat was insufferable, mosquitoes were buzzing about, and with their slow though sure attendants, fleas, and bed-bugs came in myriads to greet and congratulate me upon my arrival. Scratching and itching, itching and scratching, kept me pretty well awake all night; and then the stifled smell—the noise inside and out—the swearing and snoring of the occupants, the barking of dogs, the leaving of numberless trains of mules and donkeys outside, the cries of children, rendered the scene a perfect pandemonium—and to crown the whole, just as I had managed from sheer exhaustion to "drop off into a doze," I felt a heavy bump come up against the slender board that screened me from the street—when to my astonishment the head of a big ox presented itself, and with its cold and moist snout commenced rubbing against my knee!

I couldn't stand this any longer, and I leaped from my "slat" in the second tier.

I walked about till early daylight. But I soon found out that this was not the place to grumble or complain, or in fact to be surprised, disgusted, or astonished at anything, and I quickly went to work to establish myself as "Auctioneer."

A Mr. Montgomery had got "ahead of me" in the sale of "Brannan's store," he having offered to do it at a very low per centage—and thus the first chance of holding the hammer was taken from me.

I was, however, that day introduced to a Mr. Charles O. Brewster, who had then recently arrived from Boston, and in less time almost than it takes me to write these lines—an article of agreement was made out—our "Store" taken and leased—and I was busy painting our sign!

In those days everybody was crazy—money came and went—went and came—you knew not how and cared not where—from morning till night it was one scene of excitement and frenzy! Swearing, grumbling, drinking, and almost everybody rushing to the diggings—gamblers occupied every tent (houses there were none), and shanties where liquor of the vilest kind was sold at fifty cents per glass, and piles of Mexican ounces and silver coin covered the tables, thousands of dollars were lost and won in a single night, quiet there was none—and every one had at least to appear to take part in the general excitement.

XXIX.

THE AUCTION HOUSE OF MASSETT AND BREWSTER.

THE shanty on J street that we had hired for three hundred dollars per month, looked more like a stable than an "Auction house," and had been occupied as a bar-room by a "Monte" dealer.

With the purchase (including the good "will" and fixtures), we were the possessors of the remains of a once well stocked bar, and here I kept "open house" until our stock of liquors had vanished; the remaining "traps" we resolved to sell at auction.

My partner C. O. B. then went to the "Bay" to make some purchases of goods which we intended "offering" at night auction.

In the course of time, the goods arrived, and having painted "Night Auction" on a piece of calico, tacked it on a frame in the shape of a cocked hat, and stuck a candle inside, I stood at the door, and rang a bell, at the same time informing the "outsiders" that I was just a "going to begin" to "open" the rarest and richest stock of goods fresh arrived from S. F., and begged them to walk in.

The profits were enormous; I think our first venture was for about $1,000. We made about $2,000 on the purchase. The first night auction was quite an event. The little room was filled in every corner; the stock offered consisted in part of "Pea-jackets," blankets, socks, boots, shoes, etc. The greatest "swindle" I think on the present occasion was this: a young "Muchacho" fresh from the diggings came up to the counter, and pointing to a paper of "Jews' harps," asked the price of one (they cost about one dollar a gross), at the same time offering me a chunk of gold for it, weighing at least eight dollars—I of course took it—it was a legitimate trade—and he went on his way perfectly delighted.

Among those who composed my audience upon this my first appearance, and who if they ever read these lines will laugh, I know!—were Judge M——, Mr. P——, J. T. E——, Professor S——, Dr. D——, and others. It will scarcely be believed, but upon these occasions our profits were never less than one hundred dollars a night, and yet such was the insanity of the times, we did not think this was making money fast enough, and gave it up, to devote ourselves exclusively to "our day-sales."

The first really important one that we made, was at the far-famed "Suttor's Fort," where the gallant Captain Sutter resided with his Indians, at the time of the discovery of the gold. The Fort was about two miles from the city, and at the time of which I am writing was one of the "Institutions" of the place.

I had been introduced to a jolly fat and burly looking little Englishman, named Tom W——, who acted as overseer, and head man of the Captain's at the fort, and the Captain having concluded to sell out his stock of merchandise, I was selected by his agent "Captain Thomas White" to do the "auctioneering" upon the occasion.

We had "billed" the city pretty well, for several days previous to the "sale," I and my partner going from one end of the town to the other, I with "tacks and hammer" with the bills—which had been written by me in "very large letters," telling the public in general, that on the first of October, a large sale would take place in the above locality. The day was oppressively hot, and therefore the firm of "Massett and Brewster" took the precaution to leave their "Sale-rooms"—big word that considering the premises looked more like a large sized pigs' sty—at an early hour in the morning, judiciously dropping here and there a brief catalogue of the particulars.

Upon arriving at the Fort, I found my friend White had duly arranged the entire stock into lots, requesting me to "put through" or "hurry up" the "truck," fancy articles, and light goods, first reserving for the last part of the sale the heavy goods, such as flour, clothing, &c.

The buyers were an extraordinary-looking set, and in no other part of the world would their word have been taken for a cent.

I mounted a high stand, and with hammer in hand commenced. I am not going to laud my performances in the auctioneering line—my well-known natural modesty would prevent it, if nothing else would; but it was patent in Sacramento and in San Francisco, that at any rate I kept my customers or buyers in good humor, generally winding up my sales by an imitation of the celebrated razor-strop man, Mr. John Smith (now of the Bowery).

Upon the present occasion I had rattled through an innumerable quantity of articles varied and strange. The audience had certainly got *stuck* with molasses, *filled* with sausages, *warmed* with tea and coffee, sweetened with sugar, and tight with gin and brandy. I then came to the flour, of which there were some three hundred sacks.

I was to put them up in lots of *ten*, with the privilege of the *whole*. I was directed to get, if possible, *the cost*, eleven dollars and a quarter for a hundred-pound sack, and not to let it go under *ten*. Now it was thought that flour would "go up" to a very high figure; there was very little in the market, and many in that crowd would have liked to be the owners of the whole.

"Now then, gentlemen, we come 'on to' the flour. I shall put it up in lots of five sacks, with the privilege, &c. You are all aware of the present scarcity of this article—the 'staff of life,' gentlemen, as the Psalmist, I believe, calls it.

Gentlemen, it's a solemn fact that 'flour's rising.' Yes, gentlemen, before thirty days are over our heads, loaves (without even fishes) will be selling at a dollar apiece. (*I* paid fifty cents this morning, gentlemen, for a half-quartern!) You can't *eat* your gold dust, gentlemen. You *must have flour.* So what's offered for the first sack of a hundred pounds? Give me a bid, *if* you please. (Five dollars was offered.) Five, five, five, five, five, five, five, five—half, half, half, half, half,—narf, narf, narf, narf, narf, narf, narf. Gentlemen, this will never do. Six, six, six, six, six, six, six, six, six, six, six, six, six, six, six, six,—cutter, cutter, cutter,—narf, narf, narf, narf, narf, narf, narf, narf, narf,—seven, seven, seven, seven, seven, seven, seven, seven, seven, seven, seven, seven, seven. I cannot throw it away at this figure. Say eight. Eight I got."

"Nine," shouted another, and "narf, narf, narf, narf,—cutter, cutter, cutter, cutter, cutter."

"Ten," called out an old cock, who insisted on my knocking him down; adding that he didn't wish to be kept all day.

Now I was determined, if possible, to get, at any rate for *one lot*, the specified figure (one and a quarter), and I went on, regardless of the suggestions or advices of the crowd; and though it was pretty hard work, and what with the heat inside and the tedious nature of the sale, there being an immense amount of goods yet unsold, I was glad to get the first lot *off*,—by dint of great persuasion, and an extra amount of "gas," (an auctioneer's undoubted prerogative,) I managed to get up to the wished-for figure of "eleven dollars and a quarter" for a one-hundred pound sack. This was a big draw on my lungs, and with the perspiration streaming from every pore, I inquired, "How many will you take, sir?" fully believing I had again to go through the same rigmarole of flowery language for the balance of the lot,—when, to my utter astonishment, and indeed to the surprise of everybody, the man called out, "I'll take the lot!"

I looked at my man, who resembled more an escaped convict than a purchaser of anything. I looked at my partner, Charles B. (who was shaking from head to foot with the chills and fever), who nodded that it was all right;

when I, asking the name of the buyer, he replied, "Wolfe." I thought it was somewhat significant. I found out afterwards that he was the owner of the "City Bakery," had foreseen that flour would very soon be in great demand, and had bought up all he could. In connexion with this purchase, I will simply state that he realized, in less than three months, $10,000 from this investment, with which he returned to his home in the (y)East.

Two other incidents connected with this somewhat remarkable sale, I will briefly mention.

There were some four hundred pairs of high boots, russian leather, that I knocked down to a man at four dollars a pair. In less than two months (the heavy rains having set in), he retailed them at one and two ounces ($16 and $32) per pair, making more than $10,000 by his speculation.

I wound up the day's work by selling a live pig for $65. The animal was a fine English porker, and extremely vicious; a stout cord was attached to his leg, and it was with the greatest difficulty that I could keep him in a steady position. He evidently felt and appreciated the hornets' nest he had got into; for as I was suggesting to my delighted audience that for the ridiculously small price at which I was instructed by my employees to allow the pig to "slide," their memories of the old homestead might be refreshed and their hearts made glad by the delicious fragrance of a roast leg of pork with sage and onions! the pig, with a w-heeeeeeeekk wwekkkkee, gave a start, breaking the string, knocking down one or two of the crowd, and upsetting me in the bargain. He was retaken, and purchased, I believe, by the Baptist minister, the Rev. Mr. C., who was at that time the only professed butcher the city could boast of. This pig (whether male or female I have forgotten) was *litter*-ally the nucleus of his (the parson's) fortune; for having introduced it to one of the opposite gender, the consequence was, in the proper course of time, a large yield of juvenile porkies that realized for him an unheard-of price. And he often told me that the purchase of the Sutter's Fort pig was the first streak of fat luck he had received. His store on I street was frequently visited by me for a beef steak or chop, or a nice fresh salmon, for he was a fishmonger also; and though he was very assiduous in killing and cutting all the week, he reserved Sunday for the saving and curing of *souls!*

The amount of this day's sales was $15,000; our commission was ten per cent., making a profit of $1,500 for the firm of Massett and Brewster. This, for a five hours' job, was pretty well.

I usually wound up my sale of each article with the words (after "once, twice, three times,") "Spizeruktum bang;" and for a long time I was known by no other name.

I officiated as auctioneer in several very large sales of real estate, in and out of the city. In those days the firm of "Priest, Lee, & Co.," were the great land-owners, bankers, and merchants. They were our landlords, and consequently I was always the auctioneer selected by them whenever they put any of their city lots "into the market." Money was fairly pouring in upon us. We purchased real estate, and began to look upon ourselves as belonging to the "heavy men" of this new and flourishing city.

A proposition was about this time started to form an Episcopal church, and I was invited to be one of the "wardens," and I began to fancy how my name would look, a hundred years from thence, on the tablet over the church-door "Toney Hoope," the facetious "Baron Vaux," was another "warden," and went to church regularly. Speculations in land about this time were at fever-heat—whole cities were frequently sold by me before dinner-time, and this was the style:

A man would buy a tract of land or a "rancho" for perhaps $1000 or so—he would then have it staked out or cut up into "lots," call it a city—get some draughtsmen to make beautiful and gaudy maps thereof, insist that it was either the "head of navigation," or the nearest route to the best diggings—unsurpassed for agricultural purposes, and so on.

One instance I well remember—the place was called "Butte City," I believe the original cost was $1000. I was directed to sell as many lots as I possibly could at that figure *per lot*, and I think the embryo city yielded the fortunate speculator about $20,000—the reader need not be informed that the place was then, is now, and ever will be, a barren waste—world without end—amen!

Upon another occasion I was requested to sell "several hundred head of wild cattle," in "bands" of forty each—this was a somewhat novel proceeding—but having stated to my audience, as clearly as I could, the conditions of sale, and that the animals were roaming at large, and had to be caught by the purchasers, they commenced to bid. I was told to get ten dollars a head—the sale lasted about half an hour—and our commissions were over $500.

XXX.

A JOLLY DINNER.

THE interior of our little store was at times certainly a "curiosity," for be it known to thee, my gentle reader, that the firm of Massett and Brewster did their own cooking, made their own beds—fetched their own water—swept their own store—and indeed officiated generally.

We had bought a little stove, and for it we had paid seventy-five dollars (it could be bought to-day for two dollars and fifty cents), had furnished ourselves with some crockery, the remains of a sale we had made of several crates thereof (an auctioneer's perquisites), and I determined to give a "blow-out" to one or two old New York friends. Tone Bleecker, if he ever reads these lines, will remember the occasion. The rain was coming down in torrents—the first rain of the season, and our shanty not being waterproof, commenced to leak,—this very much interfering with our cooking operations.

I had sallied out to purchase two or three cans of preserved chicken, for this I paid four dollars a can—a pound of onions cost one dollar, and potatoes the same amount; two loaves of bread one dollar; four bottles of porter, two dollars each, ($8.) (Though our friend, Elijah W—— *did* prig a couple from W. M——'s store next door, and like a good fellow, handed it to me "over the wall!") and a lot of cigars at fifty cents apiece.

A fire was quickly built—the contents of the cans emptied into a bran new saucepan—the onions peeled, and potatoes washed and cut in slices—well peppered and salted—and *I* acting as cook—sat eagerly watching the simmering and boiling thereof. I had almost forgot to mention that I had cut across the street to my friend, the Rev. Mr. C——, the Baptist minister, who looked after the sheep—and coaxed him out of a small piece of English bacon, which I duly cut into slices to give our stew a "flavor." I had likewise found out on the shelf of my friend's store next door, some preserved parsley!—this succulent and juicy concoction was immediately sprinkled with the fragrant herb—and the aroma rising from the home-made dish, not only tickled the olfactories of every one present, but called forth the remark from my amiable partner, that I had evidently mistaken my vocation—for that as a "cook," I should certainly make a sensation. Every now and then I would lift up the lid of the saucepan, and give the contents a good stir, with a large tin spoon, used generally in ladling our gold-dust, — in answer to the bubbling, seething, and rumbling sound of the precious mixture, as if in a stew to be taken off, a fork was inserted into the potatoes, and they were pronounced "done,"—flakes of chicken, that had left the bones in disgust, jostled by slices of onion, swam about in as rich, fine, and well seasoned a sea of broth, as ever tempted the palate of a London alderman, at a Lord Mayor's dinner. The covers removed, the steam rose in clouds, and the contents were emptied into a large wooden bowl, which had seen good service, and we sat down to do justice to the "dish." Did anything ever taste quite as nice as that chicken-stew? I think not—and then washed down by the real old genuine "brown stout,"—the rain was pouring down outside, making it all the cozier within—but what with the heat from the stove, the smallness of the apartment, and the excitement of eating and drinking, and the want of ventilaion, the place was insufferably warm. Some one suggested that we should open the door—at this moment, a gust of wind gave us a look-in, and in the eagerness of its congratulations, and in a very unceremonious manner, with one puff, upset our rickety table, with its entire contents, of dishes, plates, pans, and the remains of the "soup," porter, etc.— A general stampede occurred somewhat similar to the banqueting scene when Lady Macbeth, seeing the shakyness of her lord and master, requests her "guests" to cut and run—and the last I saw of Tony B—— was the end of his coat-tail, he flying before the wind chasing his sombrero, which had left his head in a hurry on gaining the street. Upon being left alone, we cleared up matters and things as well as possible, and prepared our sleeping apparatus. I had a "hammock" hung for an occasional visitor —I sleeping on the "counter," and immediately underneath the aforesaid "hammock." An old Boston friend, Steve T——, was the occupant of the last mentioned article; and he had just succeeded, after innumerable gymnastic efforts, and sundry jerkings and pullings, to get inside of it —when the rocking consequent upon its occupancy, and the frequent potations and imbibitions of varieties of liquor, acted as a delightful narcotic, and a prolonged but not at all soft or euphonous snore gave token that he was revelling in the land of dreams. Now, however soothing and delightful to the sleeper this nasal accomplishment may be; it is not at all appreciated by those who are "wide awake,"—accordingly, I administered a gentle kick in the region of the back, that not only had the effect of stopping the noise, but of bringing him and the hammock right on the top of me!—having first been well saturated with water, doubtless from the leakiness of the roof. This came with a heavy weight upon me, my friend's "heft" being over 200 pounds—and I hardly know which of us was the most astonished or hurt.

It had the effect, however, of restoring him to consciousness and sobriety, and after having a hearty laugh over the adventures of the day and night, we composed ourselves again to sleep.

The flourishing condition of the firm of M. and B. was such that we determined to make the purchase of the lot we then occupied. Its dimensions were twenty by eighty, and the price $5,000. The deeds were drawn—the money paid—and we went on *swimmingly*—as the saying is—and the reader shall know in a very short time the applicability of this italicised word.

XXXI.

THE FIRST THEATRICAL REPRESENTATION IN SACRAMENTO.

In the latter part of the year 1849, the first theatrical representation took place in this city, at what was then called the Eagle Theatre on J street. It was a frame building covered with canvas, and though only composed of this slight material, it cost over $30,000, lumber being at that time over $500 a thousand feet. The prices were five dollars to the boxes, and three dollars to the pit.

On the opening night, which I shall not easily forget, having returned from a lengthened stroll in and around about Sutter's Fort with Mr. Bayard Taylor, I proceeded in his company to the pasteboard Temple of the Muses.

It had been raining hard, and blowing a gale of wind the whole day, and the strength and durability of the building had been sorely tried; however, as the hour drew near for the opening of the doors, crowds of anxious miners thronged the entrance, and despite the winds and torrents of rain, the place was immediately filled. By the time we arrived we found that those who were fortunate enough to have secured "pit tickets," had the pleasure of enjoying a "fresh water bath" for the same money (a luxury unknown almost in those days, as people rarely washed themselves), for by that time the water was on a level with the seats; bnt the theatrical fire raged entirely too high to be put out by any such hydraulic arrangement as this, and accordingly the curtain rose at the conclusion of the overture to the "Bronze Horse"—the orchestra consisting of the fiddle—a very cheezy flageolet, played by a gentleman with one eye—a big drum, and a triangle, that served the double purpose of ringing in the boarders to their meals at the restaurant next door. The play was the "Bandit Chief" or "Forest Spectre," in which, as the bills said, the celebrated female Tragedian Mrs. R——, from the Theatre Royal, New Zealand, would make her first appearance in California as the heroine. For this performance she received about one hundred and fifty dollars per night—

and to give some idea of the classical style of the lady's pronunciation she replied, upon the question being asked her if she would accept the hand of the bandit chief:

"Is art is as ard as a stone—and I'd rayther take a basilisk, and rap is cold fangs areound me—than surrender meself to the cold himbraces of a artless willain!"

The bills announced that the performance would conclude with the thrilling and affecting Tragedy of "Douglas," the part of "Norval" by a gentleman who had been unfortunate at the diggings, and had only recently found out the proper channel in which to display his genius. He delivered the celebrated speech

"MY NAME IS NORVAL,"

assisted audibly by the prompter, in the following strange manner, amid the shoutings, and roars of laughter of the entire house.

"My name is Norval—on the Grampian hills,
My father feeds his flocks a frugal swan—

Prompter. Swain you booby.

Swain you booby, whose constant care was
To increase his shop—

Prompter. Store—Sir—What are you doing?

"Store sir, what are you doing—and keep his only son myself at home—
For I had heard of battles, and I longed
To follow to the fields some warlike lord—
And heaven soon granted, what my sire desired—

Prompter. Denied yer booby!

Denied you booby—you moon which rose
Last night—round as a cheese—

Prompter. Shield you stupid ass!

Shield you stupid ass! had not yet taken a horn—

Prompter. Filled her horn—you darned fool—

Filled her horn, you darned fool, when
By its light a band of fierce barbers—

Prompter. Barbarians, you fool—

Barbarians you fool—rushed like a
  Torrent down upon the hills,
  Sweepin our flocks and hers—

Prompter—Herds—sir not *hers*—

Herds, sir, I said—I alone with bended
  Bow, and quivering full of arrows—

Prompter. *Quiver*, sir—

Quiver sir—I said—hovered about the enemy, and marked with a lead-pencil.

Prompter. Marked the road—you booby—

Marked the road you booby—he took

Whom with a troop of fifty chosen men I met advancing—
  The pursuit we led, till we o'ertook the spoiled cucumbers—

Prompter. Spoil-encumbered foe, you stupid ass—

Spoil encumbered foe, I meant you stupid ass—and having heard
That our brave king had summoned his bold pears and apples—

Prompter. Peers! you fool—

Peers you fool—to meet their warriors at the common—

Prompter. Carron side—

Carron side—I left my father's house,
And took with me a maid-servant—

Prompter. A chosen servant, you fool!

A chosen servant you fool—to conduct my steps—
  You trembling cow—cow—cow—

Prompter. Coward, you booby—

Coward you booby, who forsook his master—
  Returning home in a chariot—

Prompter. In triumph sir—

In triumph sir—I disdained the shepherd's slothful wife—

Prompter. Life sir—

Life sir—and heaven directed, came to—to—to—to—to—to—

Prompter. Make a darned fool of yourself, booby!

Make a darned fool of myself booby, and do the happy deed which gilds my humble name!

XXXII.

THE FLOOD OF 1849 AND '50.

THIS will be well remembered by all the old residents of Sacramento.

It had been raining fearfully for many days, and the Sacramento river was rapidly rising; the lower portion of the city was entirely under water, and our store had about two feet "in the hold." The utmost consternation prevailed; and towards nightfall a perfect panic had seized the citizens, and naught appeared visible but the tops of the houses, with a swarm of human beings on the roofs.

Luckily, at the Levee there were moored some ships, barks, and schooners, that had been emptied of their cargoes and passengers; to these the women first were carried in boats and rafts, and indeed every imaginable conveyance was resorted to. J street was one mass of water—no speck of land was anywhere visible. We had vacated our store long since in boats, and I had the felicity of seeing a trunk full of new shirts, recently received from New York, floating down the stream, together with numberless other movables. I and one or two others, having by hook or by crook got hold of a boat, it was suggested that we should pull up in the vicinity of Dr. W.'s, situated in the upper part of the city, having ascertained that the ladies of the household were entirely at the mercy of the elements, and unable to leave their "ocean-bound" residence.

Arriving there, we found the house deserted, our boat walking straight into the drawing-room, and coming bump up against the legs of the piano (the water touching the keys thereof), when, to my astonishment, I found several of my songs floating on the top, and one in particular I thought was *now* in its proper element—that was, "When the Moon on the *Lake* is beaming."

Away again down J street, bump we went against the stump of a tree—then slap into a boat—both upset—got a duck in consequence, which we duly cooked; for, strange as it may seem, and scarce as every kind of fowl was in those days, a solitary duck, in the style of "James's horseman," was taking a stroll down the street, when he was thus taken by storm. Whole families were passing on rafts —others on the back of a cow; and although everybody appeared to think that a second edition of the Deluge had arrived, and a Noah's ark the thing to erect, yet everybody seemed jolly, and thought it a good joke.

Some of my friends proposed to me to give a concert on the water, and talked of Handel's water music; but I was compelled to refuse them, after many vain attempts to anchor a boat alongside the key-board of one of Waters's pianos.

The scene at night time was truly exciting.

The full moon, like a big ball of molten silver, shone forth with an unusual brilliancy from its home in the heavens, surrounded by its twinkling and glittering companions, the stars. One vast sheet of water lay beneath, reflecting the bright flashings of the jewelled firmament; and, excepting here and there a faint light from the house tops or from the masts of the shipping in the river, there was no sign of life or humanity! It was a repetition of the first flood, sure. Patches of feathery clouds, fanned by a stiff breeze, sailed to and fro in the sky; and the leafless branches of the big trees, with their bare and uplifted arms, shook with the north wind's piping.

Morning came, and from my little window in the cock-loft of the French Hotel, the room of which I had reached by the aid of a boat and a big ladder, the scene was equally exciting, and even comical. Merchandise of every variety and description was "afloat;" rafts and boats, filled with property, and swarming with live freight, filled the streets; those persons who were lucky enough to own a house, lived and slept on the roof—cooked on the roof—made calls on the roof—drank on the roof—prayed on the roof—laughed and joked on the roof—sang on the roof—took a bath on the roof—cursed the gold fields on the roof—wished they were back in New York on the roof—got married on the roof—went to church on the roof—wrote letters on the roof—and thought they'd never get off the roof.

But they did!—and such a stampede was never seen. Property went up as the men and women got down—and the waters fell; and to show the insanity that possessed everybody, myself among the number, at this period, at a sale of real estate by Col. J. B. Starr, I bought a piece of land, *covered by one foot of water*, for which I paid $1000 in gold dust, and which I subsequently parted with for *thirty dollars!*

The waters of the Sacramento river fell gradually lower and lower, and in a few days terra firma was again visible. The flood, however, had given me a general disgust for the place, and I accordingly made up my mind to "locate" myself in San Francisco.

Accordingly, the firm of Massett and Brewster was dissolved (as the papers always announce) by mutual consent. And here let me pay a passing tribute to my valued and respected friend; for a more honorable man and delightful companion, I have not met with in my wanderings; and I am happy likewise, *en passant*, to mention, that he is not only a flourishing merchant in the City of Brotherly Love, but (very unlike his *original* partner) a happy Benedict, with a whole lot of little fledglings. Long may they wave!

I had taken a lease of a store on Jackson street, owned by Lewis & Co., and very shortly afterwards the citizens of San Francisco were startled with the ringing of a big bell, and the walls covered with bills, announcing the fact that I was about to sell some real estate on the public plaza.

It was in this year that the celebrated pianist and composer, Henri Herz, visited California, arriving hither from Mexico, where he had, it was reported, realized fabulous sums of money. His concerts in San Francisco were crowded; and upon his trip to Sacramento, I happening to be upon the same steamer, and having met him previously in New York at our old friend Adam Stodart's, he proposed that I should sing for him, and asked me what my "terms" were.

Now I had given the first concert entirely by myself in this golden land, and one or two others besides, and generally pocketed four or five hundred dollars a night; and so I asked my friend from Paris five hundred pesos. He stared aghast, and said he couldn't stand it; but, however, at the solicitation of my friend Mr. F. C. Ewer, (now the Rev. F. C. Ewer, of this city,) *the* then editor of the Sacramento Transcript, I "concluded" to sing for two hundred dollars a night. (Pretty good pay now, I think.) The price of tickets was seven dollars and four dollars, and the house, at that, was crowded.

A funny incident occurred at Herz's concert, that was greatly enjoyed by the pianist and the audience also.

In obedience to an encore in one of my songs I was requested to give the comic recitation of the "*Frenchman and the Rats.*"

A somewhat laughable little sketch illustrating the difficulties of a Frenchman in his peregrinations in an English country town, and his being aroused from his slumbers by the visit of a big rat gnawing at a piece of cheese that he had placed under his pillow-case.

When I had arrived at this point in the anecdote—two rats with very long tails ran right across the stage, and a general scrambling of the same animal was heard on the "cotton" ceiling. A roar of laughter arose from the audience—Herz being quite convulsed, and certainly up to that time I had never given this much abused animal credit for possessing such powers of *rat*iocination!

A few nights after this, having been promised the assistance of a well known, and delightfully genial and jolly fellow—Johnny Nichols, one of the then "merchant princes" of this fast growing and flourishing city, I got out my programme. Coming immediately after this well known celebrity, I felt it was a little "risky," but then I thought the additional attraction of my friend "Johnny," as we all called him, would certainly draw a large crowd.

This was my first essay in Sacramento, and I was certainly anxious that it should "go off" with eclat. Now, my friend, though he had often in private delighted the ears of his listeners by his dulcet tones and refined taste in singing a ballad, and often amused us by a peculiarly appreciative expression of his face, with his head thrown back, a gentle swaying to and fro of the body, and a nervous twitching of the thumb and finger—though, I say, often on the classic ground of K—— street, where the "Salem" boys would congregate, and peddle to the delighted miners picks at six dollars each, cans of preserved oysters for the same price, and other articles in the same proportion—though here he was often heard, esteemed, and duly appreciated—he had not "as yet" faced an audience in public.

We had a rehearsal—and I remember it well—the song "Give me a Cot" was his happiest effort, and though there were only half a dozen deal benches in the room, without any sitters, and myself, the only one present, he said he felt his heart come up in his mouth or his mouth in his heart, I forget which, and had the most horrible forebodings as to the result of the evening. He offered me any money to let him off, but I wouldn't consent, his name was in the bills, and I was responsible for the performance taking place as per advertisements.

He explained to me that he had eaten nothing for a week, in simply anticipating the dread event, that the bare thought of this being the fatal night made him deathly sick, that hanging would even be a luxury, and that it was impossible to sing upon an empty stomach!

I obdurately refused to excuse him, insinuating that we

should both be ruined in reputation, looked upon as swindlers, and probably placed on board the "Prison Brig."

He replied that he would go to his store, lie down, try and take a nap, and a cocktail, say his prayers, and be at hand at half past seven—the dread hour came, eight o'clock came, and no "Johnny,"and no—"nothing." I don't know whether any of my readers have felt the peculiar sensation experienced sometimes by public performers in "waiting for somebody to come in;" if they have, they will sympathize with me upon this occasion, sitting upon the stump of a big tree at the lower end of M—— street in a drizzling shower of rain, underneath a Chinese umbrella! Darkness reigned supreme, and excepting the feeble glimmering of a very dismal and sickly looking oil lamp over the door of the hall, no light was visible.

In the dim distance a speck of light appeared, small, but brilliant as a firefly, nearer, nearer, nearer it came. I arose to meet it, when to my delight I found it was my companion in difficulties, "Johnny," with a big roll of music, a tin can full of strong punch, and a large umbrella. He gave a faint smile as I greeted him, and when in answer to his inquiry as to whether the hall was full, I answered him that I believed it was, but felt too nervous to go and see, the effect upon both of us was painfully visible.

It was now past eight, and something had to be done. I was waited upon by the Mayor of the city, assisted by Alderman Queen, and one of the Board of Supervisors, who suggested that it was time for me "to open."

I would readily have given at that moment all I possessed to have been a hundred miles from the place.

I was informed that three or four "lanterns" had just gone up stairs accompanied by several ladies, and that there were nearly a hundred people in the room; this, considering I had not seen a living soul, was a pretty good stroke of legerdemain.

"Johnny" crept slowly up the stairs, to deposit his traps, and prepare for the event, and just as I was following him with a palpitating heart, he passed by me at double quick time, remarking that he had left his music behind, and would return immediately. I think the next time I saw my friend, was in Salem, Massachusetts, some three years afterwards.

I must do my friend the justice, however, to say, that he delegated a distinguished pianist, Mr. George P——, now, I believe, one of the most successful and brilliant performers on the Pacific coast, to play, at an enormous cost, one of his compositions on the piano, which, in a measure, appeased the ire of the expecting and somewhat disappointed audience.

Now, as the reader will perceive, though in numbers the "crowd" was decidedly a select one, the figure of admission was three dollars each, and the consequence was I was nearly $300 in hand by the two hours' exertion.

XXXIII.

"GOING—GOING—GONE!" TO THE SANDWICH ISLANDS.

UPON returning to San Francisco and finding business a little dull, I thought I would take a run over to the Sandwich Islands, a distance of some eighteen hundred or two thousand miles, I think, and generally accomplished in from ten to fourteen days, taking the "trades" with us nearly all the way.

I accordingly took passage in the schooner Emeline, Captain Howard (of New London, Conn.), bound for Lahaina and Honolulu.

One of the most delightful voyages of my life, was this trip to the Islands.

XXXIV.

THE WAY THEY CATCH WHALES IN THE PACIFIC.

CAPTAIN HOWARD, of the schooner Emeline, was a first-rate specimen of a dry, quaint, good-natured, deown-east skipper. He hailed, I believe, from New London, and though in his earlier years he had been "a wailing," he had not (to use his own expression) seen the "darned thing speout" for many a long day.

It was a lovely evening in June, and the bright red sun had just dipped its flaming body in the western horizon, leaving the sky one sheet of the most dazzling crimson, while fleecy clouds, tipped with every variety of gorgeous coloring, followed in its wake, and sailed along the heavens—sapphire, green, purple, orange, blue, and yellow commingled together in wondrous harmony—making a sunset rarely seen in other than the Pacific waters. The day had been intensely hot, and a deliciously cool three or four knot breeze was carrying us to our destined port, and I and the skipper lounging in a hammock that had been swung for us on the upper deck.

Turning to me suddenly, he cried out, "There she blows!"

"Who's *she?*" says I.

"Why the whale, of course," says he; "don't you see that thing a speouting?"

I looked, and saw in the distance, for the first time in my life, one of these sea monsters.

"Did you ever hear how they ketch them fellers?" said the skipper.

I confessed my entire ignorance of the modus operandi, at the same time expressing the greatest desire to be informed of the method by one who had been in the business.

"Wall," says he, first giving a huge plug of tobacco a good twist in his mouth, "you must know that some years ago I sailed from New London with a man named Capting

Bissum. It was my first voyage, and I often hoped, afore I got back, it would be my last. We'd been eout abeout two years without seeing a thing, and I'd had nuthing to eat but salt pork and hard bread full o' worms and uther animals, and had broke several teeth in trying to get it through my head—when all of a sudden the man at the masthead sung out,

"'Thar she blows!'

"I looked at Capting Bissum—Capting Bissum looked at me. He said nothin'—I said nuthin'.

"The man at the masthead sung out,

"'Thar—she—blows!'

"I walked right up to Capting Bissum, and says I, 'Capting Bissum, shall I lower away?' Says he, 'Simmons Howard—(that's my name, yer know)—if you sees fitten to lower—lower and be d——!' Thereupon I did lower—and I says,

"'Give way, boys, for 'ile's a rising.'

"And I pulled right straight away up to the critter, and I shoved my harpoon just abaft his blowers, and I guv him such a fluke as settled him for life; and I cum aboard, and Capting Bissum met me at the gangway with tears in his eyes—and says he,

"'Simmons Howard, you're a leetle of the smartest man as ever druv a harpoon in these 'ere suthern seas. There's my t'baccy box and my pipe, at your sarvice for the remainder of the woyage.'

"Says I, 'Capting Bissum,' says I, 'I axes favors of no man. All I want is ciwility, and that of the commonest kind.'

"What d'ye think o' that?" says he, for a yarn.

And we had a jolly good laugh at the recital.

XXXV.

THE ISLAND OF LAHAINA.

I THINK it was about the twelfth day out, that we neared the Island of Maui—of which Lahaina is the principal city. The ostensible purport of the visit of the schooner was for a cargo of potatoes and onions, these vegetables at that time bringing fifteen and twenty cents a pound in San Francisco, and only costing two cents there.

As we neared the beach in the schooner's boat, hundreds of natives came swimming towards us, throwing us fruit, etc.

Just as I was gaining the shore, and had read the words "Custom House" in large black letters on a very rickety-looking building, I heard a voice call out, "There's Steve M——."

This certainly had the effect of making me feel somewhat at home, and upon my shaking hands with my friend in uniform, I found he was the acting U.S. Consul there, Mr. Wm. Hubbard, once of Buffalo, who remembered me when at Nevin's—the reader may remember how many years ago. We "homologated" at once—my trunks were immediately transferred to his residence, which he informed me was used as the country "palace" of the Queen, Kamehameha—and surely no lovelier or cooler spot could have been selected, right on the shores of the Pacific, while groves of cocoa-nut and orange-trees shielded you from the scorching rays of the sun in the daytime.

They had two very fair hotels, where you could be accommodated at one dollar per diem, for board and bedding; but the plan generally adopted, I found out, was to hire what they call a "Grass House." These cost only four dollars a month, and are cool, and kept by the natives scrupulously clean; the furniture simply consisting of a bamboo chair, a table, a bedstead, with a Chinese mat on it, and one thin sheet, of course covered by a "mosquito net."

LAHAINA.

I had heard much in my boyish days, both in England and the United States, of the privations, the trials, the dangers, and the troubles of the "poor missionary." Indeed, I recollect of a mahogany box with a brass plate on it, that lay for years on my father's parlor table, with the significant words: "*For the Poor Heathen*" engraved thereon—and as I would *very* occasionally drop therein a heavy penny of the reign of George the Third, and give the box a gentle shake, to see how much was in it, I felt I had done something for the *copper-colored* race—and when at "Exeter Hall," at the missionary meetings, at the May anniversaries, I would gaze with astonishment, wonder, and almost holy reverence, as the chairman would introduce the Rev. Mr. So and So, from the "Sandwich Islands," to the audience. I little dreamed that I should revel in the luxuries of the delicious climate from whence they came, or witness the content, elegance, and refinement in which these self-sacrificing, disinterested, and sedate looking gentlemen passed away their lives.

Upon one occasion I distinctly remember going down to the St. Katharine Dock, in London, to witness the departure of some missionaries for the port of Honolulu—and I felt an inward conviction that they were going to certain death—that they would be cleaved right up immediately upon their arrival; and when a facetious friend of mine, who had recently returned from that portion of the globe, informed me, that at the hotel at which he stopped, he noticed one day an extraordinary-looking dish, at one end of the table, and upon inquiring its nomenclature, was informed it was "a piece of cold missionary," I shuddered at the thought of their fool-hardiness, and invariably lauded their truly Christian philanthropic and devotional intentions.

The Rev. Mr.—— of Lahaina, who had resided there at the date about which I am writing, some twenty years ago —was not only very much respected and beloved by his congregation, consisting of native men and women, but passed his days in ease, quiet, and luxury; and I was informed had amassed quite a snug little fortune; and I will here remark, not intending to pursue the subject further of the good or evil effects of the Missionary system, that in all the countries I have visited, the Missionary has been the most independent, has lived the most luxuriously, and instead of his life being one of banishment and hardship, it appeared to me to be one of tranquillity, competence, and ease.

Lahaina with its environs is certainly the principal point of attraction on the Island of Maui, it being the only seaport of this portion of the Hawaiian group.

The roadstead of this beautiful island in the spring and fall of the year is filled with large whale ships, that have come in from the various cruising grounds of the Pacific to recruit, where all kinds of supplies can be obtained on more advantageous terms, and with less detriment to the men, than at any other place in these waters.

The principal supplies, if I remember right, furnished by the natives, are hogs, goats, fruit of all kinds, poultry, vegetables, and particularly Irish potatoes, for which they receive money, cloth, etc., in exchange. Fresh beef is somewhat hard to get.

The bathing, and diversions with the surf-board by the natives, are particularly amusing. In the south part of the town, I used to wander when the sea was rolling in heavily over the reef, and observe the evolutions and wondrous rapidity of a set of surf-playing natives. The sport is immensely attractive, and to the Hawaiians full of the wildest excitement—though certainly I fancied to a novice it would be dangerous in the extreme.

As I witnessed this exciting and exhilarating amusement, how greatly I regretted my inability to swim, or to get balanced on a board just before a great big wave—and to be hurried in half a mile or so landward with racehorse speed—all the time wrapt in spray and foam—and without letting the roller break, and tumble over my head.

It seemed to me to require great strength of muscle to keep the head and shoulders just ahead and clear of the great crested wall that seemed impending over them—and threatening to bury the bold surf-rider in its watery ruin.

The natives perform this with wonderful intrepidity,

skill, and daring—riding upon the neck and mane, as if it were one of their furious chargers; and when you look to see them in their swift course dashed upon the sand or rocks, they will just slip under the belly of the wave they have ridden—and are away outside again, waiting for a sail upon another.

On the Atlantic sea-board there is wanting the delicious temperature of the water within these tropics, and I can conceive of nothing more exquisite than laving the wearied limbs in its invigorating embraces.

Speaking of Lahaina, the Rev. Mr. Cheever in his capitally written works says: "It is one of those places which you like much better as you approach or recede from it, than when you are actually in it. A little way off it seems sweetly embosomed in bread-fruit trees, and all fresh and lovely with sunshine and verdure, calmly inclosed seaward within a fence of foam, made by the sea breaking upon the coral reef. Ride over the rollers in a whale-boat or native canoe, get to the sun-burnt, dusty land, walk up a few rods, perhaps with white pantaloons, to the mission-houses, and make acquaintance on the way to your heart's content with Lahaina dust and caloric, and you will probably by that time be saying to yourself—

'Twas distance lent enchantment to the view.

"However, dirt, fleas, mosquitoes, and heat to the contrary notwithstanding, Lahaina has so salubrious and dry a climate, and advantages for healthful sea-bathing all the year round, that one who is anything of an invalid likes to be there, or, what is better, two miles above, at the seminary of Lahainaluna. It is said that the greatest observed elevation of the mercury here in Fahrenheit's thermometer, for ten years, was 86 deg.; the lowest, 54 deg. The wind is the alternating land and sea breeze. A steep mountainous ridge in the rear entirely breaks off the trades, and, receiving all their rain, carries it distilled below in a fertilizing stream that irrigates all the valley and vega of Lahaina, and is spent before it reaches the sea.

"Two or three times in a year the trades whirl over the mountain, and then woe to the man's eyes that are so luckless as to be found in it. From hill and plain there are caught up great, suffocating volumes of red dust, that envelop all the town, and even roll off to ships in the road-stead, and redden the sea. Closed doors and windows are as mere lattice-work for it. It traverses stone walls and *adobes*, human lungs and ears, and I know not but livers, and permeates every thing. If a man's eye only escape being filled and getting the ophthalmia, he is well off. But the blow is over, all is well again. The sea or the translucent Lahainaluna water is there to wash in, and, merrily making your ablutions within and without, you'll sing—

> Cold water for me, cold water for me!
> But wine for the tremulous debauchee!"

XXXVI.

THE CITY OF HONOLULU, S. I.

AFTER passing three or four weeks very delightfully here, I took passage in a Government vessel for the city of Honolulu, the Capital of the Island of "Oahu," pronounced O-wy-hee.

Two days I think brought us to our destined port. After delivering some letters of introduction, and having had my traps taken to the United States Hotel, I strolled with my friend S—— of the house of Makee Anthon & Co., (whom at this late day I wish to thank for many acts of kindness and attention), to see a few of the lions and lionesses.

I believe, at the time of which I am writing, Honolulu had a population of about 20,000—the principal building at that time was the Custom House—quite an imposing looking edifice of white stone. They also had a little theatre here, several churches of various persuasions, and numbers of quite elegantly constructed private dwellings. The varied scenery of the valley called Nuuanu, with its highly cultivated cascades, cottages, and romantic mountain sides is beautiful in the extreme. I passed some delightful hours at the residence of Dr. Judd, which he calls "Sweet Home"—and I carry with me "pleasant memories" of the charming society and kind hospitality of his wife and daughters.

Now it was suggested to me that as there never yet had been a concert given at the Islands, and as they had seen by the S. F. journals, that I had given several, "unaided and unassisted," in California, I should accordingly inaugurate the system there, and I was accordingly dubbed the "Captain Cook" of the tribe of wandering minstrels.

I was in a dilemma about a good piano, when upon being introduced to Mrs. Patteson, the daughter of Mr. Allen the U. S. Consul, she most kindly loaned me one of "Chickering's" celebrated "grand," which was duly carted to the place of amusement.

The night was oppressively hot, and the theatre crowded. The private boxes, of which there were three, were reserved for the Royal party, consisting of the King, Kammehameha, two or three Queens, and any number of Princes and Princesses. The first (and only) tier was filled with the English and American portion of the population, and the pit crammed with Kanakas, men, women, and children.

The performance had gone on smoothly enough until I came to the ballad of "The Old Arm Chair," which I was requested to sing in response to an encore. Now, not having then a very definite idea of the opinions entertained of my merits or demerits by the native part of my auditory, I was quite unprepared for the following incident, which for the moment upset my equilibrium, and threw the house into roars of laughter. When feeling in pretty good trim, I have generally been successful in operating upon the feelings or the nerves of some tender-hearted old or young lady (as the case may be) in rendering the second stanza of this charming composition of Eliza Cook, and upon the present occasion, this hydraulic phenomenon having been witnessed by two or three of the Kanakas, they all stood up, shook their fists at me, and gesticulating in the most extraordinary manner, and jabbering in the native tongue, at the top of their voices, completely upset everything for the moment. I stopped short, came to the front, and asked them what they wished. "Oliolo hale kage, boo-boo, hokey-pokey, shaggy-baggy, male-halle, poko-foko," they replied, pointing to the women who were crying upstairs. With this they ran out of the building, and swore vengeance against me. I was told that they thought by seeing the women in tears, that I had insulted them, and as they were entirely in the dark as to the nature of the performance, devoid as it was of anything particularly meretricious, they took this opportunity to vent their indignation. Order was soon restored, and at the end of the entertainment, his Majesty did me the honor to take some sherry wine with me, and invited me to the Palace on the following day.

The "Polynesian" had the following, in reference to the performance:

MR. STEPHEN MASSETT, THE AMERICAN VOCALIST.—This gentleman's first appearance at the Hawaiian Hall, last evening, was attended by His Majesty, King Kammahamaha, and the principal English and American residents, who appeared quite delighted with the rare and intellectual treat afforded them. Mr. Massett was waited upon at the close of his performance by a number of influential gentlemen, who requested him to defer his departure for a few days, to enable them to enjoy a repetition of his ballad entertainment.

XXXVII.

ARRIVE AGAIN AT SAN FRANCISCO.

AFTER a delightful run of fourteen days, I arrived again at San Francisco, in the schooner Odd Fellow, and proceeded at once to Sacramento, where I met my future partner, Mr. R. H. Taylor, of the Marysville Herald, the second paper ever started in California.

He made me an offer to purchase half the establishment, and upon mature deliberation and reflection of about an hour and a half I concluded to do so, and immediately prepared to start for my future home in the city of Marysville, Yuba county, California, and to take my seat as the junior editor of the aforementioned journal.

The Gov. Dana steamer conveyed myself and two trunks in safety to the landing at the Levee; and when I had managed, after wading up to my middle in mud and slush, to find out the office of the Herald, situated then on a barren waste, known on the map as the corner of C and Second street, I resembled more the driver of a swill cart, or a street-sweeping machine, than one of the corps editorial. Upon knocking at the door and lifting the latch, I found my "senior," wrapped in a red blanket, fast asleep, lying upon a cot, that boasted of no other ornament than that it went on "tick," and repudiated altogether pillows and mattresses. The attenuated form of the gallant Colonel lay stretched out in all the blissful ignorance of sleep, and with mouth wide open—regardless of the hammering of the foreman in an adjoining apartment, who was "putting the paper to press"—gave utterance to his thoughts and pent-up feelings in a snore that would have startled one less nervous than myself.

XXXVIII.

I TURN EDITOR.

THE office was a little wooden shanty, of a very unpretending style of architecture, and difficult indeed to describe. It had a door, a roof, and one or two windows, and was, I believe, originally one of a number of "portable houses" sent "round the Horn" by some enterprising man at the east, and by which speculation an immense amount was realized. I think ours cost about $600—(worth at home about $150.)

After waking my "sleeping partner," and meeting with a kindly greeting, I proceeded as quickly as possible to get into the "harness" of my daily business; and after some three or four days' initiation by my senior, who had to go to San Jose to report the proceedings of the Legislature, I was left in sole charge of the "sheet."

To say that I had no misgivings, upon viewing the receding form of my tall partner, as he with trowsers tucked into his cowskin boots, and with valise in hand and numberless things in his head, wended his way to the stage office to take passage for Sacramento city, would be not to tell the truth. In those days Californian editors generally slept with two or three double-barrelled pistols under their head, and the same number of bowie knives at their feet; for if an article happened to appear, reflecting in the slightest degree upon the character of an individual or individuals, corporate bodies or bodies incorporate, he, she, they, or it would immediately wait upon you "by a friend," demanding instant satisfaction with either knives, pistols, or both. Therefore, I felt keenly the fearful responsibility resting upon my shoulders.

Our paper was then a "tri-weekly;" and as the political and consequently prosy portion thereof was taken care of entirely by Mr. Taylor, it was reserved for me to look after the matters of local interest, and "do up" "the short articles, items," etc.

The year of my residence in Marysville passed away so

delightfully that I really regretted the thought of leaving; still, as restlessness and change were the order of the day, and I fancied the offer made me for my interest in the journal a good one, I made up my mind to sell out; intending to return to New York, prior to a brief trip to Europe, and being at this time master of a larger sum, in cash and real estate, than I had ever been before or have been since.

Many interesting incidents and adventures took place during my sojourn here; and from a little memorandum book of my brief Notes, I will jot down a few of them.

XXXIX.

AN EDITORIAL CONCERT.

UPON one occasion, the business of our paper led me again to San Francisco; and having (as was usually the case) been very successful, not only in swelling our subscription list pretty considerably, but in collecting large sums for advertising, I thought I might do a little business profitably on my own account, having been solicited by many of my New York friends (amusements being at that time rather scarce) to give a concert.

I accordingly went over to the "Alta" office, and got out a programme. The prices were—boxes, five dollars—side boxes, three dollars—pit, three dollars.

The bellman, to whom I had paid five dollars for ringing in the people, and calling out at the top of his voice the nature of the entertainment, had just informed me that the house was full, and it was time for me to begin, when, all of a sudden, I found I had forgotten the piano.

Now as there was no orchestra, and I always accompanied myself in my own songs, the reader will perceive I was in a "fix." However, great was my delight and relief in the premises, when at the eleventh hour I found a gorgeous Chickering grand at my disposal, which Mayor Selover, of the Union Hotel, was kind enough to loan me. An apology was made by me for the delay, and all went off well; I netting $600 by the labor of one hour and a half.

The day after, the city was reduced to ashes by one of the largest and most destructive fires on record; theatre, hotel, piano, and everything else being fuel for the flames. The next day I received a letter from my esteemed partner, who remarked that he thought it was "rather derogatory to the dignity of an editor to be going about the country giving exhibitions of his vocal and imitative powers;" but that he wouldn't have any material objection, provided I would *halve* the receipts!

So much for my "Editorial Concert!"

XL.

THE GREAT FIRE—AN INCIDENT AT THE BANK.

At this time T. Butler King, Esq., was Collector of the port, and running for U. S. Senator. Our paper supported his election, and the consequence was, a very "fat" advertisement fell to the lot of the proprietors of the "Marysville Herald," to the tune of $1800, which amount was duly handed to me in octagonal fifty dollar gold pieces, and which was lodged for safe keeping at the banking-house of Burgoyne & Co., at the corner of Montgomery and Washington streets.

The deposit was made the day after my concert had taken place, consequently I had about $2500 "on call" there at the time.

I was standing at the top of "Clay" street, near "Pike," when the fire was raging at its height; block after block of buildings were caught in the fiery embrace, Union Hotel, Theatre, El Dorado Building, all, all were swept away, and at last the flames caught the Bank of Burgoyne & Co., whose building was considered fire-proof. It was seemingly inclosed in sheets of flame, and many a heart quailed in expectation of losing every cent there deposited, for the heaviest accounts in the city were kept at this pet banking-establishment. If my friend J. R. C. ever reads these lines, he will *recollect* the query I put to him, as to whether he thought the "place" would stand!

On that night everybody slept in the open air, on the top of barrels, bales, or anything else—there did not seem a vestige of a house left. Utter desolation and despair reigned supreme. About ten o'clock on the following morning, Mr. Geo. Plume, one of the firm, upon going to the safe (one of the celebrated Herring's by the way) handed me my buckskin bag of gold, with even the sealing-wax not melted!

So much for a good safe, and my luck!

Before I left Marysville, it was suggested that I should have a "farewell concert." The following "correspondence" upon the subject appeared in the daily papers:—

Marysville, Nov. 29, 1851.

To Stephen C. Massett, Esq.

DEAR SIR:—Before you break the final link, and bid us farewell, we earnestly solicit you to give to the ladies and citizens of Marysville a public concert,—in order that they, as well as ourselves, may once again have the gratification and pleasure of enjoying and appreciating your excellent voice and musical talents.—You will thus add another to the "pleasant memories" we shall ever have of you, and, we hope, also, increase those which you kindly say you will take away with you.

We pledge ourselves to give you a bumper, and with the sincere desire that happiness and prosperity may ever attend you,

We are, dear sir, With every consideration, Yours most faithfully,

Hon. S. M. MILES, Mayor.
EDWARD S. WOODRUFF,
President of Common Council.

E. Garst, Ald. 1st Ward.
F. W. Shaeffer, Ald. 2d Ward.
D. W. C. Rice, Ald. 3d Ward
Howell & Co.
Blanchar & Garst.
Col. C. S. Kasson.
S. T. Watts, M.D.
Chas. Ball.
Thos. Bennet, M. D.
Roberts, Packard & Co.
King, Pierce & Co.
R. H. Taylor.
Cuningham & Brumagim.
Packard & Co.
Henry P. Watkins.
J. H. Adams.
W. Willson Smith.
Stephen J. Field.
James Cushing.
Samuel A. Wheeler.
Capt. A. Pinnix.

Marysville, Dec. 1. 1851.

To the Hon. S. M. Miles, Alderman E. Woodruff, Alderman Garst, and others:

GENTLEMEN:—Your very kind and flattering letter has just been received by me, and I assure you from my heart I thank you for your good wishes. I shall be most happy to give a Concert in Marysville ere I leave, and I have the pleasure to inform you that I have been promised by Messrs. Van Reed and Alderman McDuffie, the proprietors of the El Dorado, the new brick building erecting on D street, the large room, on the night previous to their opening, for that purpose. Due notice will be given of the evening the concert will take place.

Assuring you, gentlemen, that I shall ever retain the liveliest remembrance of your favors,

I remain your obedient servant,

S. C. Massett.

On the 2d of March, 1852, I left San Francisco in the Pacific M. S. S. "Northerner," Captain Randall, for Panama; and a most delightful trip we had of it.

After enjoying myself to my heart's content once again in dear New York, and receiving the congratulations of friends upon my safe arrival from the Land of Gold, I made up my mind to pay a visit to my relations in England, and make a brief trip on the Continent.

I accordingly presented myself at the office of C. H. Marshall, and engaged a passage in the packet ship "Great Western," Captain W. G. Furber, for Liverpool.

We left New York on the morning of February 17, 1853, and landed at the Victoria Dock, Liverpool, on the 7th of March, after a delightful run of only 16 days.

XLI.

SINGULAR SENSATIONS UPON RE-VISITING ENGLAND.

If I have succeeded in interesting the reader sufficiently in these reminiscences and sketches, to have kept in his memory the date of my arrival in New York from England, he will find that about seventeen years of my life had passed away since I had left my "native heath;" and certainly my sensations upon my return, as may be imagined, were of a very peculiar nature.

I had left England a boy, arriving in the New World with no fixed purpose or intention, had led somewhat of a discursive life, and certainly a very different one from that carved out for me by my beloved parents.

How many and shifting were the scenes I had passed through. How many changes had taken place; what views of the past greeted my mental vision, as I gazed through the long vista of the departed years, and my heart lingered with pleasure and with pain on the "pictures of memory," that flashed for a moment before me, as I trod once again the shores of my native land! Pleasure at the thought of meeting once more with the few that remained of our once extended family circle. Pain as I yearned for

> "The touch of a vanished hand,
> And the sound of a voice that was still!"

XLII.

MY FIRST DAY IN LIVERPOOL.

It was exactly half-past four o'clock on the afternoon of Tuesday the 7th of March, that I landed with my baggage at the Victoria Dock, and proceeded to the depôt to be examined.

This I found (contrary to my expectations) to be a very easy matter, the officer simply passing his hand down each side of my trunk, and taking my word that there was nothing in my hat-box but my new "Genin."

I then took a "car," as they called it, and drove to the "Adelphi" Hotel—one of the best taverns in England—to the porter who carried my luggage from the steamer to the baggage office, I gave two shillings (or 50 cents), to the "cabman," one shilling and sixpence.

I found a "book" (à la Americaine) in the hall of the hotel, in which I registered my name, and was shown to a very comfortable room (No. 18) by a very pretty little chambermaid.

The bedstead and fixtures generally amused me exceedingly—so different from ours in America! It was ascended on either side by a step-ladder—it was surrounded by huge damask curtains—a fire made ready for lighting—

guard, fender, poker, shovel, and tongs; these trifles brought up most strangely to me the "days lang syne!"

Now, I do not intend in these brief "glances" at places and people, to give any very extended sketch or account of the surroundings, or of my sojournings,—the thing has been done to death from the year *one*, up to the present time; and I shall content myself by saying in reference to *Liverpool*, that I think it one of the most gloomy looking places I have ever visited, and that I felt that I could "do" it in one day quite easily, and to *my own* satisfaction.

Towards night I strolled a little through the town. The first thing that struck me was the "street-singing," two blind men were walking hand in hand, in the gutter, looking as blind men invariably do, right up in the sky—singing "Rejoice greatly in the Lord," whilst in another street an awful specimen of humanity—stone-blind also, shuffled along, with a tract in his hand, which he kept constantly thrusting nervously at the passers-by, singing out in the most doleful manner, "Moore's Almanack," only a "apenny!"

At the Theatre Royal (a miserably dirty looking place—that after the luxuriousness of "Wallack's," "Laura Keene's," "Niblo's," or the "Academy," was really intolerable) I found they were playing the "Enchantress."

The audience was slim, and I did not see a pretty woman in the house.

I paid four shillings—(one dollar) for my seat in the "dress circle"—the upper boxes were three shillings; the pit two shillings, and the gallery one shilling.

The singers were Miss Louisa Pyne, Mr. Harrison, and Mr. Borrani.

The lady I thought bore a strong resemblance to "The Queen"—and has one of the first voices I ever heard, she sang superbly. Harrison, with decidedly a fine voice, was harsh in his style, and occasionally sang out of tune—he is a large muscular good-looking fellow, a little like "Wood," and a handsome likeness of "Gardner," who played at the Park some years since. Borrani's voice grated on the ear—he seemed to have no method—he is a very Jewish-looking personage.

The orchestra was led (as the bills say) by Mr. Fitz-william, son of the actress—and was wretched—and to my astonishment the "first fiddle" was played by a "colored gemman"—yes, a regular woolly-headed mulatto.

I stood two acts, and turned my steps to the "Amphi-theatre" where they were playing "Uncle Tom's Cabin"—stood about five minutes of that—for the dirt, dust, heat, and fleas, were not to be endured. I accordingly adjourned to a thorough English looking Oyster Saloon—being a room about four feet wide by six deep. Here a very civil, fat, rosy-faced man, with "bib and tucker" on, opened me a "couple of dozen of Natives," his wife cutting me some thin "bread and butter;" and washing it down with a glass of very indifferent ale, I paid my bill, and toddled to the "Adelphi," followed and beset by beggars, old women with bills of the play, distressed seamen, and *abandoned* females.

Arrived at the Hotel, I had a very pleasant interview with the composer Mr. George Barker, known in America as the author of "Mary Blane," the "White Squall." After a "strong cup," I adjourned to my cozy chamber and *high old bed*, the top of which having reached I seemed to fall through an ocean of feather beds, covered by at least a bale of blankets, and several hundred yards of the choicest Irish-linen—it having first been subjected by my pretty chambermaid to the operation of the warming pan, the reader can well imagine I did not suffer much that night from "cold."

Thus ended my first, and ("I guess") last night in Liverpool.

XLIII.

ALL ABOUT THE CITY OF LONDON.

THE next day I took the Express Train for London, paying one pound seventeen shillings for a first class ticket —this is about twice the amount that would be charged for the same distance in America. I arrived at the Euston Square Station at about four o'clock, and proceeded at once to the residence of my nephew Dr. F. C.W—— in Great Coram St., Russell Square.

* * * * * * * *

Once again did I find myself in my native city.

How difficult I find it to describe my feelings as I obeyed the request to "Knock and Ring" that stared me in the face, at the house of my relative! When I left England he was a boy at school. I return to find him a practising physician, with a little family of youngsters! and then the greeting! the mental surprise of each at the change! the eagerness with which I sought to catch the faintest remembrance of the past, either by glancing at the portrait, or a piece of furniture, or by questions innumerable—with these sensations few of my readers will sympathize—and I will proceed at once to "jog along" in my own way with my doings in the big city.

If the reader imagines that I am going to *describe* London particularly or any other city, town, or hamlet, I may have to mention, he or she is greatly mistaken; and as I said at the commencement of these "reminiscences," I intended to be guided by no rule, in the construction of this book, but just to "jot down" scenes, incidents, and things—as they occurred in my brief sojournings in the different portions of the globe, I have at various intervals visited.

It seems to me that the sensations of a person on his first arrival in London will be those of intense curiosity. They may not partake particularly of the feeling of wonder or admiration; because the visitor may probably, at a distance, have been accustomed to attach a vague idea of importance and grandeur to everything belonging to this City—and the places and objects that may first meet his gaze—as in my case—may not possess so much externally to recommend them to his notice, as many towns which he may have passed through on his journey.

For instance, a person coming by any of the Eastern suburbs, will be sure to form a very different idea of the vastness or opulence of the great Metropolis, from that conceived by another who comes to it by a western road, and takes up his residence at a West-end-Hotel—but most assuredly, wherever he alights, he must immediately receive an impression of the greatness of London, and it seems to me that his curiosity to explore it will be immediately excited.

My advice, in the first place, to all visiting the "Great Metropolis," is to take apartments in some nice quarter of the town—in the vicinity of Piccadilly, or thereabouts, say in Old Bond Street, St. James's Place, or Duke Street, and get your meals when and where you please. Hotel life in London is not only extremely expensive, but to an American I should imagine anything but desirable. Indeed I have often heard Englishmen remark, that the American system of charging a certain fixed sum per diem is a great deal the best.

"Simpson's" in the Strand, nearly opposite "Exeter Hall," is a first-rate place to dine—at about two shillings and six pence cost, including your pint of porter. If you happen to be a little further west—the "Albany" in Piccadilly, or the "Waterloo" in St. James, will answer equally well; at either of these places, you can get a capital dinner for three shillings, or seventy-five cents.

Added to this there are innumerable "chop-houses," such as the "Cock," "Bolt-on-tow," "Dr. Johnson's," the "Goose and Gridiron," "Dolly's."

Now as I have stated above, the plan is much the best to hire a sleeping apartment in a good location, for which you will pay one pound one shilling or five dollars a week, or even less, if you do not care to be in so fashionable a locality, as for instance in "Cecil," "Surrey," or "Catharine" Street in the Strand, a very snug and cozy lodging can be had for twelve shillings per week.

Thus it will be seen, that a person desirous of economizing can reside in the big city for one pound ten shillings or seven dollars per week.

XLIV.

THE "FIELDING"—MR. THACKERAY, ETC.

It was during my connexion with the "Marysville Herald," that I made the acquaintance of two young Englishmen, travelling in California, whom I subsequently met in London, and to whom I am indebted for many pleasant introductions.

I was introduced by one of these gentlemen to the "*Fielding*," a literary club (now I believe defunct) situated in Henrietta street, Covent Garden.

Of the notables I met on my first visit, "Thackeray," "Douglas Jerrold," and "Albert Smith," were the most conspicuous.

Thackeray had just returned from America, where he had been very successful with his Lectures on the "Georges."

I had been presented to the author of "Pendennis," by a member of the club—a Sir George A——, which, doubtless, had the effect of inducing the learned satirist to cast one of his patronizing glances on so unimportant an individual as myself.

Now at this club, and at the "Garrick," (about which more by and bye) there seemed to obtain among the members a perfect "free-masonry" of feeling; and badinage was indulged in to any extent.

Thackeray had just entered, and was thus addressed by the "business man" of Albert Smith, "Well, Thackeray, you got on very well with your 'show' in America; have you seen ours?"

Thackeray seemed at first to take no notice of the remark, but walked slowly to the fireplace, sat down in an arm chair, crossed his legs, adjusted his spectacles, and with the tips of the fingers of each hand meeting, and looking straight at a piece of Liverpool coal, replied in the following curt manner:

"I never had much opinion of your brother's talent; but I admire his good fortune!"

The fact is, he did not "see" the applicability of the word "show," or like the free and easy style of interrogatory indulged in.

XLV.

COMICAL SCENES IN A POLICE COURT.

The police regulations of the metropolis are admirably adapted for the maintenance of peace and order, and are very much superior to the old fogy system of "watchmen" and constables. The chief office of the Force, I think, is in "Guildhall," in the city, and I was informed the total number of men, including sergeants and inspectors, etc., was over 7000.

One of the most celebrated of the police offices is in Bow-street, Covent Garden. Here upon one or two occasions (as the reader shall know) I enjoyed a hearty laugh.

The "Court" is open to the public each day, while the magistrate is sitting, and presents to the reflective observer, many scenes of varied character, which make a lasting impression on the mind. The First Case was

Mr. Doddles and his Donkey.—James Doddles and his wife were charged with disorderly and riotous conduct under the following unpleasant circumstances:—Mr. Doddles presented a most chilling appearance, for his clothes were wet through, and his hair, matted with mud and blood, clearly showed he had not had an opportunity for the use of a comb for some months past. His better half—in more senses than one, for she was twice his size—stood before the Bench, with her nasal organ entirely enveloped in plaster and rag. The couple altogether presented an appearance which could not fail to create a smile even from the Bench. The evidence of the police was to the effect of their having seen both defendants at daylight this (Saturday) morning very much the worse for plentiful imbibings, and in company with a —— donkey, who apparently shared in Mr. Doddles's frolics, if he had not in his drink, for he was incessantly kicking up his heels at every drunken attempt they made to load him with their wegetables; and once on finding that a fine bunch of carrots, which they had slung across his neck, was within reach of his grinders, he speedily displaced and nearly devoured it, to the great amusement of the lookers-on, before he was detected. Ultimately it was found requisite to remove James and his wife to the station-house, for they created a great disturbance, besides wallopping the donkey unmercifully.—Magistrate: What are you, Mr. Doddles?—James: Your honorable vorship, I sells wegetables and all kinds of green stuff.—Magistrate: And where do you live?—James: Vy, I lives close alongside of Borl's-pond.—Magistrate: What pond do you mean?—Officer: Ball's-pond, Dalston, sir.—James: To be sure; but I alvays goes to Common-garden-market for my goods, vet or dry, vind or no vind, and precious vindy it vos this morning, I can tell you, and no mistake.—Magistrate: Come, now, tell me how you and Mrs. Doddles got into this state, and be quick, if you please?—Mrs. Doddles: Go it, Jim, tell his lordship all about it.—James: So I vill. Yer see, yer honor, this is my wife—my Sarah—(putting his hand on her head to force her to curtsey.)—Mrs. Doddles: Now then, Jem, mind my nose. (Much laughter.)—James: Vell, sir, as I vos saying, Sarah and I goes to Common-garden on the donkey.—Magistrate: What, both! it must be a famous strong one, then.—James (seriously, and holding up his finger): Yer honor, it's the werry best "moke" as ever had long ears. (Great mirth.) Well—we goes there safe enough—and in course I'll tell the truth. We had a drain or two afore we bought the stuff, and a drain or two arter. Now, I don't know how it is, but my Sarah and me often drank twenty times as much, but it never got so far ahead on us before. Then the "moke" couldn't stand on his legs, and vonce he threw us both clean off him.—Magistrate: What, threw you both off?—James: That's it, yer honor; "up goes the donkey, and away goes Sarah and me." (Renewed laughter.) I cuts my head open again a scraper, and my Sarah breaks her nose. Well, then, I owns as I did it—yes—I vollopped the "moke," and—and—that's all of it.—Magistrate: Is your wife's nose much injured?—Sarah: Your lordship, the doctor sez as how the cartlid (cartilage) of it is werry nigh broked. The donkey threw us away flying, and I fell vith my nose between the rails of a grating.—Subsequently, and amid continual merriment, the defendants were dismissed—his Worship thinking no doubt that they had suffered enough.

The Second was

THE TAIL (TALE) OF A JACKASS.—From the era that Saul went forth to seek his father's asses, and from the intelligent *donkey* which reproved Balaam, down to the veritable *Lumber Troop*, *asses* have formed a continuous link in the chain of human society. Mahomet rode on one to Mecca. Peter Pindar wrote an epistle of some two hundred lines or more "to his ass, Peter." Sterne moraliseth over the truly sentimental dead "Neddy," at "Nampont." Mr. William Wordsworth says mighty fine things of a *temperance*-looking donkey, drowned in his own beloved lake (see the Excursion, Book iv., Pedlar, etc.) and brays as eloquently as poor Sancho Panza, when his "dumb animal!" went astray in the mountains—not to mention the "Golden Ass of Apuleius." The ass of Hampstead-heath, however, distances all other animals.

John Jobson *vs.* Timothy Brown.—This was an action for the recovery of a donkey, price 12s., sold by John Jobson—commonly known as "Jack Sleeky," to the defendant, Tim Brown, for the aforesaid sum of money.

First Commissioner—How will you pay, Mr. Brown?

Mr. Brown—Not no how, if so be I nose it—(laughter)—his donkey's a reg'lar wishous one, and I couldn't manage him not no how—(laughter.)

Third Commissioner—Well, sir, you shouldn't a' bought him.

Sleeky Jack—Now, then, jest year me speak, an' ill up and tell you. This year hidentical donkey as he speaks on, used to run on Hampstead-heath on a Sundays, along with another one; this year tother one died through severe weather, and the donkey as I bought took it so much to heart as I never seed afore—first he took to biting, then he took to kicking, and at last one o' our chaps on the heath said as how a change of hair 'ud do him good, so I took the hanimal down to Blackheath and sold him to Tim Brown, as kept donkeys for women to ride on. (Roars of laughter.)

First Commissioner—Well, and what passed?

Sleeky Jack—Why, Tim Brown axed me how he'd go —trot him out, says I—and werry well he trotted—then he ses, ses he, what's he carry? anythink, ses I, as he stands under—(laughter)—werry good, ses he, but I ain't got the ochre—(money)—oh, as for that 'ere, ses I, 'taint no matter —so we 'greed for 12 hog (shillings), and said as how he'd git it out of him (the donkey) afore next week, and fork out the browns like a man of honor—(roars of laughter)— werry well, I left the donkey—he never did—and I never set eyes on him, not till sich times as I met him in the skittle ground at the back o' Hog-lane.

Second Commissioner—Now, Mr. Brown, what do you say to this?

Tim Brown—Some on it's true, my lord, and some on it's not true. Fact is, somehow or other, he managed that ere mawnin as he speaks on, to get the donkey inter a werry good temper—in fact, I yeard 'em a conwersing together, whilst I turned round to Bill Smith about a harness, and I suspect werry much he'd bin a givin on him some wittles. —(laughter.) No sooner was he (Sleeky Jack) gone, than the hanimal set up such a huniwersal holler, as set all the t'other asses a goin, and we couldn't quiet 'em not no how —(it wos a downright reglar munity (mutiny), and nothink couldn't stop it—nobody couldn't ride him—I wallopped him—no go;—tried him at a hayband—no go; twisted his tail—just the same, my lord; so arter I was tired on him, and couldn't knock no sense in him, I let him go, and I

8

never set eyes on him since; and it's my opinion he come to a bad end, as all obstropolus asses does—there. (Roars of laughter, in which the commissioners joined heartily.)

After a short consultation, it was decided that half the sum should be awarded with costs. So much for an ass—we can fancy old Dogberry, chanting to the favorite tune of one of the renowned Lumber Troopers the "Lass of Richmond Hill."

The third all about a hot savvilor (or sausage) and a baked tater:

LAMBETH-STREET.—A charge of assault was preferred before T. Walker, Esq., by a sleak greasy-faced eatinghouse keeper, against a thick-set hungry-looking mechanic.

"Please your vorship," began the complainant, "I sells cook'd *wittles;* and this here chap comed a Saturday in my shop, and said he was 'werry *peckish*, and should like *summat* nice.' 'Vot can you have nicer,' sis I, 'nor a hot savvilor and bak'd tater?'—'Vell,' sis he, 'I'll have a hot savillor with some mutton gravy.' So as I was a dipping into the pot for *von*, I seed him prig a piece of roast *wheel*. 'Cup,' sis I, 'that's *no go;*' and I ax'd him to drop a *bob* for the weal, when he said he'd hadn't got a *mag* more than twopence to pay for the savillor. Then I jumps over the counter, and ketches the *weal* out of his fist, and claps it back agin into the dish. Arterwards I *werry gently shoved* him out of the shop; and while my back was turned, he fetches me sich a nasty kick behind, that I vent smack agin a saucepan of hot weggetables."

The defendant, when called upon to explain the aforesaid kick, declared that the complainant had not only commenced the assault, but had used "wiolent langvidge."

"That ere's false," said the complainant, "for I'm always werry pertikeler *never* to give *nobody* no *sarce*."

The magistrate considering the assault proved, fined the defendant 1s. and discharged him.

XLVI.

THE LONDON SHOWMAN.

THE next thing in order of my reminiscences of London will be a sketch of a personal encounter with a veritable "showman," and the proprietor of a "Punch and Judy."

I was walking on Tower Hill one morning, when I saw a man, dressed in a tight-fitting spangled dress, endeavoring to make a circle among a crowd of ragged men and boys by throwing a large ball attached to a long rope in their midst; upon going a little closer, I found that a variety of performances were about to take place.

On the steps of a big one-story yellow house, with two windows with red curtains and a door with a brass knocker, resting on four large wheels, some three or four feet from the ground, stood a man, of the most singular appearance, "hollering" out at the top of his voice, at the same time slapping the side of the show with a short rattan which he held in his hand.

He was a sort of "Bill Sykes" looking fellow, and had evidently been little addicted to paying much attention to his toilette.

Upon closer inspection, I noticed he relieved the monotony of singing out the nature of the exhibition, and the thrashing thereof with his cane, by blowing on a certain instrument, known in that locality as a "mouth organ," made of reeds of different sizes, joined together, and fixed in a leathern case, stuck in the top of his waistcoat, immediately under the chin; at the same time, with both hands beating a tremendous drum, and moving his head, with puffed-out cheeks and screwed-up mouth, up and down the reeds, his eyes fairly starting from their sockets with the exertion of blowing, and having the appearance of a man in the last stage of strangulation.

On his head he wore a very dismal looking white hat, with the crown knocked in, and a dirty pipe sticking in the hatband thereof; a fustian jacket, very oily and greasy, covered the upper part of his body, while a portion of his fat legs were encased in a pair of highly-polished corduroy knee breeches, the remaining part being covered with a pair of thick worsted hose, with laced ankle jacks, and iron specks to match.

At the top of his voice, which it seemed to me you could hear for miles, he held forth in something of the following style:—

"Now then—vork up, vork up 'ere, and see the vonderful 'Amabarcadoria' or Great Physician from Bengal, in the Vest Inges; he persesses the most unparalleled and inestimated medicines; and can cure any incident to humanity, from a corn to a consumption. We has a long list of cures he has performed (hif you'll step inside) by his grand, eliptical, Asiatical, piratical, puritanical, nervio cronio machine, but will only read you three out of 30,000. Here is the first:

"'Dear Sir—I was jammed to death in a linseed-oil mill at Faversham. Cured with two bottles!'

"And here is one which is the vonderfullest of all.

"'Venturing too near the powder mill at Hammersmith, I was, by a sudden explosion, blown into a million of atoms. By this unpleasant and unforeseen haccident, I was rendered quite unfit for business, which were a butcher's; and hearing of your grand bilious cordial, I was required to make a trial thereat—when, to the astonishment of my family, the first bottle united my stray particles, and the second eradicated an entire cure.'

"Vork up, vork up—this is the Regular Booth, and inside is the Principal Emperor of the Carcasses Mountains.

"He can take a red-hot poker, and run it into a barrel of gunpowder, and it will not go off.

"He will then load a blunderbuss with some of the dentical powder as would not explode, charged with twelve ledden bullets, and will fire it full in the face of any of the spectators as pleases, vithout there being hingered.

"He will borrow half-a-crown of any of the company, vitch he vill never return to them, vithout any motive whatever. He will then introduce you to the three celebrated brothers—

"Halley, Muley, and Hassan, from the Calaboose Islands, from which he was originally a native. Halley will take a lighted torch in his hand, and jump down the throat of his brother Mulley, who will in his turn take another torch, and jump down the throat of his brother Hassan; and though Hassan the elder is encumbered with the weight of his *twa* brothers, Halley and Muley, yet he will take another torch, make a flip-flap, and jump down his own throat, leaving us all in the dark!"

I could not stand it any longer; so I went in. I forgot to mention, that on one side of the house, upon a piece of canvas, was displayed a painting of a "Fat Boy."

Immediately upon entering, the showman, pointing with his short stick to a perfect mountain of fat, proceeded as follows:—

"Master Villiam Fiddes—or the Hinfant Goliar! He is the seventh son of Joel (that's me) and Helizabeth Fiddes, who is industrious and respectable persons, as resides in Manchester, which was in the month of November he was born. He is only six years of age, and is considered one of the greatest vonders wich this world as ever produced by the Supreme Being. Ladies and gentlemen, when this Fenominer of nature were born, he had four regular teeth, and very shortly after that possessed twenty-two teeth.

"He is a remarkable helthy child when he is well, and is very amusing, and possessed of very pretty features.—(Show the gents your leg, Billy.)

"His food consists of a common and wholesome description, and is generally boiled in hot water, as the doctor says his hinside requires soft things, and is considered the greatest wonder of the world. It would be morally unpossible to describe everything belonging to this great wonder of nature, as he is endowed with every necessary qualification vich adorns the human frame, as such should be produced, and is mild, sensible, and pleasant.

"This wonder of thousands has been universally admired by all classes in the kingdom for his gigantic proportions—

(show your bust, Billy!)—which hexceed to a pre-himinent degree any other of the human species in the universe."

Stepping down, he desired me to look through the hole of a peep show box, resting on tressels, magnifying several highly-wrought colored engravings.

"Now then (said he), vipe your noses, and don't breathe upon the glasses. First scene in the grand mis-representation of the battle of Waterloo. Look to the right, and there you may perceive His Grace the Duke of Vellingtine mounted on a vite hontire. To the left you will see Town Major White all in the act of delivering despatches to his Grace. Says Town Major White—says he, 'Lead on your troops to wictoree, or b' dad you'll lose the day.' Says Velentine—says he, 'D' ye think I'm a going to be dictated to by the likes of you, all on these 'ere plains of Vorterloo? No! I'll be —— if I do!'

"Next is—Grand Fight between the Scotch Lion Vallace and Six English Bulldogs, for fifteen thousand sovereigns aside. To the right you may perceive the properietor of the lions a-encouraging hof they. To the left you may perceive the properietors of the dogs a-encouraging of those. There you will see von of the dogs nibbled in the rear by the lion, vile he is a visking out the hye of another vith his fiery tail.

"Eighteen thousand spectators is a looking on in the most magnanimous and facetious manner; the whole forming a grand and malignant spectacle never vitnessed in this or any other country.

"Next is—The Greenland Vale Fishery. See the man a standing at the brow of the boat—strikes the vale vith the arpoon—vile the vale is a making off for the land, a sprouting up blood and vorter, infinitely higher than the man's ed to the left.

"Next is—The Cock Pit of His Royal Majesty's Line-of-battle Ship Wictory, of 1029 hundred tons, at the memorable occasion of the battle of Traffalgar, February 57, 1488. Look into the hole of the ship, and there you will see His Royal Highness Lord Nelson in the hagonies of death, surmounted by the principal Hossifers of His Majesty's Fleet, assisted by a Corpse of Ryal Moreens; vilst in the back ground the crew is otley pursued by the henemy, the Hadmiral of the French Fleet in the hact of horling down the colors to the flower of the British Navuy, vitch forms the alligator of Brittania Rules the Vaves!

"Next is—The North Pole at Sunrise! as seen by that celebrated Navigation Captain Cook, R.N., of the Royal Navuy, drawn upon the spot by a beutiful and genteel young lady, only seventeen years of age, who fell a lifeless wictim to the infernal arts of a wiley she bear, one of the properietors of that icy region,—sent down for that express purpuos by His Royal Highness George 3, vich God persevere to the right.

"To the left there is a party of hardy tars attaches the bear behind his rear unbeknown to him, corsing him to forgo his lovely and accomplished victim, vich am sure of, and his lifeless tract is a crimsoned vith his gorge; vilst in the back ground there is a party of shemale cubs, a congregating after their manner, a sucking of their offensive young, regardless of their future destination or revord, which nature has produced.

"Next is—Battle of Bunker Hill. Look to the left and there you will perceive His Royal Highness Lord Vashingtine of America a buttoning up his royal coat and a bobbing up his hed up and down, in order to awoid the canon balls (small blame to his reverence!)"

(Little boy sings out) "Please, sir, vitch *is* General Vashington. I can't see!"

To which the showman replied—"Jim, bring up that piece of shammy leather and vipe this boy's glass. He can't see!"

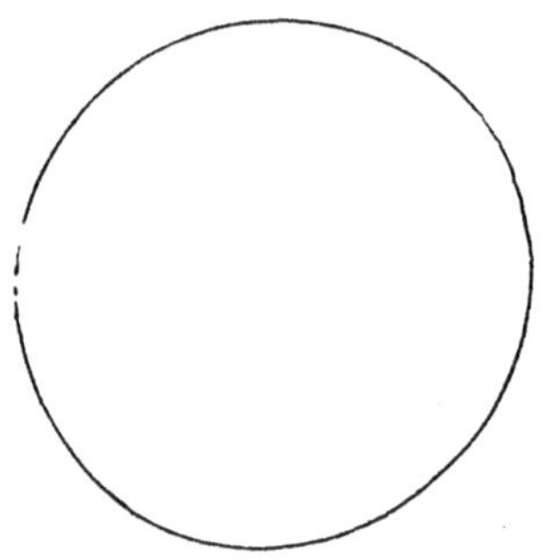

XLVII.

PUNCH AND JUDY.

I HAD been for several days listening in vain for the well-remembered cry (a sort of cross between the shrill squeak of a pig and a penny trumpet) that invariably precedes the approach of a Punch and Judy, when one morning, in the vicinity of Manchester Square, I suddenly pounced upon one.

I was delighted. I had not seen one since I was a boy.

But then there was no audience. In vain did the showman, having slipped from his shoulders his portable play-house, and looking up and down the square, and up at the windows of the houses, announce to the inhabitants his arrival. Nobody appeared. At last I stepped up to him, and asked him how much he'd "show" for?

This seemed to surprise him; when, eyeing me from head to foot, he replied—

"Vell, seeing as 'ow you're all by yourself, I'll give you the whole thing for eighteen pence, cos I may pick up a few 'a'pence besides."

To this I assented; and accordingly he jumped inside of the show box, and let down the curtains.

For the benefit of those of my readers who have not seen one of those "institutions," I will endeavor to give a brief description.

It appears, as I was informed, that they first made their appearance in the streets of London in the reign of Charles the Second; and have a charter from that monarch, giving them the privilege of exhibiting in any portion of the city without molestation.

The consequence is, that their audiences present a pretty miscellaneous appearance, and are generally attentive and quiet, consisting of fogies (old and young), chambermaids, nursery maids, servants (in and out of livery), boys and girls (of every age and size), and now and then a stray policeman.

The show is about eight feet high and three feet wide, made light, and very portable. A box, containing the movable figures, consisting of Punch, his Judy, the Doctor, Nurse, Undertaker, Thief, Grave-digger, etc., as also the Gallows, Coffin, Houses, Watchman, and other characters and "fixings," is usually carried by another man, who assists in the performance *outside* by asking and answering the questions of Mr. Punch et al. *inside.*

The top part of the show represents a stage, the figures of which are worked by a man inside with wires, upon which appear in quick succession Mr. Punch, with a big stick in his arm, Mrs. Judy, with a dirty cap on, who is instantly greeted by her lord and master with several whacks, with the big stick aforesaid, on the back of her wooden head, one blow of which on an ordinary skull would be "death to nature." She, however, rises immediately, as if refreshed by this gentle memento of her lord's affection, and seizing the stick from his hand, commences wolloping him in the same style. In vain Punch hollers out peccavi. She's got the upper hand now, and continues to pommel him most unmercifully. The audience are in ecstasies. The usual striking scenes of a five-act melodrama take place. A house is erected, containing one door and a window; the latch is thrown open, a head pops out from the second story, and disappears immediately beneath the heavy blow of a stick from a wooden man in the street, who is seized by a wooden watchman, with a dark lantern made of paper. In the course of the play, somebody is killed, and the murderer happening to be Mr. Punch, he is sentenced to be hung. A gallows is erected, and the murderer executed, and afterwards placed in a coffin. At this critical juncture, when the audience suppose him to be really defunct—he jumps up, gets hold of his stick, and knocks down parson, undertaker, and his weeping relatives, friends, gallows, and all—makes a bow to the audience—gives a farewell w-eeeeekk! and the play is over; and he jumps into his box, to delight another portion of the inhabitants of the big city.

The following is not a portrait of Punch, but the latest *carte de visite* of a civil old fellow immortalized on page 181.

XLVIII.

SOMETHING ABOUT LONDON BOYS.

THE "showman" is generally followed by a crowd of boys—and it seems to me that London boys are as peculiar to their locality as the Palm is to the East.

They delight, especially in "Fisticuffs" and "Punch and Judys,"—very fond of rabbits and birds, white mice, and pigeons; always out of the elbows, addicted to screeching, whistling and singing, great proficients on the Jew's Harp, faultless at peg in the ring; able to knuckle down before all other boys in the universe; fond to destruction of apple-peel and pocket-knives, tyrants over their juniors, but plucky to their seniors; born with a very great contempt for young swells, and all descriptions of old ladies; witty beyond their years, and as vagrant as the London sparrows for which they set traps upon the smoky house-tops; they may be found in swarms wherever there is a sight, or an accident, or a water-cock turned on. They delight in everything dangerous. You may see them running their hardest along a parapet, or climbing over the spiked railings of the park. Keen sportsmen, they wander with an old tin shaving-pot, a short stick, thread and hook, to enjoy a day's fishing for stickle-backs in the Hampstead ponds. They are the mortal enemies of butterflies and cockroaches. Democrats to the heart's core, they keep up an incessant warfare against boys of gentle birth. They glory in their corduroy. The vagrant habit that in after-life will prove their curse, and accomplish their fall, grows fast upon them. The want of their parents makes them old as soon as they can walk. Sent to fetch the beer, when other and more fortunate children are laughing upon gaily painted rocking-horses—taught to look sharply upon the world, to see that they get good weight and full pints; cuffed for every fault, and rewarded for any service by the permission to play about the streets—they are as wild as the offspring of the woods.

XLIX.

KENILWORTH CASTLE.

I HAD been greatly fascinated when a boy by the delightful description in the "Sketch Book" of Washington Irving, of his visit to "Stratford-upon-Avon," and had long cherished the idea of paying my individual respects to the landlady of the "Golden Lion Inn." Accordingly on a bright June morning, I took the train from London to Coventry, en route to Kenilworth, Warwick, and Stratford.

Stopped at Coventry just long enough to see the old-fashioned looking house of "Peeping Tom," and take a glass of "home-brewed," and I thought I'd take a quiet stroll towards the primitive town of Kenilworth.

The walk from this point to Warwick was indeed lovely —the distance, I think, about five miles—the whole country looked like a magnificent flower-garden—the quiet depths of the meadows, and the mossy roots of ancient trees, with their bright leaves waving on high their "plumes of green;" the sheep-bells tinkled in the distance, the cowslips, buttercup, and primroses, peeped up to greet me as I passed; the sweetest little marygolds gemmed the ground in every direction—lovely daisies with a pupil of gold, and an iris of snow-white petals, like a pale glory surrounding it, followed in its wake by the sweet violet, accompanied by a trumpet-shaped flower, of delicate construction, and of a pale blue color, that held up its slender head with a decidedly elegant and thorough-bred air,—dotted about here and there was a little red flower that crimsoned with a blush much richer than the reddest coral, as I crushed its dew-charged leaves beneath my careless tread—then there were some little meek white flowers nestling modestly away in the sheltering grass, betraying their graceful presence by a languid perfume, faint, but very sweet;—then came the cottages, with the pretty little gardens in front,—and the roses creeping round the porches,—the bleating of the little lambs—and from this lovely spot, over which leaned the uplifted blue of a cloudless sky, a world of bright-winged things sent up their hymn of praise!

And now a "word or" so about Kenilworth and its renowned "Castle."

Most interesting was my ramble through the venerable remains of the once magnificent dwelling of Royalty, and it seemed to me there could not be one more deserving of notice, or more worthy the admiration of the lover of picturesque beauty than this same Kenilworth Castle.

I entered at a little gate, inside of which was a sort of "porter's lodge," and there I found a very civil sort of spoken old fellow, who at every word kept touching his hat, replying to my numerous questions in the most obsequious manner.

The principal places pointed out to me were—The Inner Court—and "Grand Court," Cæsar Tower—The Three Kitchens—The Strong Tower—King Henry's Lodgings—Sir Robert Dudley's Lobby—The Presence Chamber—The Great Hall, or Banqueting Room—Mortimer's Tower—Secret Postern—The Swan Tower—"Amy Robsart's Bower"—The Plaisance, etc.

Here then, I thought, had walked, driven, rode, sat, eaten, slept, drank, laughed, scolded, frowned, and smiled the haughty Queen Elizabeth—my thoughts flew thick and fast.

I was imagining what sort of a looking cove the Earl of Leicester was, when a vision of Sir Walter Raleigh, spreading that velvet coat out for the Queen to walk on, would come to me. I had hardly thought of this, when phantoms of Sir Walter Scott, Rebecca, Amy Robsart—and even the "Bowery Theatre!" Blount, Tressilian, etc., floated in my brain—and I seemed thus as if by some spell, to be brought in close review with the halls, the ceremonies, the tournaments, the banquets, the domestic usages, of people who had lived hundreds of years ago!

The scenery around and about Kenilworth is, as I have before said, beautiful. On the night of my arrival all was quiet repose and rural beauty, beaming with cheerfulness and felicity, and though the Castle of Kenilworth is now only a pile of venerable ruins, still it is magnificent in its decay, and still the glory and the pride of the place in which it stands.

L.

WARWICK CASTLE.

On reaching the little town of "Warwick," I quickly "made" for the "Castle." Upon arriving in the town I was told I should find it very difficult to gain admittance, as it was after the hour that visitors were allowed to enter. I thought, however, I'd try—accordingly I rattled away at an immense lion-headed knocker—three times as large as any "Lord's" in Grosvenor square—and the big gate quietly opened—a very pleasant old lady presenting herself at the entrance.

She said it was impossible for me to see the Castle that day—as the "Earl of Warwick" was *not at all well.* I then asked her if she would take my "card" to his "Lordship," upon the back of which I wrote as follows:

"An American would feel greatly obliged by the Earl of Warwick's permission to take a hasty (*plate of soup* I would have liked, for I was mighty hungry)—glance at the Castle, as he will soon leave for America, and not probably visit Warwick again."

This had the desired effect—for having waited in the "Lodge" some time, my female friend returned with his Lordship's permission.

Away I went through bright yellow gravel walks, rows of stately trees, bowers of loveliness, fragrance, and beauty, until reaching another gateway, and descending a flight of steps, a large door was opened, by a very good-looking, portly, grey-headed man—the steward—who told me his name was "Gregory," and that he had been in the Earl's service fourteen years.

This magnificent castle is one of the noblest specimens of ancient grandeur, I am told, that England now possesses, and is of extreme antiquity.

The approach to the outer court of the Castle, is through

a winding road cut out of the solid rock, extending upwards of one hundred yards, the sides of which are most luxuriantly draperied with evergreens, ivy, etc.

This emerges into an open space covered with vegetation, from amidst which the two turrets rise frowningly from a slight eminence, and with a degree of wildness in the scenery around, that indeed raised in me a feeling of awe.

An embattled wall, in the centre of which is the gateway, flanked by towers, and surrounded by another bristling arch, connects the two towers. I went over the drawbridge, through the gateway, which is beautifully clothed with ivy, entering a passage which ushered me into the "Inner Court," where a scene novel and bewildering was presented to me. Then I came to what they called the "Keep" or "Mount," crowned with battlemented walls, and interspersed with a verdant mass of foliage. To the left was the inhabited portion of the Castle with quite a modern entrance. Then I saw the large windows of the Chapel, and to the right the massive walls which bound the soft and verdant sward in their inclosure.

I entered the Castle through the great hall, leading to the suite of apartments shown to the visitor, containing paintings of extraordinary beauty and value of Vandyke, Rubens, Michael Angelo, and any quantity of curiosities, etc.

While walking about this room, a servant entered carrying in her arms an infant of some four months old. "That," said the steward—"is the future heir to the estate." If he lives he will be the "Earl of Warwick." It was the infant child of Lord Brooke, the son of the (then) present Earl. The nurse let me take the future Earl in my arms. I patted his pretty face, said unintelligible things to it, and it ended in the young 'un's setting up a squall like the war-cry of a Tuscarora brave.

Among many articles of interest, I was shown here the saddle used by Queen Elizabeth, when going to Kenilworth, the Virginal (or Harpsichord) given to her by the Earl of Leicester, with the Royal Arms of England on it, it is a very curious instrument, somewhat resembling a banjo—a pistol given the present Earl by Col. Colt of Hartford.

Queen Elizabeth's silver dagger—as also the bed upon which Queen Ann reposed.

LI.

STRATFORD-UPON-AVON.

AND now for my pretty little village of Stratford.

How I peered out for that "Spire" of the church, where rest the remains of the immortal poet. How I was charmed with the perfect quiet—the repose, the tranquillity of everything as we entered the village, so beautifully described by my friend Mr. Brady, in a speech that he made two years before—at the Dramatic Fund Dinner,—as being "asleep!" for so indeed to me it appeared.

How charming the quiet of the cozy little front parlor, of the pleasant little inn ycleped the "Golden Lion," kept by a right merry fellow I assure you, Mr. Henry Heartly by name, and who very kindly offered to be my pioneer to the places of interest in and about the village.

Accordingly I first went to pay my respects to the "Red Horse," or rather to the little parlor thereof, immortalized by Washington Irving in his Sketch-Book, and as all good travellers ought to do, asked for the celebrated "poker" which he called his "sceptre."

The landlady very good-naturedly said, "Oh, sir! I'll fetch the poker immediately, all the Americans wish to see *that*—but I have to lock it up to preserve it!"

Presently she brought it in, with all the pomp and ceremony imaginable—having the words "Geoffry Crayon's sceptre" engraved on it.

After wetting our lips with a draught of mild ale, we returned to the "Golden Lion," (tourists, make a note and stop there) and dined.

My landlord has the most perfect collection of theatrical portraits perhaps in England—upon the walls of the room in which I was sitting, I noticed paintings of the elder Wallack, Edwin Forrest, Macready, Kean, Booth, Charlotte Cushman, Charles Kean, Ellen Tree, Farren, Faucett, Mathews, Elliston, etc., etc.

After dinner we strolled to the house where the "Poet was born;" reaching it—I stood for some minutes gazing with admiration and wonder.

On a board, on a mean-looking edifice in Henly street are rudely painted the words:—

"The immortal Shakspeare was born in this house."

I passed into the little shop, a dismal apartment indeed, with rough stone pavement, and a lot of old iron hooks sticking in the wall—the place seemed to be about eight feet square—presently out popped a little woman—a Mrs. Stanley; quite a pleasant chatty body—very amusing indeed, and she really seemed to take great pains in describing the relics.

She said: "There 'av been four or five hof your countrymen ere to day, sur. Some werry nice people, sur—you're from Hamerica, sur, I think—haint yar?" I assented. "I knowed it, sur, by your 'at; you'll hexcuse me, sur, but the Mericans wear such broad rimmed 'ats." We then went up a narrow dingy staircase to the chamber where William Shakspeare first saw the light, on the morning of April 23, 1564.

It is a moderate-sized apartment, very low roofed and dirty, having but one large window in it; every inch of the wall, the door, the ceiling, and indeed every available place was covered with names; she pointed out to me, Edmund Kean's, Schiller's, Lord Byron's, Sir Walter Scott's, Washington Irving's, Tennyson's, etc. I tried to find a place whereon to "fix" my humble name, but my pencil broke when I commenced the "M," and it *led* me to think of the folly of it.

How great the difference, I thought to myself, between the proud walls and towering heights of the Castle I had just visited, and this humble dwelling! and yet, when even *they* shall fall beneath the destroying hand of Time, and crumble into nothingness, will this little spot be worshipped, cherished, and revered—and his great memory be as green and fresh in the hearts of all, as when first his bright genius flashed upon the world!

Among the few articles of furniture in the house—none of which can be considered as belonging to the home of Shakspeare—is a chair whose history has been admirably drawn by Washington Irving in the following words:

"The most favorite object of curiosity, however, is Shakspeare's chair. It stands in the chimney corner of a small gloomy chamber, just behind what was his father's shop. Here he may many a time have sat, when a boy, watching the slowly-revolving spit with all the longing of an urchin, or of an evening listened to the cronies and gossips of Stratford dealing forth churchyard tales and legendary anecdotes of the troublesome times of England. In this chair it is the custom of every one that visits the house to sit; whether this be done with the hope of imbibing any of the inspiration of the bard I am at a loss to say—I merely mention the fact; and mine hostess privately assured me that though built of solid oak, such was the fervent zeal of devotees that it had to be new-bottomed at least once in three years. It is worthy of notice, also, in the history of this remarkable chair, that it partakes something of the volatile nature of the Santa Casa of Loretto, or the flying chair of the Arabian enchanter, for though sold to a Russian princess, yet, strange to say, it has found its way back again to the old chimney corner."

We visited the Grammar School, in which it is presumed he received his education. Saw the desk at which he sat, the scenes of his youthful meditations—the sports, familiar to him in early and mature life,—the site of the house, where, with a sufficient income, he passed his latter years—and the church where his mortal remains were consigned to the grave.

I was then introduced to a Mr. Thomas Heritage, who is the fortunate possessor of the "Marble Fount," used at the christening of Shakspeare.

It is indeed a rare curiosity—kept at the end of his pretty little garden, and as is the custom, we drank from it some wine, I (with his permission) cutting from the pedestal some moss for presents.

No money would buy this extraordinary relic: he has been offered for it large sums at different times.

Leaving the very friendly roof of Mr. Heartly, I heard a man crying out something about an "auction sale;" and having, once upon a time, done a little in that line in Sacramento, I thought I would at least look *on* in Stratford; and now, to give you—or Austins and Spicer, or Priests, Wilmerding and Mount, of your city—some idea of the immense trade of this quiet little nook, I intend giving you a verbatim copy of the bill of sale at the aforesaid auction. Here it is:—

"UNICORN INN,"

☞ *Stratford upon Avon.* ☜

TO BE SOLD AT AUCTION,

BY MR. BROWN,

ON WEDNESDAY JUNE 22d, 1858,

The following valuable property!

VIZ.:

1. A pair of Gents Black Slippers.
2. A driving Rug.
3. One Carpet Bag complete.
4. Shaving Box and Brushes.
5. One pair of Braces—3 Shirts—4 Collars—2 pairs of Stockings—3 new Maps—1 Warming-pan—1 Boot-jack—a Toasting-fork!—a Gridiron, and a map of Scotland, New York, and the East Indies.

Cards of admission to see the goods, to be had on immediate application to Mr. William Savage.

We then went to "Anne Hathaway's Cottage." Crossing the fields to the west of Stratford, by a well-frequented footpath, brought us to the sweet little hamlet of *Shottery*.

Oh! how beautiful it looked, with its green lane, picturesque, timber-ribbed, thatched cottages, babbling rush-fringed brook, and pretty wooden bridge. The house is of timber and brick, two stories, with thatched roof, and looks like two joined together. I looked up the central chimney, and saw the letters I. H., 1697. Up stairs I was shown an old carved bedstead, of the real old Elizabethan period, supposed to be the one upon which Anne Hathaway slept. The room below shows traces of the good old times; the rude stone floor, low ceiling, heavy beams, oaken wainscot, and rough plastering. The wide fire-place, with the cozy chimney corners and supporting beams, where the wood-fires must have often crackled and blazed on the ample hearth. Here, too, was the seat, with the straight high back, that rested on the porch outside the cottage, now quite porous with age—upon which ofttimes, doubtless, during the long summer nights, did our poet and his first love while away the hours; and who knows, but upon this very bench, some of the most impassioned of his verses might have been written.

In coming back to the town, I strolled by the banks of the Avon—crossing the river near to the church, in the chancel of which rest his remains. It stands on the margin of the river Avon. You approach it through a long avenue of lime trees, the boughs of which are so interwoven, as to produce a striking colonnade, and the effect is peculiarly pleasing. To-day the weather was exceedingly beautiful; little children were playing in the grave-yard, and dancing on the tomb-stones—the pleasant low murmuring of the river was grateful to the ear—boys were fishing in the stream, and birds were carolling away from the branches of the bright green trees; and as I for the last time looked up at the pretty spire, towering to the skies, I thought of the graphic words of Washington Irving, in his well known "Sketch Book"—which, if I do not quite correctly subjoin, I most humbly beg pardon, but I fancied them somewhat appropriate:—"How would it have cheered the spirit of the youthful bard, when, wandering forth in disgrace upon a doubtful world, he cast back a heavy look upon his paternal home, could he have foreseen that before many years he should return to it covered with renown; and that *lessening spire*, on which his eyes were fixed in tearful contemplation, should one day become the beacon, towering amidst the gentle landscape, to light the literary pilgrim of every nation to his tomb!"

It had grown quite dusk by the time we returned to our little inn—the stillness of death reigned around—by and by the moon was sweetly smiling through my pretty gothic window, on the sills of which were some plants of geranium and mignonette, and the fragrance of them was sweet to me—and I felt more and more the beauty of my friend's words, that the little village of Stratford upon Avon was—asleep!

In the book kept in the bed-room at Anne Hathaway's cottage, for the registering the names of visitors, I found the following:

July 13th, 1849. E. L. Davenport, America; Fanny E. Vining, London; Anna Cora Mowatt, New York; James Mowatt, New York.

"The three Americans above named hold their pilgrimage so far, as lightsome and gay to find so much reward in being able to view all these early associations of the 'immortal bard' in *their* land, if possible more adored than here. In the above sentiments, the true born English woman 'Fanny,' begs to join heart and soul."—Good!

LII.

THE "GARRICK CLUB."

It was my good fortune to be elected an "honorary member" of this celebrated club, after a pleasant introduction to some of the members by Mr. A. Arcedeckne, known as the "Commodore," and certainly some of the most agreeable hours were passed by me there.

The Club is situated in Hart Street, Covent Garden, and has more the appearance of an old-fashioned private residence than anything else. Inside the appointments are most comfortable and luxurious. Here you can breakfast and dine in the most gorgeous style imaginable, and not only a great deal better, and with more comfort than at a Hotel or Restaurant—but much cheaper.

In the "smoking room"—a sealed apartment to all but members—you meet with some choice spirits. Albert Smith, Walter Lacy, Lyster O'Brien, Shirley Brooks, Mark Lemon, Thackeray, Charles Dance, Sir Edwin Landseer, were amongst the notables who patronized the cozy retreat. Upon the walls are some superb paintings—presented to the club by some of its members—one I think by Landseer, and the other by Stanfield.

I never can forget the great kindness experienced by me at the hands of all those whom I had the honor of meeting here—but as I have some further reminiscences of this delightful association, occurring during my second visit to England in 1858, I shall refrain from any further "Jottings" until that time.

LIII.

THE LITTLE CHAPEL IN CANNON STREET.

In this street, not far from the celebrated "London stone," and at the end of a little court yard, you will read the words "*Salter's Hall Chapel.*"

It was raining hard on Saturday afternoon. I had to meet a friend in the vicinity of London Bridge, and being a little earlier than the hour appointed, I strolled along this well known thoroughfare, and rested at the gateway of the little court leading to the chapel.

I have always cherished the greatest fondness for old scenes, old faces, and associations, and though I had not set my foot upon the stones of that courtyard since I was fourteen years of age, I seemed led by an impulse I could not resist to revisit the well remembered spot.

The reader will be kind enough to understand—if he or she is interested in these memoirs, that the *last* time I had visited this place of worship was with my beloved mother, and the particular occasion I cannot forget, for it was upon her leaving the chapel with me, after the morning service —and for the *last* time in her life, that the first symptoms appeared of the disease which carried her to her grave.

* * * * * *

Everything in the little chapel was unchanged—the green baize door opened freely—and there was the selfsame pulpit—its cushion covered with "brown holland" to preserve it from the dust of the week,—the vestry, with its framework of glass—the clerk's place with raised desk—and there were the pews—the one she occupied—but where —oh, where are the worshippers!

I walked up the aisle, as if led by an unseen hand, and stopped at the pew, where so often I had sat with her—the cushions, hassocks, and little box for the bible and hymn book, seemed to be just as I had left them; the rain pattered against the window panes, and the moaning of the wind was a fitting accompaniment to the gloom around me, and my own thoughts.

Seventeen years have passed away, since I was with her,

whom I loved better than all the world beside, on that very seat.

Oh! how the changes, the vanities, the toils, trials, vexations—and even the aspirations of my life, vanished into thin air, in the meditations of that quiet scene; the past was only a dream—the future a mystery—and in the present, I seemed to be bathing once again in the fountains of youth—the memories of whose bright era were now so strikingly awakened.

I could hear again the little quiet voice with which *she* joined in the congregational hymn (for there were no *paid* singers there); the attentive look at the minister, the moistened eye, the head bent low at the time of prayer, I then beheld again, and placed my hand upon the book of hymns that she had so often touched; I opened it, and bursting into tears, felt that we were again reading it together!

Oh! if for those who have gone before to the other and the better land, it is permitted, either in spirit to revisit, or from their heavenly dwelling to behold, those whom they loved in life, she, whose pious teachings and tender solicitude were then renewed within me—she, whose hand in the dread hour of dissolution I was the last to clasp, the last to feel its pressure in return—she, from the "fields of light above," must have felt that the seed sown by her affectionate counsellings had not been entirely wasted, and that the promises of youth were not altogether unfulfilled!

I was awakened from my revery by the appearance of the old pew-opener, an aged matron, busy in dusting the chapel for the service of the morrow, who, upon telling my name and the object of my visit, appeared strangely affected.

I passed out once again through the little green baize door, down the courtyard, into the street, and stood at the gateway—alone. Her feet or mine will pass there no more. I felt how little sympathy there was on earth. There I was, alone—a mere speck in the crowded thoroughfare of that big city. But I reflected, in my loneliness and desolation, that there were many, even among the noble and the great, who might envy the peaceful sensations and holy emotions aroused within me while revisiting "The Little Chapel in Cannon Street."

LIV.

LONDON TO PARIS.

FRIDAY, April 8, 1853, started for Paris, by the way of Dover and Calais.

I left the London Station at about nine in the morning, and arrived at the hotel in Paris at about eleven o'clock at night—a distance of about 315 miles, costing about £3. To Dover it is 80 miles, and took two hours; over the channel, 23 miles, in about two hours; from Calais, through Lille, Amiens, and lots of smaller towns, the train reaching Paris a little before eleven o'clock.

I went first to the Hotel Meurice, but finding it uncomfortably full, proceeded to the Hotel Choiseul, kept, and capitally too, by Morin, at 325 Rue St. Honoré, very near the Place Vendôme.

Now there is so much to dazzle, bewilder, and delight one in this city of cities, that I find it difficult to know of what first to write, or to give any particular description of my impressions.

It would take a residence of several months—I was going to say years—to appreciate fully the wonders of this mighty capital; consequently, one passing only a few days therein cannot be expected to know much about it.

First of all, I would advise the visitor, upon the morning of his arrival, to consult the article headed Strangers' Diary, in the daily English newspaper called Galignani's Messenger, taken at all the principal hotels, and whatever is to be seen on the day of publication is invariably mentioned.

My first effort was to find out the whereabouts of my nephew, a student of medicine, in the quarter of the town called the Rue de l'Odeon. Succeeding in the search, we "peregrinated" together "sight-seeing."

We first went to the Louvre and Luxembourg gardens and palaces. Readers will be surprised when they are informed that only a few hours were devoted to these renowned places of curiosities and art; but the fact is, I never had any especial taste for galleries of paintings, mosaic pavements, marble vases, or gorgeous specimens of sculpture; and even if I had the inclination or the ability to go into the details of a description of the wonderful things to be seen in these ancient and renowned museums, it has not only been done so often before, but in Galignani's Guide Book, which everybody possesses, a full, true, and particular account is given; therefore, I shall content myself (and doubtless please my readers better) by simply clipping from my Diary a " brief item " of what I "saw" and " did " each day.

LV.

PLACES IN PARIS FOR THE STRANGER TO SEE.

SHOULD these lines fall into the hands of those who intend to remain (like myself) only a few days in the French capital, they may perhaps find some benefit from perusing the following List of Places, arranged in the order which is most convenient for saving time:

1. Palace of the Tuileries and Triumphal Arch of the Carrousel.
2. The Louvre and its Museums.
3. Column of the Place Vendôme.
4. Obelisk of Luxor, and the Place de la Concorde.
5. Triumphal Arch at the Barrière de l'Etoile.
6. Chapel of St. Ferdinand.
7. Chapelle Expiatoire.
8. Church of the Madeleine.
9. Palace and Galleries of the Palais Royale.
10. Church Notre Dame de Lorette.
11. Exchange.
12. Bibliothèque Nationale.
13. Church S. Vincent de Paul.
14. Strasburg Railway Terminus.
15. Conservatoire, Arts, Métiers.
16. Abattoir of Popincourt.
17. Cemetery of Père la Chaise.
18. Column de la Bastile.
19. Cathedral of Notre Dame.
20. Hotel de Ville.
21. Palais du Quai d'Orsay.

22. Legislative Assembly.
23. Hotel des Invalides.
24. Artesian Well of Grenelle.
25. Musée d'Artillerie.
26. Church St. Germain des Près.
27. The Mint.
28. Ecole des Beaux Arts.
29. Church of St. Sulpice.
30. Palace of the Luxembourg, Picture Gallery, etc.
31. Hotel Cluny.
32. Pantheon.
33. Church of St. Etienne du Mont.
34. Gobelins Manufactory.
35. Garden of Plants, Museums.
36. Fontainebleau.
37. Cloud.
38. Abbey of St. Denis.
39. Sevres China Manufactoiy.
40. Versailles.
41. Vincennes.

LVI.

PARIS NOTES.

I do not agree with my friend Belle Brittan that "the women of Paris are *not* handsome." I think, as a general rule, that they are. But I do agree with Col. H. F., that there *is* something indescribably neat, trim, and fascinating about them; and that they take much more pains to please, *in little things*, than either the American or English women; and to me there is a certain indescribable witchery of manner about them wonderfully irresistible, and a *style* perfectly enchanting. Comparisons, I know, are "odorous," but give me a French woman before any other!

Gad, it's enuff to drive any nervous man into 1853 fits a minute to look at 'em! For take the veriest and most ordinary waiting maid, and even if not pretty, she will have a deliciously fitting dress, with such a pretty little waist, and look so trim, clean, and neat, with a little white "cap a 'top,'" put on so wickedly, that it requires a "great deal of nice consideration," as John Brougham says, to pass 'em by, without *wishing them a happy New Year!*

The weather is now lovely, and oh! how shall I describe

the beauties of the gardens, the walks, the drives, the thousand and one sights of this earthly paradise! Come with me for a moment to the *Toolaries*, now beginning to look beautiful, the trees just out in leaf, all fresh and green, cut and trimmed so as to form groves, shady bowers, and quiet nooks. Hundreds and hundreds of chairs, and benches without number, invite you to "take a seat," and every day and evening, up to nine o'clock, it is filled with all sorts of pretty women and children. Then the *Cham-d-Lyssees*—whether on a Sunday, or at night—equally strange, fascinating, wonderful. Charivaris, walking theatres, dancing monkeys, vendors of everything, portable concert rooms, fitted up gorgeously with flowers, mirrors, and bright gas-lights, the singers "fixed off," as if just going to the dress circle of the Astor, in days gone by; half-a-dozen, or a dozen, complete orchestras, all firing away, and neither putting each other out, and the whirl of excitement, the mass of people, and then so much civility and order; no jostling, no rude "rubbing up" against you, no shoving, pushing, *as in London*, no treading on the toes, without the pleasant salve, "Pardon, monsieur!"

Then the *Bull-e-vards*, o' night, with the multitudinous caffes, thronged with men and women, the glare of gas, the brilliant shops, the myriads of black, blue, and every colored eye, perpetually flashing upon you, the tightly fitting little French boot, the elegantly turned ankle, the indescribable *raychercha* way they have of raising the dress, about two inches and three-quarters, as near as I can recollect, and last, though not least, that *walk*—oh! my nerves, it's really orful, and I have to run down a back street, to get out of the way, it's too much for poor human natur.

Then the *Theatres*—all order and politeness—no fighting and rowdyism, no scrambling for places—you just leave your glove, or piece of paper, or a playbill, to show you have occupied a seat, and nobody disturbs it. Then the acting, and the scenery, and the orchestra, and the *toot-on-somble*—oh Lord! it's ruinous. I have heard Der Freyschutz, 'I Puritani, Sonnambula, William Tell, Lucia di Lammermoor, as I never expect to hear them again—no boisterous applause—no hi-hi-ing—no ridiculous *encore*-ing—no *ill-timed* brava-ing, or anything of the sort.

The night before last I went to a place called the *Jardin Mobile*, eclipsing anything of the kind I had ever seen—Niblo's is a *leetle* in the style. Well, here were beautifully laid out, hard gravel walks, just like marble to the feet—magnificent lamps, of variegated colors, hanging from trees, and trembling in the air—fountains, beauteous in form and design, gushing, spouting us, and watering plants and flowers, whose perfume fairly intoxicated you. Seats and sofas formed of cut grass and moss—quiet little retreats, and such cozy shady nooks; and then right in the centre, in a kind of Aladdin's palace, was the orchestra, while a portion of the visitors were enjoying themselves in the giddy dance—waltzing, polkaing, or *mazoorkaing*, as the fancy dictated. The admission was two francs—about forty cents. But the fact is, there are so many places of the same sort here, that it is foolish to particularize. Then the night was so lovely, the scene a perfect blaze of enchantment and beauty, that it seemed as if Mr. Mahomet's heaven had broken loose, and taken a fit to give us poor mortals the "latest style of the fashions."

Anne Hathway's Cottage.

LVII.

THE FRENCH ACTOR LEMAITRE.

May 26.—To-day " Yankee Silsbee," the eccentric comedian, called on me, and in the evening we went together to see the great French actor Lemaitre, the original " Robert Macaire," I believe. He was performing at the Porte St. Martin.

The theatre was crowded, and going in late, we had a poor place. Our stock (united) of French was extremely limited, although my companion informed me, that he would translate the plot, &c., to me as the play proceeded.

This was quite satisfactory, and by the time we were ready to leave the theatre, I ascertained that an old soldier (one of the Old Guard, kind of " Maid of Croissy" piece), with a knapsack, had just arrived from Morocco, I think, with a large stick in his hand, and dusty shoes and gaiters; that he walked about until he came to a table, and a stool—that he sat down, and with raised hands cried, "Mon Dieu! Mon Dieu!"—that the audience applauded—that he then toddled off, looking very much like Nickenson of the Olympic—that the audience applauded again—and this was Lemaitre, the great French actor, as I am told he is, and which I do not of course doubt. Well, it was something to have *seen* the man, and therefore my thanks are due friend Silsbee for his conducting me thither, and translating for me the plot.

A FAC-SIMILE OF A BILL OF FARE IN THE PALAIS ROYAL.

I used to dine very often in the Palais Royal, where are some capital restaurants.

At the " Restarong de Paris, Galerie Montpensier, 23 Et. Roo Monpensier 18," kept by Godin, is one of the best of these, and on his bill of fare he has such extraordinary English, that I asked for one, so that I might give a verbatim copy.

DINNERS FOR 2 FR. A PLATE.

May be hadi soup four dishes at choice as meet fish, poltry, gam, sveet dainty dishes which pastry, one dessert, bread at direction, and ½ a bottle of wine of Macon, or Chabblis, or a bottle of beer. Half a oyster can be had to suppy a dish.

OBSERVATIONS.

Dishes of supplement 40c.
The Soup is never replaced.
Is shote be made a diminutiod of 50c. for every bottle to the persons who shall call for some fine wine insted of their ordinary wine.
The dinners are not to be shored! (shared).
But no diminutiod in the dinners price.
It will be perceived 30c. by child for bread 40c.
For dessert supplement 30c.
Sweet meas for dessert 20c.
Only a portion of fowl will be hat for dinner.
One bottle seltz water supplys one plate of coffee.
The dessert can be replaced a glass french liquor.

LVIII.

AN INTERVIEW WITH A CORN DOCTOR.

I WAS in my bed the other morning, looking over a bundle of "Spirits," just sent me from London, when a gentle tap, tap, tap, at the door, interrupted my pleasant reading. Well, in walked a large, broad-shouldered, stout feller, about six feet and a half in height, who, with a bow, and hat in hand, delivered himself as follows:—

"Good morning, sare."

"Morning," says I.

"I'se called to see you, gentlemens, as I vood vish to know, as you have any like to have your *caron* (I understood him) taken out?"

"My *what!*" said I. "I don't understand you. You must have got into the wrong room. Who are you? What the d——l is it all about?"

"No, no, sare, my name is Doctare Koke—and I am ze first *ca-r-o-n*"—

"What is that?" says I.

"Vy (pointing to his toe), cor-un—vat you call c-o-r-u-n, eh! You no vat I mean? for your toes? Now I take 'em out, as never vos, and they never com no more. I vill show you ze patronage I has got, from ze first gentlemens and Lords of ze vorld; and, sare, some Americans. I got a certificate of Doctare Permniman—you know him, sare? —from New York"—

"You mean, perhaps, Mr. Penniman," said I.

"Yes, sare, that's him—Mr. Pennman; he gif me his certificate. I took out all his coruns, and his family's, likewise out of the Prince Saxe-Meinger."

Here is an extract from his printed certificate—

"Dr. Kock, inventor of entirely new process for to take the radical cure of corns, bunions, nails who have entered the flesh, without fear of return, or pain or cutting, a few minutes in the operation being performed.

"Dr. Kock has had the pleasure of employing and using his peculiar method upon numerous patients, who, after years of suffering, have been enabled, after he has operated on them, to walk with ease and pleasure, and wear the tightest shoe, which ever could have been made."

Then follow these crack-jaw names—

Prince de Ligne,	Princess Hypsholandais,
Prince Holek,	Princess Stephanie,
Prince Gluka,	Princess Lucien Bonàparte,
Prince Sckarcatine,	Duke of Monterfel,
Prince Galikis,	Duke of Albadie,
Prince Sangusrko,	Duke of Chevreuse,
Prince Kosgerbey,	Duke of Noailles,
Prince Jerome Bonaparte,	Duke Georges of Meklinbourg,
Prince Herman of Holanberik,	Dr. Perminman of New York,

And several Thousand others too Numerous!

LIX.

THE "NOTRE DAME."

FAIL not to attend high mass at the Cathedral of Notre Dame, or at the churches of St. Roche, St. Eustache, or

Notre Dame de Loretto, at ten any Sunday morning, for you will there witness a most imposing spectacle, and be delighted with some superb music.

THE BEST PLACE TO DINE.

The best dinner I got in Paris was at the "British Tavern," Rue Richelieu.

LX.

HENRI HERZ CONCERT.

Monday, 18*th April*, 1853.—Strolling along the Boulevards I met "*Henri Herz*," had not seen him since I sang at his Concerts in Sacramento.

We had a hearty laugh over old times, and inviting me to come to his concert on the following evening remarked, that he didn't think I should see *any rats* running across the floor!

Next evening went to 48 Rue de la Victoire, where I found a brilliant audience assembled. Heard for the first time, Tamburini—was disappointed; fancied he must be getting into the "sere and yellow." The tenor, Gardoni—good. Sivori (heard often in the United States), superb (though not, I think, equal to Vieuxtemps). Felix Godefroid, on the harp, perfectly enraptured the people. Laborde sang delightfully.

After the Concert, I was presented to *Auber*, the composer; had a brief and pleasant chat about America, and an invitation to call and see him.

Wednesday.—Heard Sophie Cruvelli—to me one of the most fascinating singers I have ever listened to in "Semiramide."

Belletti was there also. The opera was superbly given. I have never heard such an orchestra. On the following evening heard Der Freyschutz at the Grand Opera, with Mad. Nau; and a portion of "Lucia," in which Mad. La Grange sang divinely, she being called out *five times!*

Left Paris at half-past 10, per rail, for Chalon-sur-Saone; paid two Napoleons for a first class ticket (about eight dollars); dined at Dijon at 6, and arrived at Chalon at 9—put up at Hotel de Parc.

The French railways are admirable. The carriages comfortable and luxurious, the conductors invariably polite, and the punctuality of the trains astonishing.

As I left Paris my eye was charmed by the exquisite beauty of the scenery of the surrounding country; snatching a hurried glance at the world-renowned Forest of Fontainebleau, and envying the content and peace of the peasantry, so happy and cheerful, women, men, and children working in the fields together, reminding me of Macaulay's beautiful lines:

"Now let there be the merry sound
Of music and of dance;
Through thy corn-fields green, and sunny vales,
Oh! pleasant land of France!"

And also of the rhapsodies of old Cardinal Richelieu, in the lines so graphically given by Forrest:

"My island France! My wedded wife, sweet France!
Who shall proclaim divorce 'twixt thee and me!"

Thursday, 21.—Left in steamer for Lyons. The "Saone," a beautiful river, a good deal like the Rhine. Scenery matchless.

At Lyons, stopped at Hotel de Nord, to which place I and a Mr. Repka, of Philadelphia, had been taken by the "Courier."

Strolled through some of the silk factories, and accidentally "came across" my old friend "Toot G——," of Philadelphia.

His astonishment was great on seeing me. "Why, Pipes, where the d——l did you come from? I thought you were in Marysville, California, buried in a gold mine!"

Well (I replied), the fact is, I have been engaged by the manager of the Theatre to play a *round of my Shaksperian* parts, and so I thought I'd open in the most popular one, which is "Claude Melnotte," in the Lady of Lyons!

"You don't say so," says he, "by golly, I'll come and see you to-night!"——

I saw him about four years afterwards in Chesnut street, Philadelphia.

LXI.

LYONS.

WENT to the Theatre; a beautiful building, fitted up elegantly. The orchestra, consisting of about sixty performers, was capital—six violoncellos, four double basses, twenty fiddles.

I have forgotten what the play was about, but I know, that *out of France*, I have never seen pieces so well put upon the stage—never heard such an orchestra—never seen acting so good—and never looked upon such stage scenery!

* * * * * * * * *

Went up the heights of Fouvier, from which place I had a splendid view of the Alps and Mount Blanc. Registered my name, and saw the signatures of J. T. B. and L. G. C.

Start for Avignon in steamer at six in the morning. Passed down the Rhone, gliding by some of the most beautiful vineyards I had ever seen, arriving at Avignon about four.

This is a very ancient and antique looking city, and somewhat celebrated, I am told, as being the Chateau of the Popes. We dined here very nicely, at seven taking the rail for Marseilles, arriving there at half-past nine at night.

LXII.

MARSEILLES.

STOPPED at Hotel d'Orient. On the next day, had a very pleasant interview with Mr. Hodges, the American Minister, who invited me on the following day to dinner.

Marseilles is a very bustling, business-looking city, and, I believe, the largest seaport in France. The quays, docks, and wharves are swarming with life and motion, and the fleet of vessels, and the smoke-jacks of a score or more of steamships, is most refreshing to the eye of those who have passed the greater portion of their lives in "big cities," and, as my friend "Col. Fuller" remarks in his spicy book:

"The city is flourishing under the new impulse given it by Louis Napoleon, who is everywhere breathing the breath of life into France."

LXIII.

NICE.

Monday, 24*th April.*—Left Marseilles at nine, per Diligence, for Nice, Italy, travelling all night. Entered the Sardinian territory about eight, Tuesday. Stopped at Hotel des Etrangers.

I was delighted with this place, the situation right on the shore of the classic Mediterranean. Perfectly beautiful.

The weather at this season of the year was lovely. There are here about 40,000 people, among whom are many English, those whose limited income renders it a more convenient place of residence than in larger and more expensive localities.

The town is situated at the foot of Montalbano. This city and its environs are greatly celebrated for a pure and healthy air, the climate even, I was informed, in the middle of winter being very mild; accounted for by the situation of the neighboring mountains, which are connected with the Alps, and protect the place from storms.

Start for Genoa at seven, again by "Diligence"—oh! horror! The scenery on this route surpassed everything in grandeur I had ever dreamed of.

28*th April.*—Arrived at ten, and put up at Hotel de la Croix de Malte sur le Port.

This is emphatically a City of Palaces, through many of which I wandered, and was, of course, delighted.

LXIV.

A REMINISCENCE OF GENOA.

THE second day after my arrival I was fortunate to meet with a young Italian, from Palermo, who spoke pretty good English, and finding that, like myself, he was waiting for the Leghorn steamer to take him to Rome, we joined company, and I very gladly availed myself of his offer to show me some of the places of interest in and about this ancient and interesting city.

He proposed first that we should visit the "Pallacini Gardens." These are distant some four miles from the city.

It is the country-seat of a wealthy Italian Marquis, and the house and grounds are open for the inspection of visitors at certain times of the year.

To give some idea of their vastness and extent, our guide informed us that five hundred laborers and mechanics were constantly employed in the different departments every year, making improvements and keeping the grounds in order.

Imagine to yourselves, then, a palace of tne purest white marble, of the most elaborate style of architecture, the main entrance to which is ascended by innumerable steps of the same dazzling material, looming up, as it were, from a bed of roses. The view from the summit was surpassingly grand, and my eye was fairly feasted with every variety of scenery.

Mountain, hill, valley, and dale—artificial lakes, with gilded and gaily colored pleasure boats—water-falls, fountains, bowers of loveliness, cool and shady nooks—exotics, and flowers of every name, odor, and color—aviaries of birds of the richest and most glorious plumage, pouring forth the sweetest melody, fairly intoxicating the senses.

Sunday, 1st May. Left in French steamer for Leghorn:

—Put up at Hotel Victoire, a capital house, beautifully kept, clean beds, lots of water, large towels, civil landlord, who speaks English (or did), and gave us a capital fare, and well furnished rooms.

My first intention upon arriving here, was to buy a "Leghorn hat," a thing I had never seen since I was a boy; but failing in this, I was attracted to the Plaza, to hear the finest band that I ever remember listening to; I refer to the "Austrian"—composed of about a hundred musicians—each performer a professor of the instrument upon which he plays.

They stood in the middle of the Grand Plaza, by lamp-light, the conductor standing in the middle of the space, baton in hand—the band was composed entirely of wind instruments—and played divinely.

The following day went per rail to "Pisa," and (of course), up the *Leaning Tower!* The scenery on the route was exceedingly beautiful, but upon arriving we were beset by a perfect swarm of beggars, or, as they are called, lazzaroni, half-starving, starved, maimed, halt, and blind, whose supplications for "carita, signor, carita," beat anything I had encountered in Malta.

The tower, it appears, was built in the twelfth century, and it leans eight feet from the top to the base, and is reached by a flight of one hundred and ninety-six steps. My sensations upon going up this *slanting dicular* tower were most peculiar, and though it has been standing more than six hundred years, and has braved the "battle and the breeze" in the shape of earthquake, storm, and wind, I felt that it was going to fall down with my weight!

At the top were large bells, rung upon the occasion of the execution of criminals, or a fête day.

We then went to the cemetery—the "Duomo," or Baptistery—returning to Leghorn at four.

LXV.

CIVITA VECCHIA—TO ROME.

From Leghorn I went by steamer to Civita Vecchia, put up at Hotel "Orlandi," very good, and very expensive. This is, I believe, the only seaport in the Papal States—and I should think it very fortunate for the residents of the dominions of his Holiness, that it is so—for another such place would be the death of any one, whose business called him thither; though Civita Vecchia is certainly one of the numerous places which steam navigation has raised from comparative insignificance.

Numbers of travellers land here on their first entrance into Southern Italy; and the lines of steamers which regularly touch here on their voyages between Marseilles and Naples have given a slight importance and spasmodic activity to the town, which it never could have acquired by any other means.

I should imagine it to contain 5000 souls.

They have a theatre here, and I saw *La Sonnambula* very badly performed.

Tourists are never permitted to land, until the captain has shown his papers, and passports are carefully examined.

Directly after we landed we were beset by porters; but we had made our bargain before leaving the steamer.

Two "pauls" (or 50 cents) for landing is quite enough. Before we left the town our baggage was twice examined, amidst the greatest "fuss and feathers."

These annoying and ridiculous impediments give an early acquaintance with the greatest drawback to travelling in Italy.

On Tuesday, May 3, I started by Diligence, at half-past eleven A.M., for Rome—arriving at half-past seven in the evening—paying therefor 20 pauls or $5.

The first view I obtained of St. Peter, was about 17 miles from the city, where the great dome loomed up in the distance like a big balloon—the postilion, cracking his whip, and "hollering out" *voilà! St. Petar!*

Now, I think I have before hinted to the dear delightful reader, that my visits to all these wonderful places being very much on the "Will o' the Wisp" order preclude the possibility of a very extended "mention;" and indeed, were it not so, it has been done to "tatters" by thousands of tourists who have preceded me—and so the "Eternal City" will be disposed of as follows:

I had put up at the Hotel d'Allemagne, in the Via Condotti, kept by "Franz"—and I was told, it was considered one of the best taverns in the place. I think I found this the most expensive place I had yet visited in Italy; my hotel bill was about $4 a day.

The following letter I sent to the "Knickerbocker Magazine:"

"Hotel d'Allmeyne, Rome, May 8, 1853.

"MY DEAR KNICK.:—At last the feet of Mr. PIPES have reached the seven or eight-hilled city, and from a capitally-furnished room, only six stories high, with a magnificent prospect, is he penning these few lines to you, a keind frend promising to mail it from London, as that will save you at least a hundred dollars postage, this bein' very deer in the Papal States. Now as I have seen and gazed at sum werry curious 'things' on this side the worter, and have only a short space to report 'em in, I shall pick out a phew 'PIPE-stems' for those of your Reeders who have done me the honor of glancing at my ill-spelled yarns. Fust of orl comes Mrs. HARRIET BEECHER STOWE. In each of the cities and towns through which I have pass'd, I have seen in various languages, the announcement of 'Uncle TOM'S Cabin' for sale, and in two instances the name was spelled thus: 'MISTRESS, HARRIET BEATCHER STOVE!' In PIEDMONT, I saw it akted, and the Italien who took the part of UNCLE TOM affected the audience to tears, the women crying like sixty!

"My edication being sadly neglected in the 'classikal line,' wen a young child, prevents my givin' you any very extended notis of this world-renowned citty, or interesting anekdotes of Mr. CÆSAR, Mr. TITUS, Mr. NERO, or POMPEY'S Pillar, and the like; but a few of the 'things,' providing I can spell 'em right, I will 'jot down.' Among the foremost I would menshun 'The Colluseum,' where BIRON used to lie on a stone, and right 'Child HAROLD.' It is in vast preservashun, though wonderfully goin' to ruin. I sor the place were the wild beastesses used to cum up through a iron grateing, while Mr. CÆSAR and his family used to look on. SAINT PETERS is decidedly larger than our church in Barclay-street, take it orl round on an average; then, it has got a ball, so high that the bats can't fly up to it; whitch makes 'em very cross, they say. I sor the POPE, who is a very mild-looking gentleman, dressed in various colors. Peeple generally kiss his toe—I disremember which one—but I didn't. He goes to Bed about eight bells, and gets up immediately before breakfast. I visited the late residence of NERO and TITUS, still standing. Some of the fresko's, though painted three thousand years ago, are yet visible; they were done by various painters, such as VANDIKE ROOBINS, Sir JOSHUA REYNOLDS, MICHAEL ANGELO, TITMARSH, MORELAND, ELLIOTT, INMAN, and RAFFLE. I am not quite certain, but I think these are sum o' the names.

"Then I went to the VATIKAN—one thousand, four hundred rooms; sor statuary, mummies, (no daddys,) regular original ones, done up in linen; then I went to the theatre paid two pauls entrance, (ten cents English;) the play was 'MARY, Queen of Scots;' didn't understand a word of it, corse it wos hurried up in Italien. It appeared that Sir WALTER REALLY got into a muss with Queen ELIZABETH, but I an't quite certain. Then I went to the 'Pantheon,' or the 'Pantry' I forget which: this wos built twenty-five years B. C., and is still standing: there is a large hole at the top, which admits light and rain, sometimes both: I think they show you the pew St. PAUL used to occupy, but I'm not quite sure. Then I went to the arch of Mr. SEPTIMUS SEVERIOUS, carved all over in real stone; then to the Pyramid of CAYIUS CESTIUS; then to the arch of CONSTANTINE, and Temple of VESTA, where the first waist-coat was made; so they said, but I an't quite certain. I didn't see any regular, real Romans, like they used to be in the old times: they all wear tail coats, now, and patent-leather boots, and gold shirt studs. I sor the Foram, but I don't think they were sitting; I an't quite certain. On my way to Rome, having to stop at Leghorn for two days, I took a run per Railroad to PISA, and went up the Leaning Tower; and I fully expected it would fall down every minit, bekorse I wos there, but I believe it is yet standing. Pisa is in Tuskany, or Tuscaloosa, I forget which.

"Yesterday, I sor a copy of the 'KNICKERBOCKER,' of last month or the month before, at the English Reeding-Room of Mr. PIALE, Number Seventy-Nine, Piazza di Spagna, and there were half-a-dozen 'Merikans waiting to get a sight at it. There was the nice blue cover, the pictur of 'Old NICK,' in the easy chair, and in a moment, there came to me such 'pleasant memories' of the past, of 'chats' and mild 'brewings' 'now and then' in the sanctum, of sundry visits to Nassau-street, and the polite and gentlemanly Mr. H——, when a bright, fresh copy would be handed me; and pleasing indeed to me was the thought that I might soon meet you again!

"Trooly Yours,

"JAMES PIPES, of Pipesville."

When I inform the reader, that I met a gentleman upon my first visit to the Vatican, who informed me, that he had visited Rome regularly for eighteen years—passing three or four months there each season—and did not imagine that he had seen *half of it*, I need make no further apology for the brevity of my remarks, considering, I fancied *I* had seen it in four days.

My English friend was horrified when I told him of my flying visit. The other day I got hold of rather a funny specimen of English composition. Here is a *verbatim* copy: it is the advertisement of one of the Hotels: "Hotel Meloni, Rome. This handsome and extension hotel, situate on the beutiful Piazza del Popolo, on the side of the magnifical walk of Mount Pinio as also the benefit of being in most of its parts warmed by the sun near the English church, and possessing fine points of view, together with the salubrity of the air. The Hotel is directed by the proprietor himself who neglects, no, thing, in his establishment, to reduce it, one of the most, comfortable houses in Europe, as well for the distribution of its apartments, and finery of its furniture, as for the uttermost cleanness, and reasonableness of prices, as so many Royal family, and many other of equal distinction who have had the goodness of honoring it might verify."

On the 10th of May, I found myself again in Genoa, on the 11th I left, by diligence and railroad, for "Turin," the most *modern* city in Italy.

Put up at the Hotel "Feder"—at the Theatre, I saw "Uncle Tom's Cabin" performed—an Italian personating the woolly-headed African—and even with this transmogrification—the audience were "moved to tears."

Next day left for "Chambery," the capital of Savoy—crossed the Alps by way of the "Mont Cenis"—bitterly cold—the scenery beyond description beautiful.

LXVI.

A SCENE TO BE REMEMBERED.

I SHALL ever remember a little incident that arrested my attention, upon reaching one of the highest points of the snow-capped mountains of the Alps, where we for a brief time rested to change horses.

Now I like the Catholics; for to me, there has always seemed to be so much real sincerity and heartfelt devotion in the followers of this creed—on the mosaic pavements of the magnificent cathedrals, that in many lands I had visited, alike kneel the rich and poor, the noble and the peasant, no "stalls" for the titled, no $1,000 "pews" are rattled off by your fashionable " auctioneer" for his kid-gloved and lavender-scented "communicant." Here they are all on a level—and let their belief be right or wrong—they show, I think, by their profound and devotional reverence for the Supreme Being when in his Temple, and by their charity for the poor, the weak and erring, a brighter pathway to Heaven, than the followers of many other creeds, who look upon *them* with derision!

We were descending—the sun had just risen—steeping in the bright red light the snow-capped hills, as far as the eye could reach.

Our diligence had stopped to get fresh horses—and we were just on the point of starting on our downward track, when from my seat in what they call the *banquette* or top of the vehicle, I saw on one of the projecting pieces of rock, on the right hand side of the road, what appeared to me to be the remains, or ruins of an old chapel, with a "cross" before it—*and a peasant woman kneeling there!*

Little did she dream that she was seen by *mortal* eye!—and thither had she gone to offer up her simple prayer. It was intensely cold—and the danger and difficulty of the ascent must have been indeed great. How intense the devotion of a soul thus praying! how fervent the prayer—how sublime the spectacle—how acceptable to the Omnipotent!

LXVII.

GENEVA.

On the 14th I arrived at "Geneva," and put up at the hotel de Corrane, on the Lake, and felt like singing the song,

> " I have crossed the proud Alps,
> I have sailed down the Rhone," etc.

Lake Leman lies before me, and from the window of this charming hotel the scene is perfectly enchanting.

One of the most interesting reminiscences connected with my brief sojourn in Switzerland, was the following.

I had rested for a day or so, at one of the little villages on the banks of Lake Leman, near the far-famed town of Zurich, and I want to tell the reader of my meeting with

THE LILY OF THE VALLEY.

The reader is aware, that, in some parts of Northern Europe, the English language is spoken; indeed, in many of the Swiss Hotels, it is quite common. I was in one instance, however, fortunate enough to meet with a family who talked good old Saxon, the head of which was the host of the pretty little village inn at which I rested. Here, as in other lands, the children have their "May Day Festival;" and, though I was not quite in time to witness their merry-making, I was in time to inhale the fragrance of the flowers—in time to tell you of the exquisite beauty, even though withered on the stem, of "The Lily of the Valley." What a lovely day it was—as, looking from the window of my Hotel, I watched the bright sun-beams, as they danced and sparkled on the clear blue waters of Lake Leman! The breeze was crisping the waves, so that they danced and gently tossed about the tiny boats, with milk-white sails, that glided on its surface.

A very compact little vessel was hired for a moderate price, and as she fluttered her wings to the wind, I seemed fairly to revel in the quintessence of quiet and repose. The first summer rain had just fallen, and the valleys, hills, and dales, refreshed by the showers, seemed to send up a song of thankfulness to Heaven, while the trees, filled with blossoms, some just putting forth their leaves, looking so green and lovely; and as far as the eye can reach, it was one vast panorama of matchless beauty.—On nearing a little village, the name of which I have forgotten, not very distant from the far-famed Zurich, whose waters have been immortalized in story and song, I observed, as I thought, an unusual gaiety and liveliness of the people, and I was about remarking to my companion that I imagined it was some fête day, when he informed me we had arrived just in time to see the last of the Swiss May Festival. Children's sports are to me always interesting, and so away we went, through innumerable groupings of lads and lassies, and vine-yards, bowers, and gardens of surpassing beauty, the air seemingly laden with the perfumes of a thousand exotics, when, suddenly, in the distance the well known May Pole was seen. But the dance had ceased; the little twinkling feet that so lately had trodden on the spring blossoms, had disappeared; but the Lily of the Valley was there, and its fragrance was sweet beyond description.

A little blue-eyed girl, of some seven summers, had just plucked the flower, and placing it in her bosom, began to cry. This attracted my attention, and I went to her and asked her to tell me the cause of her grief. She said that her little sister, whom they used to call the "Lily of the Valley," had been taken from them, and she was going to send this flower with her to Heaven, to be planted there! I need not say I became much interested, and followed the little stranger for some distance; but, in the throng of children, I soon lost her.

The little ones that, on my arrival, were grouped together in the very height of glee and excitement, as I fancied, were speaking in subdued tones, while the peasants looked sad and gloomy.

Musingly I strolled to the inn of the village, where I learned the cause of the ceasing of the festivities. Here, also, had they a "May Queen," one they were wont to call the "Lily of the Valley." For three summers had she reigned over her little flowery band, when suddenly she was called away to bloom in the fields of light above.

But listen to the story as they told it to me:

The sun never beamed more gloriously than upon the May-morn about which I am writing; the last crowning of the "Lily of the Valley," and though its little head was bent in sickness, the genial sunshine, it was thought, would revive, and the merry-making and excitement prove beneficial, rather than injurious. And so they placed her upon her floral throne.

The shoutings of a hundred tender voices went up; processions were formed, and garlands, wreathed by little hands, were tossed in the air. All eyes were turned towards the throne of roses, and her crown of pure white lilies, that she loved to wear, was placed upon her brow. She looked so lovely there, in her dress of buds and blossoms; but she was *very pale*, and her eye looked up to Heaven! Could she have heard them calling her away? She smiled so sweetly, she could not be in pain; and then she tried to raise herself, but the exertion was too much for her, and just waving her little hand,

> "She fell in her saint-like beauty,
> Asleep by the Gates of Light!"

The color returned not to her cheek, and thus this tender floweret, in the very height of its May Day glory, was taken to be transplanted into the heavenly nursery!

The May Day dance was over. Garlands and wreaths of flowers dropped from slender hands, that in their glee had held them—and tears flowed like rain; and, where so lately smiles, laughter, and the joyous strains of music floated in the air, sobbings now were heard, and rejoicings were at an end.

I thought it was a glorious way to die,—ere the young heart had grown familiar with the paths of sin. While even the spring flowers budded, bloomed, and blossomed on her very breast—while the shoutings of innocent voices greeted her—her spirit passed silently away.

This is the story that they told me; and now I will tell you, my reader, *what I saw.*

There was no coffin—no pall—no raven plumings—none of the trappings and sombre liveries of the grave, seen there;—but upon two pieces of *cedar wood*, bound tightly together with boughs of evergreen and myrtle, forming a sort of trellis-work, the body was placed, dressed in a garment of plain white, with a single flower—the "Lily of the Valley"—resting on the breast. The scene was most imposing. It was night; but the moon shone full upon that lovely face; it was so light—so very light—it did not look like *Death.* And, then, it seemed to smile, as though a pleasant dream was her's;—or, perhaps, she was talking to the angels. And, then, each of the children kissed those little lips, so still now, and cold, and their hearts seemed breaking. I could hear their sobbings;—and they called her "Lily;" and they seemed to think *that she could hear them!* and one said she knew she smiled when they called her—but now she had gone to God to be a Queen among his little angels! She was so very beautiful! And then they sang a hymn; and its distant echo among the hills made me think that it was answered by cherub voices;—it was so distinct, so very clear, that it startled me;—and, then, I saw them turn away and weep, for the "Lily of the Valley" had passed from their sight for ever!

In connexion with the preceding, I have great pleasure in introducing the following stanzas, presented to me by Dr. Keyes, the husband of the fair writer, when on a visit to Montgomery, Alabama, March 10, 1859.

THE SWISS MAY QUEEN;

OR

THE LILY OF THE VALLEY.

An incident, related by Stephen C. Massett, in his travels in Switzerland, suggested the following lines.

There was not a bud or flower so fair
In Zurich's lovely dale,
As the gentle little maid, they called
The Lily of the Vale.

Three years a gay and youthful band
Had crowned her Queen of May,
Who ever hailed the coming
Of the glad and joyous day.

Another May-morn came again—
All hearts were beating high—
The air was soft—and brightly beam'd
The azure of the sky.

The maidens, with their garlands,
Had gathered on the green,
And were waiting for the coming
Of their loved and gentle Queen.

Lily was drooping, but they thought
The sunshine bright and warm,
Would bring again to blooming life
Her fragile little form.

She came, and then they placed her
Upon her floral throne—
Decking her brow with blossoms white,
Flowers that she called her own.

She looked around, smiling with love
Upon that fair young band—
But the bright and fragrant wand she held
Was trembling in her hand.

Then, the angels must have called her—
To heaven she turned her eyes—
And her gentle spirit, upward borne,
Soared fluttering to the skies.

At night the moon in glory shone
Upon the scented bower—
Again they gathered to the grave
In the tranquil, silent hour.

A bier was made, all covered o'er
With flowers for a bed—
Again the lilies of her choice
Were bound around her head.

Queen of the angels, now she reigns
Queen of a lovelier throng—
And with that minstrel band above
She sings her May-day song.

Weeping, below, the maidens turn
From the dark and saddened scene—
No more they'll clasp in warm embrace
Their own loved May-Day Queen.

St. Andrew's Bay, Fl.
Feb. 19, 1855.

Back again in Paris. Been gone only twenty-six days, during which time I think I have not been idle.

24th May.—Yes, while in London the big Tower guns are firing, and hurrahs are rending the air; variegated lamps in the shape of V's and A's are trembling and hanging from the house-tops—for this is Her Majesty's birthday. While all this is going on, here I am sitting once again in my pleasant room, after my rattling journey.

Just returned from visiting the Museum, Palace, and Gardens of Versailles, and therewith was I delighted. The day was lovely, and providing myself with a valet de place, made for the rail depot, from which place we started at 10 A.M. Versailles is quite a large city, containing, I am told, some 60,000 inhabitants. There is always an immense number of troops here; but of course the principal object of interest is the Palace and Gardens, I accordingly made the best of my way thither. Before we entered the principal court of the chateau (if these *French words* are spelled wrong you and your readers will pardon me) I was struck with its really beautiful iron palisading. It offers to the view an extent of 117, or thereabout, yards, divided into eleven parts by iron pilasters, terminating at the two extremities by pedestals bearing trophies. The suns which surmount the gilt lyres decorating the iron pilasters, are to be met with at every step in the different embellishments of the chateau. Louis the XVI., I am told, chose this planet for his emblems. The Palace is approached from the town by the Place d'Armes, about 800 feet broad, on one side of which are the stables erected under Louis. They present semicircle fronts, with courts inclosed by handsome iron railways, having lofty gateways, ornamented with trophies, &c. They afford accommodation to 1000 horses. The Grand Court is about 400 feet in breadth, and separated from the Place d'Armes by stone parapets flanking an iron railway, richly chased with gilded ornaments, with a central gateway, surmounted with the ancient crown and shield of France. At the end of this railing are groups of figures in stone—on the right representing France victorious over Austria—on the left victorious over Spain. In front are sixteen marble statues of Richelieu, Bayard (I could not help thinking of one of the editors of the Tribune), Colbert, Turenne, and others. In the middle is an immense equestrian statue of Louis XVI. It is magnificently executed. I almost fear to say how many rooms I walked through, filled with exquisite paintings; but I believe there are some four or five hundred. With the Chapel I am particularly struck. The interior, I am told, was restored by Louis Philippe to its original splendor. It was here that in 1769 Louis and Marie Antoinette were married. The pavement is of the most costly marble, wrought in mosaic. The balustrades of the galleries are of marble and gilded bronze. The paintings in the Chapel of the Virgin are most exquisite. Service is chanted here every Sunday morning. I went then to the Theatre. Fourteen columns, fluted and gilt, separate the upper boxes, fronted with balustrades richly gilt. The other ornaments are in crimson and gold, with lots of mirrors and chandeliers. This is only open on presentation of one's *passport* and a small fee. I then went to the *Grand Apartments.* The king's are lofty and large, encrusted with marbles, and loaded with a perfect profusion of massive and gilded ornaments. The queen's are in white and gold, and look exceedingly rich and chaste. But how shall I tell you of the Park and Gardens? Of the variety and effect of the plantations and water, or of the immense number and beauty of the statues, vases, and groups. Here are two beautiful vases in white marble, ornamented with bas-reliefs—then come the oblong basins, upon the borders of which repose, I forget how many, magnificent bronze groups. At the end of the terrace are two fountains, adorned with groups of animals—all sorts of flowers, rich and rare, are to be found in profusion. I could fill my sheet in talking to you of this place of enchantment; but as I have other things to chat about, let me leave Versailles. Come and take with me a quiet stroll into one of the many beautiful public gardens of the Champs Elysées, I forget the name of *this* one, but I am told it ranks first. Well, a light iron frame front leads you to a spacious vestibule, the vault being supported by eight columns, and from thence to a very large garden completely *roofed with glass*. A range of iron pillars runs all along the interior, supporting a light and airy gallery filled with lovely flowers, the space below being laid out as a garden, with orange trees and all sorts of rare exotics—great big basins in the form of enormous sea-shells, cascades, statues, and groups; the bloom, perfume, and beauty of the scene my pen fails me to describe. There is even an aviary here filled with beautiful birds, warbling away; and in the centre of the garden a grassplot leading to a romantic grotto. While the walls that connect portions of the iron framework are coated with mirrors! Verily a scene did Mr. Pipes witness the other night. And though he wandered gloomily and alone, through this earthly paradise, yet he fully appreciated the delicious situations of many of those around him; for, taking advantage of the beauty of the night, the magic of the scene, the witchery of the music, and the soft and inviting shades of the mossy bowers, than which, nothing more lovely could he imagine Eden's garden to produce, were many of both sexes, and "eyes replied to eyes that spoke again." It seems to me (to be a *leetle* poetical) that words, breathed in places like this, come with ten-fold power upon the imagination, and the guards to the heart are unconsciously lulled to sleep, and the simple-hearted one is too apt to fall a victim to the insidious arts of the vicious and depraved.

Once again—and perhaps for the last time—on the Boulevards! Oh, street of streets, how shall I write about thee! Broadway is great—Regent street, Oxford street, Piccadilly—are nutmeg-graters; but these same Boulevards are the greatest. Countless numbers of trees on either side—the dazzling beauty—the luxury of the shops—the restaurants—the lofty houses, some of beautiful architecture—the crowds of well-dressed persons—the glittering of thousands of variegated lamps among the trees—the sounds of music and the roll of carriages, all form a perfect medley of sights and sounds to the eye and ear, not a little perplexing, though not unpleasing to the visitor who walks there for the first time on a fine evening. Forms, stools, chairs, in any number, filled with men, women, and children. You pay *two sous* each for a seat. Then there are puppet shows, Punch and Judys, pantomimes, rope dancing, dancing, dancing dogs, anything, everything! The scene, as I last evening took my farewell stroll, was indescribably wonderful and exciting; a confusion of colors and images burst upon my vision, the whiteness of the houses, broken at intervals by dark masses of verdure, formed a beautiful contrast to the blaze of light issuing from the splendid cafés and club houses, while the glaring gas lights without illuminate the groups seated round the little marble tables; cabs, elegantly ornamented coaches, and carts, rush almost noiselessly by, on the newly macadamized carriage-way, and all seem perfectly entranced in the pleasure of idleness. How I yearned to "parley-voo-de-dingdong;" but 'twas of no avail, and so with a last lingering look I turned down the Rue de la Paix, to the Place Vendome, into the R-o-o-o St. Honoré, and thence to my hotel.

On Sunday I saw the Emperor—the late Mr. Louis Napoleon. He was on horseback, dressed in a blue frock coat with a velvet collar, grey check trowsers with a dark stripe down them, patent leather boots, and a shiny hat—that Genin brought out for him. He looked pale, touched his hat occasionally, sometimes took it off.

26.—Left Paris for London by way of Boulogne per rail. The place is a sea-port in the channel at the mouth of the little river Liane. The upper town, or what they call Old Boulogne, is built on the summit of an eminence, and encompassed with walls. The lower town is partly situated upon declivities, stretching down from the ramparts and the slopes of the beautiful hills which line the harbor, flanked on either side by two long piers. The suburbs of Boulogne are indeed lovely, and I should imagine that no continental town can vie with the numerous advantages which it possesses; it is so near England, its situation and environs so beautiful, and just for all the world like Rockaway; it has a sandy beach, rendering it a most agreeable bathing-place and summer resort. Here, during the season, are any quantity of English; and I assure you I feel, after my journeyings, where for weeks I have not heard a word of my own tongue, that *at least* I can understand and be understood, for, though a *French* town, it is decidedly *half English.* Signs and sights like these greet the eye: "*Mrs.* Susanna Taylor, Butcher"—"John Buck, from London"—"Good Beds, 1s. 6d."—"Chops, Steaks, Liver and Bacon, Cold Cuts, Brown Stout and Table Beer, *The Era taken in*"—"Shaving 1d." —"Muffins and Crumpets," and the like. Quite refreshing this, after reading, or trying to read, all sorts of jim-crack words and quirly-gigs! And then you see "young" and "old" England to great advantage; see on the Pier o' mornings and evenings short waistcoats, large feet, striped trowsers, short bosomed shirts with three black studs, gaiters, narrow rimmed *'ats*, a *Murray's* guide book, a spy glass, and a thick stick; then you hear the Queen's Hinglish walked into pretty considerably, such as "Wen did you git 'ere?" "I 'ad such a lark yesterday harfternoon!" and "'ow did you like the hopperar, hay?" etc. But I like Boulogne much—the hotels are capital, and I have been most kindly treated.

Just received a very pleasant note from Mrs. Henry Russell (the wife of the celebrated vocalist and composer), inviting me to call at the Chateau Lettsom, Maquétre.

Passed a delightful day there with her charming family.

LXVIII.

AN INTERVIEW WITH BRAHAM AT THE AGE OF EIGHTY-FIVE.

AND now for an incident that happened to me at Boulogne. First, I would premise that I have been most lucky in my travelling companions, always finding some nice gentlemanly fellow, who would, if I needed it, translate for me, or give me some bit of valuable information. About half way from Paris to this place I found but one gentleman in the car besides myself, and this one having the *almost* universal bit of "red ribbon" stuck in his buttonhole, I felt satisfied it would be in vain for me to suggest a remark, either about the "weather" or anything else; accordingly I folded my arms, and commenced musing. My companion, however, asking me if I objected to his smoking, changed the current of my thoughts, and I soon found myself chatting away, on all sorts of topics. Accidentally mentioning California, I was asked if I had met with a Mr. T——, of San Francisco, and upon my replying in the affirmative, my companion presented me with his card, stating that he was his brother, and inviting me very kindly to his house. Upon the arrival of the train at Boulogne he insisted upon driving me in his very elegant carriage to the hotel from which I am now writing, and through him I found out the residence of a lady, whom years ago I had met in New York, and who, when I called on her here, received me most cordially, and it is she I have to thank for the great pleasure I afterwards received, in calling on and passing the evening with the *veteran* Braham! Yes, the veritable Simon Pure—the seemingly imperishable.

Now I shall try and give you as exact an account as possible of what was said and done, and as good a description as I can of his appearance—for he is certainly a *living wonder*. There were present a Mr. Westmacot, brother he told me to the sculptor, and uncle to an old acquaintance of ours, a doctor of the same name, who formerly lived in New York; Miss Bolton, the sister of the late Mrs. Braham, my friend Mrs. R——, her daughter and myself. I was not a little surprised to see Mr. Braham walking about the room without any support—no stick—and when I was introduced he gave me quite a good shake of the hand, saying, in a most jovial manner—"Take a chair, sir; happy to see you—we are just taking tea, will you join us?—I want to chat a little about New York."

He was dressed in black, and with the exception of being a little thinner than when in New York, had not changed one particle in fourteen years; when I last saw him he was standing on the steps of the "Astor," whistling for his dog!

And he was actually letting grow a *little moustache*, which has an indescribably ludicrous appearance on a person of eighty-five.

Having with me the programme of one of my own concerts given in California, I showed it to him. He took it, and though the print is very small, he read *every word of it*—seemingly to wish to show us that he *could*—without spectacles! He then turned to me and said—"Come, sir, will you sing me a song?"

"With pleasure, if it will afford you the least amusement," said I.

Accordingly my *pipes* were set a going—and when finished—the veteran singer, going towards the piano, said to me—

"Now, sir, you have done me the favor to sing me a song, I will give you one of mine!"

He sang the "Death of Nelson" gloriously! I never heard him give it with greater power and effect. It was a treat, I assure you, and was so unexpected. But I think his reply to me, upon my asking him quite seriously, of course, if he intended *again visiting America*, is the greatest thing on record—"Why, sir, I can hardly say, *but I may!!!*"

He spoke of many in New York—and of the old Tabernacle, where he made his debut—said he was glad the Americans seemed to like Alboni so, and made this remark, or as near as I can remember, in reference to her matchless voice. "I never heard so fine a voice—it is like a *gum-tree*, sir—it oozes out like, and in her pathetic passages would draw tears from stones!"

He spoke too of our excellent friend, Mr. Timm, saying how beautifully he accompanied. I passed a most delightful evening, and now, on leaving Boulogne I would say—Go to the "Royal Hotel," kept by Mr. Hughes—capital eating and drinking, excellent beds, and lots o' water and *large towels.*

In this town, in 1848, I believe, the celebrated romance writer, Le Sage, died, and was buried. Here also, in 1844, Thomas Campbell, the English poet, died, as did Churchill also in 1700 and something.

Some delightful walks, promenades, etc., are to be found

here. The jetty seems the most fashionable, especially towards the close of the evening; when it is high water, hundreds flock to the pier, to watch the vessels as they enter or leave the harbor.

Left Boulogne per "City of Paris" steamer, for London.

On Wednesday, June 29, I left Liverpool in the steamship Atlantic, Captain James West, for New York.

On Saturday, November 5, I started on my second trip to California in the steamship Illinois, Captain Hartstein.

To be a faithful chronicler of my individual fortunes and misfortunes, it becomes necessary to inform the reader (if he or she has had the courage to follow me thus far in my biography) that, when I arrived from California, I had a tolerably fair competency; and that with a little proper nursing, and prudent investment of my "funds," I might take my ease for the future. Certain it was, that I had a larger amount of "cash" than I ever possessed before, and I began not only seriously to think of building a house in the Fifth Avenue, but of paying daily visits to Wall street to look at the "stocks"—with what profit the reader shall presently know.

In those days there was a stock called "Madison and Indianapolis." Now, it was suggested to me by a distinguished member of the "Board," that it was not only the safest thing I could invest in, but that it paid a tremendous dividend, or "words to that effect," as my friend Judge B—— says.

About this time I had several thousand dollars in the Chemical Bank.

(I always had a high regard for this institution, partly from the fact of the highly respectable looking class of old fogies whose ingress and egress I had often noticed, and partly from once having been nearly apprenticed to a chemist and druggist.)

The day I drew out my "balance" from this highly esteemed repository, was a sorry one for me. I was the most wretched man alive, and I think I not only felt in my pocket a hundred times to see if the check was there, but I walked up and down by the door of the broker's as many more, before I presented myself at the desk of the entry clerk.

The stock, I believe, was purchased at 109—and from that moment it gradually descended in the scale of railroad securities.

The correspondence I have had in regard to this investment, would alone fill a volume; and the agony I endured for months as, day by day, I saw the hopelessness of my "case" in the lowering of the figure on the Stock Board—never having *once* known the refreshing sensation of a "rise"—can be better imagined than described. Indeed, it makes me sick to think of it; so I will simply add, that this being the state of affairs, I resolved once again to woo Dame Fortune on the shores of the Pacific.

LXIX.

ALL ABOUT "PIPESVILLE."

IN the month of January, 1854, I made the purchase of a piece of land on the "Old Mission Road," in the city of San Francisco, the full particulars whereof are contained in the following sketch, written for the California Chronicle, then edited by my friend, Frank Soulé:

I think it is nothing more than fair, and justly due to my individual friends, and the public in particular, that I should give a distinct, succinct, and faithful account of the purchase, settlement, rise, and *fall* of the suburban retreat yclept "Pipesville." In doing so I must go back to first principles, and the reader will be kind enough to take a peep at me, seated at my desk in the office of Col. J. D. Stevenson, a little wooden shanty, surrounded by water, on Montgomery street, where now stands the brick store built by J. B. Bidleman. It was the month of April—say the *first* (most ominous incident!) in the eventful year 1849. Now I had never in my wildest dreams of prospective wealth and independence, entertained the idea of being the actual possessor of any "real estate"—had never before cared to inquire the price of a "20 × 80" or "50 × 160" lot in my peregrinations through the streets of dear old New York, or indeed in any city, hamlet, or town, that I have visited in any part of the globe. I had imagined that "*lots*" were originally staked out and *salt*ed down by Adam, as a first rate investment for future generations, should they "hold on" long enough, and that by some genealogical hypothesis, the present "owners" had obtained rightful possession. The reader can then in a small degree imagine the excited state of my feelings, upon being informed, on a very foggy and misty morning in the aforesaid month of April, that I was the actual possessor of *two lots* 100 feet wide by 200 feet deep, in the "beautifully situated" and flourishing city (!) of New York—of the Pacific!! My first impulse was to pack up my trunk—not a very difficult matter just then—consisting as it did of only one suit of very seedy black clothes, three shirts, and one odd sock, and proceed thence immediately and settle, as I was assured by the enthusiastic proprietor that the trifling investment would be a fortune for me and mine in a very few months, the property being so very near the proposed "City Hall," the "Public Schools" (oh! Lord), and the "Railroad Depot," to say nothing of their contiguity to the water, *i. e.* the city front! The deeds were made out and duly "recorded," and by *myself* at that, for be it known to thee, my worthy reader, Mr. Pipes, in those days, was a Notary Public, invested with all the privileges, rights, and emoluments of that exalted, high, and honorable calling, and by a no less distinguished individual than Brigadier General Governor Riley, attested by H. W. Halleck, Secretary of State!—and for the curious in those matters I have the original document to show them. I accordingly credited myself with ten dollars, the price of recording, locked up my deeds in a large tin box, purchased at a great expense of my friend Mr. Smith (now Smith Brothers & Co.), and not only got up several times in the middle of the night to see if they were safe, but foolishly thought every visitor that entered our office on business or otherwise, came to make me "an offer" for them. I will not tell you how often I have strained my eyes, in looking at a large map that was tacked up against the wall (?) of our wooden shanty, to find out the precise whereabouts of my two lots, until I had, in a feverish state of excitement, with my perspiring finger, made a dirty streak all along the beautiful surface of this splendid specimen of caligraphic art, drawn at an expense of $200 cash by my fellow clerk, Mr. Rowe! How, with mouth wide open, I had listened (until I had swallowed a lot of flies) to the startling accounts of several returned missionaries (to whom lots had been presented by the liberal proprietor, upon their promise to *build good and substantial houses within sixty days!*) who had well-nigh fallen victims to the prevailing epidemic called "fills and cheever," or "tickled to death" by mosquitoes! or how, in my own imagination, my property fell, when I found that other purchasers were glad to back out of their first investment and "let it slide," not feeling any desire to make further payments—how it would again rise, upon hearing the Colonel state, in his eloquent style, that it was the "*head of navigation, and must be the grand depot of all vessels bound to the Pacific! and that he had sent to New York for 'one hundred iron houses,' which would arrive before 'next spring' or 'the fall,' I forget which!*"—and with what mental anguish I used to proceed, again and again, to the beach to look out for those ships, which were never heard of or seen! But this suspense I could stand no longer, and accordingly departed, one bright morning, in a small schooner, to look after my property. The crew consisted of the skipper (a thorough Down Easter), two men, a small boy, and myself. We were informed that the place of our destination was situated at the "junction"—I'm certain that was the word—of the San Joaquin and the Suisun Bay, rivers—that it was impossible to mistake the locality, as it was *the head of navigation!* Our skipper (who had evidently expected to see a flourishing town) had fortified himself with several large charts, quadrants, compasses, maps, and telescopes; but on the *tenth day out* he seemed to be in great doubt as to the precise whereabouts of the "city," and I noticed that he walked the deck in a very nervous and excited state, muttering to himself in detached sentences: "Well, neow, I swow, if ever yer ketch me on to another woyage of diskivery sich as this, I'm darned! Whar in thunder is the plaiçe? I don't see no bildin's—nor nothin! I guess we've got the wrong side o' the river!" Upon which I pointed out to him a small hut, about the size of a hog-pen, suggesting at the same time that probably it was the landing-place. *Jee-roo-sa-lem!* cried out the capt'n, giving me a look not easily forgotten, and with a w-h-o-o-p, and a scream of laughter, he tried to make for the landing. In doing this we were nearly all drowned; how I got on shore I know not (the "lots" never entered my head once), but I *do* know that I hollered out to some men to take me off in a whale boat, I cared not whither, for what with the excessive heat, the swarms of mosquitoes, and the utter desolation and dreariness of the prospect (?) death seemed more preferable than a "stay" in "this horrible place."

The *schooner* thought otherwise, and remains to this day,

high and dry, on one of the "water lots." My property was on the corner of C and Second streets, right opposite the (imaginary) court house!—but the only vestige of humanity, or of animal life, that I could discover, was one bullock's head, very much flyblown, a very dirty looking Digger Indian, and an old shoe. The improvements since that time, have not been of a very extensive character; and though I still "hold on," it would be quite difficult accurately to arrive at its present market value, or its precise location.

THIS WAS MY FIRST "REAL ESTATE" OPERATION.

The reader will be good enough to proceed with me to the Levee City—Sacramento—and step into the office of "*Priest Lee and Co.*," on the corner of J and Second street, who, at that time (October, 1849) were immense merchants, land owners, and speculators generally. It was here then, that on an October morning bright and early, long before breakfast (I'd 'a got up in the middle of the night, if their office had been open), I laid $5,000 (five thousand dollars) on their counter, in good dust, for a lot twenty by eighty on I street that had been sold some months before for $100; at the same time I was quietly informed by my plausible landlord, that it would be worth $20,000 in a few weeks. The second edition of the *first flood* soon followed, the waters entirely covering my land *outhouse!* and I *barely* escaped with my life, on the *back of a large cow.* that was swimming down the street! I felt now perfectly satisfied that real estate had received its death-blow, and that I had better sell out my interest immediately. Accordingly I intimated to my excellent partner, Charley B., one of the best fellows in the world—that he could take the lot back at a fair price, which he readily agreed to, giving me the money. Now mark what I did—at the old "Sutter Hotel," there was one day a large sale of "Real Estate" (the water at the same time covered the entire city, do not forget that!) The auctioneer, Col. J. B. Starr, was offering some valuable *corner* lots on 7th and R streets, emphasizing particularly *usually* in his eloquent, and fascinating, and glowing style, the fact of their being *corner lots*, the witty Col. adding, "See, gentlemen, you can cut them up into sixteen *beautiful building* lots—property *must* rise—after the water leaves us—I assure you the depression is only temporary—millions are coming from all parts of the earth to settle in this highly favored land—and *this* is the spot they will choose!" Thus spoke my friend with the "hammer." I was very wretched —knew not what to do with my money—I couldn't eat it —I had no place to put it—and it wasn't a sufficient pile with which to leave the country, and what to do, I did not know. Some cove bid $1,001 for the "corner," *I* bid $1,002. This lot I sold in about sixteen months after to Jesse H. for $30 (thirty) dollars.

THIS WAS MY SECOND OPERATION.

I then bought two lots on K street for *twenty-five hundred* ($2,500), and was at one time offered *ten thousand dollars* for them, and ultimately sold them for eight hundred ($800).

THIS WAS MY THIRD OPERATION.

In despair, disgust, and a fearful description of mental torture, that I hope never again to experience, I came down to San Francisco, thinking, perhaps, to recover myself by making a small investment in a "water lot;" everybody imagining his fortune made, could he obtain one. I accordingly, at a sale of real estate of the property of Alcalde Geary, now Col. John W. Geary, made by Kendig, Wainwright and Co., (Ned Byrne assisting,) paid $100 cash for a "valuable piece of property," as the bills said, somewhere near "Rincon Point." This I sold for $120 to my friend Sam W——, and it is now (probably) worth $50,000 or $60,000! Peter Simple title (clear and confirmed).

AND NOW FOR MY FOURTH AND LAST OPERATION!

The purchase of the piece of land known as "Pipesville," situated near the large marsh, right by the bridge, on

Mission street, has entirely cured me of any further desire to invest any extra change I may have at any time in "real estate." I sicken at the very word—and yet I am not sorry I made the purchase. The circumstances are briefly these. Upon my return to California in December, 1853, I still felt that I would like to take a small chance, once again, at "Land," by which so many, since my absence from the country, had become rich; and having at the same time more money than brains, I made my desire known to a large and successful land owner, and personal friend, who, in reply, most kindly remarked, that he would "keep me in his eye." This, I thought, most liberal and considerate, and I felt perfectly safe, and sure of a speedy turn of good luck. The day at length came, the purchase was made, and when with this announcement my disinterested friend informed me (in answer to my query as to the exact location of the property,) that there was a *house* included in the purchase, my enthusiasm knew no bounds. The idea of *owning a house* in this expensive country! I could neither eat, sleep, nor drink; couldn't even wait for the omnibus, but footed it immediately to Mission street, arriving at the "Bridge" in a profuse perspiration. Now the only houses visible were Mr. Moss's elegant mansion, known as "Beverly Lodge," and some white cottages on the other side of the "creek," owned by some distinguished members of the "stock and buckskin." Of course, I did not venture to pull the bell of the lordly castle of the first mentioned gentleman; but I *did* think that one of the three or four white cottages had, by one of those peculiar twists and turns of California luck, fallen to my "lot." I tapped at the door of one or two, inquiring if they knew of any sale having been lately made of a valuable house and lot in that vicinity? When one of the neighbors, pointing to a patch of land, seemingly in the centre of the swamp, with a thing that looked like a pigsty in the middle of it, remarked, that a Mr. S—— had the other day sold *that* piece of property, at P. and D.'s auction rooms, and he presumed it was the house (!) and lot in question. I instantly rushed, or tumbled down the hollow, to look at my purchase, and my spirits fell ten feet deeper than the lot, which was at least sixty feet *from the grade of the street!*

Still it was something; it had a door, which actually opened; a window, with three panes of glass in it, and a small bench in front to sit down on; and I consoled myself with the thought, that it was a *step*, perhaps, towards a fortune, to be the rightful owner of an establishment, even humble as this in California. Time flew by, my property did not nor has it yet risen one cent in value, and I have bravely got over my caring if it ever *will*. I do not now get up at early morn, and sit on the old fence, or the railing of the bridge, for hours together, waiting for it to "look up." I indulge no more in vain and useless speculations as to when they will *commence*, to say nothing of completing, the "Market Street Railroad." I care not whether the "toll" is abolished or not; I would not give a fig to know whether it is out of or in the "city limits;" or if it is covered by the Bolting and Barren, the Ly-mantour, or any other claim. It is sufficient for me to know that it is *mine*, by right of purchase; that it is all paid for, and by money honestly earned by me in this great and glorious country; that the "city and county" taxes are all paid; and that I have a faithful and trustworthy German "retainer" (doubtless some exiled nobleman), who is supposed to pay me one dollar a month rent (cash), but which, by some extraordinary system of *hocus pocus*, I never receive.

And now, dear reader, permit me to tell you that your humble servant is himself the nomenclator of this pleasant spot. It pleased me to call it "Pipesville." Have you any objection? And once upon a time I thought how jolly and cozy it would be to have a little "cottage" of one's own, eh?—to read, chat, write, smoke, and think in! The idea was no sooner entertained, than I found myself at a "carpenter and builder's," and in a short time my little "snuggery" was finished.

And here I am—not exactly rich, but, thank God, in good health, tolerably happy, and at ease. From my little window, the view of the bay, the shipping, and surrounding country—the range of hills of the Contra Costa, with the high peak of old Mount Diablo looming up in the distance, is exceedingly beautiful, and I feel while dotting down these (perhaps to you tedious) random thoughts, that there is something pleasant in life after all, and that a good many of us, at least, are the makers of our own miseries. I am now a fixture; this is my homestead—and from this snug little ten by twelve room, my friends, and the public, if they please, shall occasionally have a "word or so" from their obedient servant,

JEEMS PIPES OF PIPESVILLE.

P. S.—My "Ranch" was broken into a short time since, and this is, to inform any future thieves, robbers, housebreakers, etc., that there is nothing here of the slightest value, nothing but my books, papers, and writing materials, which ought to be left *stationary*. So they may spare themselves the trouble of again breaking my door open. Should, however, they still persist, my retainer (a stalwart German), who now sleeps inside, is fully prepared to give them a *warm reception*. J. P. OF P.

Dated from my Ranch, "Pipesville," Mission street, San Francisco, Cal., April 20, 1855.

Upon my return to San Francisco, I entered the law-office of "James Doyle, Barber & Boyd," remaining with them some two years. Many and exciting were the scenes that occurred during that period, some of the more important of which I will briefly refer to.

Somewhere about this period, the greatest consternation seized the owners of "real estate," in reference to the confirmation of the "different claims" by the Land Commissioners.

Now, as my property was purchased *entirely unbeknown to me*, by my distinguished, disinterested, and wealthy friend, Squire P. Dewey, Esq.,—my superior officer, Horace P. Janes, Esq., generously offering to advance me $800 of the purchase-money—I had not the slightest doubt as to the "title"—indeed, I had no opinion about the matter either one way or the other. But it was suggested to me, that there would be no harm in my writing a business letter upon the subject to General James Wilson—a particularly worthy and pleasant gentleman—and having preserved a copy, I herewith present it to the reader:

It appeared in the San Francisco "Herald," 26 January, 1856:

LETTER FROM MR. JEEMS PIPES TO MR. LIMANTOUR.

"PIPESVILLE," Near a large Marsh, right by the "Bridge," Mission street, Yellow Cottage, San Francisco.

MY DEAR SIR:—The state of mind to which I am driven by the fact of the confirmation by the Land "Commission Merchants" of your claim to all the lands running from the Bay of Biscay to Point Lobos in the North, and to Mason and Dixon's line in the South, may be by you conceived, but certainly cannot be described by me; and I now take the earliest opportunity to state my case, calling your attention first to my

☞ ABSTRACT OF TITLE: ☜

which, though being rather complicated, and entirely unintelligible to myself, may be sufficiently "satisfactory" (as the noble order of E Clampus Vitus gentlemen observe) to you to induce you to respect my claim.

ADAM AND EVE, to CANE, ABELL & CO.	Deed dated 1st April, 02. Recorded liber A, page (R. G. & Co.) Consideration—(a good deal.)

James Grants, bargains, sells, and confirms, all that uncertain piece, parcel or lot of land, situate Lying, and being in the City of San Francisco. Describing the same by long and short metre.

CANE, ABELL & CO. to GENERAL WASHINGTON.	Deed dated 1776. Never recorded. Consideration—the U. S.

GENERAL SANTA ANNA, to THE PEOPLE OF THE UNITED STATES.	Deed (of blood) dated 1846. Recorded (in History.) Consideration—$786509876598543 2987607070760.

Grants, bargains, sells the whole of Oregon, California, (including "Pipesville," mind that,) Rincon Point, Mission Dolores, and the

Pueble; commencing wherever the United States commences, and ending where it ends!

City, State and County taxes are all paid.

THE PEOPLE OF THE UNITED STATES, to B. F. STERETT.	Deed dated 1852. Recorded in liber B (p. 179.) Consideration —$ (a large sum.)
B. F. STERETT, to JEEMS PIPES.	Deed dated January 1854. Recorded in liber D (p. 199.) Consideration—$ (a large sum.)

Hoping the above abstract will, with the assistance of Doctor Watts, enable you to—"Read my title clear,"

I remain, *Deer* Sir, yours truly,

JEEMS PIPES, of Pipesville.

The gallant General immediately sent me a "clear deed," and the proper documents from Limantour—for which he will, at this late day, accept my thanks.

LXX.

A PIKE COUNTY WEDDING.

ACCEPTING the invitation of a friend to join him company on a brief trip to the "Sulphur Springs" of Sonoma Valley, on a bright October morning of this year; I left this city of "wind and dust," for the quiet little town of Benicia, proceeding thence to Napa, where of course (excuse the joke) I slept—arriving at the "Springs" duly the next day.

I found out at the Hotel, that a wedding was "coming off," or "going on" in the evening, to which I and my friend were invited; and as it was my first introduction into real genuine, Simon pure, "Pike County" society—it not only amused me greatly—but I will try and give my readers the benefit of my observations.

About eight o'clock the bride and groom entered the room, looking pale and agitated—but apparently completely resigned.

It would have been a matter of very little difficulty to have driven a moderately-sized horse and cart between them, so great was the distance they stood apart. The bride was dressed in a green silk gown, very short-waisted —high-necked, with short sleeves—showing a pair of red arms, with long hands attached, squeezed into a pair of large-sized "men's 8's."

The groom wore a blue coat, with buttons that once were gilt—and (for it was warm weather) light pants of a very dubious cut, with long straps, surmounted by a very short waistcoat.

They were then requested to seat themselves upon the sofa, which they accordingly did, one at each end.

The minister then stood up, placing a chair before him, poised upon two legs—and leaning on the cushion, commenced the ceremony by saying, in the most peculiar *nasal* tone of voice—

"*If thar air any parsons here who kneow any jest reson why these teou couple shood not be united, in the bounds of holy wedlock, let 'em speak right eout!*"

An awful pause ensued, interrupted only by the parson himself—singing out,

"I pronounce you man and wife!"

Then commenced any quantity of kissing—the brother-in-law of the bride becoming so fearfully excited, that he rushed to embrace the *bridegroom first.*

Soon after this, supper was announced, and the wedded pair proceeded to the supper room.

When seated at the table, the waiter asked the bride what she would take for supper.

The bride replied, "I should like ter know what you have got, first."

"Beef and pork," says the waiter.

"Well, I don't mind if I do take a small chunk of your pork," says the bride.

The waiter rushed to get the desired "titbit," when a man, coming in an opposite direction with a large dish of apple sauce, lumped up against him; both tumbling down with an awful crash, the bridegroom turned sharply round, and wished to know, "What on airth they were doing on?"

Some fruit being on the table, the bride reached forth her hand to get some grapes, when her husband, with a look of intense horror, cried out—

"Ma–ree, don't yer eat them 'ere grapes, coz you've had the diaree, and 't aint good for yer!"

The reader can imagine the feelings of the company.

Supper ended, they proposed a dance; the band, composed of one fiddle and a small fife, playing the "Arkansas Traveller."

We then retired for the night.

In the morning, bright and early, a buggy was standing at the door, ready to take the "happy couple" away.

"Good morning, bride," said one of the ladies, as the blushing wife appeared.

"*I haint no wife neow neither*," said she.

"Well, that's a pretty compliment to your husband, anyhow," rejoined the lady.

"*Haint got no husband neither*," said the lady from Pike.

This the bridegroom couldn't stand, so coming up, he cried out,

"*Yes yer have, Ma–ree—I've got the certificate.*"

"Whar?" says the bride.

"In my trowses pocket!"

A general laugh followed, during which the pair "bolted."

LXXI.

SKEDADDLING OF BANKERS.

WONDROUS and astounding were the events in the monetary and financial world about this time. Bankers, monetary agents, exchange brokers "busted" entirely, and the community seemed paralysed with the announcement that the banks had suspended.

First went Page, Bacon & Co., then Adams, then some of the smaller fry, such as the Miners' Bank, Savings Bank (?), etc.

Some ludicrous scenes occurred on the 17th and 23d of February.

At the first run on Page, Bacon & Co., their doors were besieged, crowds pressing in with looks of horror depicted on their faces, intending to draw out their little all.

Men, women, and children, cabmen, merchants, longwharf Jew slopsellers, piemen, candymen, tailors, barbers, actors, priests, circus riders, water carriers, omnibus drivers, editors, saloon proprietors, Frenchmen, Germans, Italians, Greeks and Swiss, "fancy women,"—pushed, shoved, crowded, jammed, raved, and stormed—bumping up against one another, the perspiration rolling down their faces in streams.

One woman rushed down in a cab, carrying with her two sacks in which to place her cash. She leaped over the heads of everybody, and jumping upon the counter, demanded her money, which was, as soon as possible, counted out to her; the amount was *ten thousand dollars*, and she went on her way rejoicing.

Some there were who, in their agony of doubt and suspense, offered to sell their certificates of deposit at a great reduction; and I was told of two or three instances, where five, ten, and fifteen hundred dollars were made in a few minutes by an *hombre*, who had greater faith in the "house" than the holders of their paper had, by buying up for cash, at a fearful discount, their money certificates.

I noticed some who were lucky enough to get their money out, even then, wearing the most forlorn faces. They knew not where to go, what to do with it, or with whom to trust it. Up and down the streets they wandered, running this way and that—the weight of the *oro* annoying and troubling them.

With uncertainty, fear, and trembling, they looked at *all* the banking institutions of the city—who *was* solvent? "Mine Got, vat a guntry!" sang out the Jew. "Sacre nom de Dieu!" cried out the Frenchman; while the Englishman insisted, that "Hhif 'ed sent his money to Hold Hingland, as 'e hort to 'a done, it 'ud been all right." In this the Yankee partly agrees with him, except that he thinks "*Uncle Sam's Treasury Notes* would have been a *leetle* slicker investment!"

LXXII

THE PANAMA RAILROAD.

THE great event of the year 1855 was the completion of the Panama Railroad.

Now, instead of the trouble, annoyance, and danger of muleback riding, you are wafted from ocean to ocean in luxurious cars.

No more rivers of mud, nasty mule traps, broken pieces of pavement—no more donkeys perpetually stumbling over and against rocky, narrow, and dangerous defiles—no more extortion of the filthy natives or the detestable steamers on lake or river.

These are now forgotten, and the eye is gladdened by the sight of the iron bands and wooden ties of the rail.

The completion of this railroad should be regarded by all Americans as a grand national triumph.

For a long time past the most powerful European nations schemed, talked, and planned of the best mode of effecting this enormous undertaking; but it remained for American enterprise and genius to complete, in a few short years, a work that baffled the skill of the older powers of Europe to undertake.

The name of John L. Stephens will never be forgotten.

He first deemed the scheme feasible, and in the marshes and dismal swamps of the Isthmus he labored until stricken with disease and death.

He was followed in this great work by Colonel Totten, of the U. S. Corps of Engineers, as Superintendent of the Road, who first joined the enterprise in its infant state; and most faithfully has he performed his duty; sparing no energy—always at his post—kind, attentive, and humane to those under him, he has won the sympathy, good will, and love of all; and now the great desire and wish of his life is triumphantly consummated at last.

Passengers cross now in four hours; it took me, in 1849, eight days!

LXXIII.

A BANK "BURSTS," AND I LOSE MY MONEY.

AGAIN a victim. In the general panic that now seized hold of the banking institutions, I found myself slightly interested, and without entering more minutely into particulars (for the concern, on account of some private reasons, shall be nameless), I will simply state, that by the "closing" of one of the Montgomery street banks I was rendered penniless; and, at the suggestion of my friend J. T. D——, gave a concert at the Metropolitan Theatre.

I believe it was generally conceded that a more brilliant assemblage was never seen in San Francisco; and when the reader is informed that a number of my personal friends took $50 of tickets apiece—to the amount of $1000—and that at the door over $1500 were received, some idea may be imagined of the "quantity" of the audience, to say nothing of its "quality."

The success of this night determined me to give "public entertainments" on "my own hook," *à la* Russell, Dempster, or the late Albert Smith; and as this fact changed once again the current of my life, and with a four years' experience in various parts of the globe to the "method thereof," I wish to say a few words to those who essay the task of giving "single-handed" or Monologue Entertainments.

LXXIV.

MY FUTURE COURSE.

IF any person thinks it an easy thing to entertain an audience for *two hours alone*, let him go and try it—that's all!

Now, I do not make this remark because I think I have been successful in accomplishing this, or for the sake of self laudation, but to undeceive those who vainly imagine that it is an easy or quick road to travel to obtain a "fortune."

"Fame" may possibly be obtained, but I think it will be conceded that a "fortune," as the result generally speaking of the peregrinations of a "wandering minstrel," is the "exception."

Having determined, then, to adopt for the future the above mode of earning my daily bread, I started once again for Sacramento, got out my programmes and posters, secured the Rev. Mr. Benton's church, and was comforted by the following pleasant notice from the Union, the leading daily journal of the city:

"Stephen C. Massett, pioneer concertiser of Sacramento, poet, and by no means unknown to fame as the author of many humorous effusions over the signature of 'Jeemes Pipes, of Pipesville,' is to give a grand ballad concert this evening. The programme is brim-full of variety, consisting in part of comic and serious readings, songs, selections from the poets, recitations and representations of amusing scenes and characters, &c., &c. The versatility of talent possessed by Mr. Massett is an undoubted guaranty that the entertainment will be attractive. Mr. M. is contemplating a tour through all of the mining and agricultural sections of the State, and has resolved to devote himself for the future exclusively to this profession; and none who know the man will for an instant doubt that it is the one for which he is in every respect fitted. The concert is to be given in Rev. Mr. Benton's church, and tickets, which have been placed at the low price of one dollar, are to be obtained at the music stores, hotels, and the door.'

It would be tedious, difficult, and, indeed, unnecessary, for the reader to follow me, either to commiserate me for my losses or rejoice at my successes in my subsequent trip through the Northern mines and Oregon, and I shall content myself by simply giving a very brief account of my ramblings as a public performer—relating one or two rather amusing incidents—until the period of my departure for Australia.

LXXV.

SOME OF THE TROUBLES OF A WANDERING MINSTREL.

I THINK one of the most painful and decidedly uninteresting sensations experienced by those resting entirely upon their own individual merits for the attraction of an audience, is the one of *doubt*, as to whether there will be a large or small number to greet him. Now, as I have felt this sensation in a greater or less degree as often as most young beginners, the reader shall be initiated in some of the mysteries of the feeling.

I was at a place called Oroville, then a dismal looking mining town, but rich with the "gold that perisheth," a few wooden houses, innumerable tents, any quantity of lawyers, hotels made of canvas, streets knee-deep in mud, bar-rooms innumerable, and of course a theatre—called the American.

It was in this building that my "Concert" was to come off."

I had been congratulated upon my arrival by several friends known before in Sacramento, who appeared quite delighted at my advent, expressing at the same time not only their belief that the house would be crowded, but the promise that *they* would be at hand with all their friends!

I suggested that it looked like rain, and that the streets were almost impassable from the mud and slush, and that the "ladies" (I think there were about six in the town) would find it impossible to "*piroot*" thither. To this they replied, that that didn't matter, they all wore "jack boots," and cared nothing for rain, mud, thunder, and lightning!

This consoled me for the time. Now, I wish to inform the reader (and I know in this I shall get the sympathy of my "professional brethren") that, without a single exception, it has *invariably rained* on the first night of my entrance into any new locality. Yes, from Botany Bay all the way to the Hanover Square Rooms, London.

My "Hotel," if such it could be called, was "located"

immediately in front of the Temple of Thespis, and accordingly I could watch the pulse of the public pretty well, without being diskivered, or subjecting myself to the vulgar gaze of "*Pike*," a very peculiar institution in those days.

To those of my readers not exactly "up" to the meaning of the word *last* italicised I would say that to the best of my information and belief, there is a county of that name somewhere in Missouri, from which locality many thousands have emigrated to California. Now, these "Pike countyans" are a most extraordinary looking set of people, and though, I suppose, as the world wags, there are as many "decent folk" among 'em, as in any other portion of the globe, they certainly, in their appearance, manners, and talk, are entirely *sui generis*, and unlike any other human beings I have met with in my travels.

The men are, as a general thing, hugely and squarely built, broad-shouldered, very long arms, large coarse hands (whose "grip" I would ad-*vice* persons to avoid), lanky legs, with a thigh so long that when they sit down, half a dozen children could squat thereon with ease. Their spare-time is occupied in "whittling" and "chewing,"—the "arm-chairs" in the different bar-rooms, hotels, and "loafing" places, bearing pretty strong evidence of their "cutting" and "slashing" propensities. They affect slouched hats, generally with a hole in the top (either to hang it up by, or to let the wind in or out), and turned up in front. Peeping from beneath a very ill-shaped and dirty looking patched coat, you will see a portion of a dingy colored shirt, once perhaps red; the nether appendages encased in a pair of tight fitting badly cut "pants," the entire suit prevented from falling to pieces by a big leather "strap" round the middle with a clasp in front with the letters "U. S." engraved thereon; a knife, a pistol, and dirty buckskin bag for gold dust complete the appointments; the feet—about the size of a small cradle—are shoved into the largest sized pair of "high lows," sockless, and unwashed; the beard is worn, as nature originally intended it should be, and the hair—of every indefinite color—is matted, shaggy, and uncomfortable looking.

Your "Pike" countyian is not very communicative, and is apt to look upon everything and everybody with suspicion; seldom speaking to you, unless addressed first, and even then his replies will be extremely laconic and unsatisfactory.

A couple of these worthies, I noticed from the windows of the tavern, were reading the "Poster" on the door of the theatre, and as I thought I could quietly walk by and hear their views, without being "spotted" as the unfortunate "showman," I crossed over the way, as though accidentally strolling by, when Pike No. 1 relieved himself as follows:

What in thunder's a "Ballad *Consart?*"

Pike 2. Wall—a guess it's a "kinder show" and play acting.

Pike 1. "By Jeems Pipes of Pikesville." Whar's Pikesville, I wonder?

Well—guess we'll have to go—tickets two dollars. By golly—he'd ben glad to got a shilling in Missouri!

With this comforting consideration I returned to my

"quarters" to ruminate upon my chances of success in the evening.

"Hotels," in the mining towns at this period, were peculiar institutions.

The dining-room was immediately entered from the street door, the furniture consisting of two or more long deal tables on tressels, with benches on each side; up in one corner was a washbowl with a jug of water, a very dirty towel hanging from the wall, and a comb and brush attached to a string, swinging to and fro like the pendulum of a clock from frequent usage.

A "Chinese gong," or an immense "triangle," at the hour of twelve announces to the crowd that dinner is ready. Instantly a rush is made, and the greatest disorder prevails. "Roast," "boiled," "baked," "stewed," "fried," fat and lean, disappear with lightning rapidity, gallons of water are swallowed, plugs of tobacco are thrust into the mouth, and the teeth picked with a large jack knife, and all is over in about fifteen minutes.

The "sleeping" apartments are not of the most elegant description.

The one I had was furnished with a narrow cot, with a bed of straw encased in a red blanket, a broken pitcher containing about half a pint of water, a quarter of a yard of a dirty looking piece of cotton for a towel, and half an inch of a tallow candle, stuck in a bottle, completed the furniture of the apartment. The price was two dollars a day.

The reader can imagine there was not much in the surroundings of my habitation to inspire me with a very great deal of enthusiasm for the labors of the night. Well, the hour arrived, and the rain, as usual, was on hand.

I mustered up sufficient courage to cross over about a quarter to eight, peeped in at the door, and saw about a dozen fellows in the pit smoking, spitting, reading the programmes, and one or two indulging in remarks not at all complimentary to me (there was a woodcut of me on the bills, that resembled more the head of a murderer, or disappointed pickpocket, *as appears* in the Police Gazette, than anything else), some were gazing with intense interest at the drop curtain, and speculating as to who the figures were intended to represent; one insisting that it was "William Penn," making the treaty with the Indians, another with a fearful oath knew that it was Captain Cook, as he appeared immediately before being eaten by the savages, and a third that it was Adam and Eve before being snaked out of the Garden of Eden.

The last man was right—and at the tinkling of a little bell, our first parents, the snake, the trees, Captain Cook and William Penn, were rolled up into as fine a dumpling as ever faced a baker's oven.

I had a "Melodeon" in those days (as pianos were difficult to obtain) upon which I accompanied myself in my songs. Now this has not a very lively effect, either upon the performance or the audience—the music emitted therefrom being a sort of cross between an accordeon and a barrel organ—at the same time, I have to keep in the wind by a perpetual movement of the right foot on the "pedal," ah: if for a second I miss, the "bellows" indignantly resigns its office—the machine gives a feeble and dying squeak—and I am left to the tender mercy of my audience.

It was during a very pathetic rendering of the opening song, "When the Moon on the Lake was beaming," that this fatal casualty happened—and to add to the miserable state of my feelings—which I do trust will be fully appreciated by the reader—I was requested to "dry up" by somebody in the pit.

Now whether this suggestion had anything to do with the hydraulic nature of the ballad in question, I know not; —but considering it was only the *commencement* of a two hours' performance entirely unassisted, I think my situation deserved some sympathy.

I managed to "get through"—and though the affair was not pecuniarily successful—upon the whole it went off very well—and upon each succeeding occasion—particularly when my audience was of that peculiar quality, I gained greater confidence, and cared less for the trifling annoyances.

My trip through the Northern Mines was upon the whole a pleasant and successful one.

I visited "Shasta," "Downeville," (where I was very cordially greeted by my old partner Mr. now Judge

Robert H. Taylor), "Grass Valley," "Weaverville," "Yreka."

Crossing the "Trinity Mountain" by mules to "Yreka," this latter "City" is about five hundred miles from San Francisco.

LXXVI.

LOLA MONTEZ.

At "Grass Valley" the late Madame "Lola Montez" was residing in a very picturesque little "villa" guarded by a large sized "Bear," sundry dogs, parrots, cats, etc. She and Johnny S—— received me very hospitably, and the evening passed with the Countess of Landsfeldt, and the merry groups, there and then assembled—among them were "Gus. S——" of this city, and Gil. M——, of Baltimore—will ever be remembered by me with pleasure.

LXXVII.

OREGON.

Before leaving for "Australia," I determined to make a brief trip to Oregon.

Accordingly on the morning of July 21st, I left San Francisco in steamer "Columbia," for this remote portion of "Uncle Sam's" dominions.

We stopped first at Crescent City, where I had the pleasure of greeting Mr. David (now County Judge of Klamath) McComb of New York, then connected with Wells, Fargo and Co.'s Express—the steamer coming to an anchor about three quarters of a mile from the beach in an open roadstead. The boat was lowered away, and we started for the beach.

In making a landing here (there were no wharves then), at certain seasons of the year the surf is very dangerous, and some most amusing scenes occur, particularly among the ladies, in their attempts to land dryshod; and the Chinamen, in their passage to and fro from the mines, to prevent their tails from becoming wet—for all Chinamen wear their hair very long, and have a very religious horror of wetting it. The wind was blowing a gale from the south-west, and as we neared the bar the prospect was such as to make us feel very shaky. An amusing scene occurred in passing the passengers from the boat to the steamer. Among the females was one from the rolling "Zider Zee," a delicate miss weighing about three hundred pounds, more or less, including a small and ugly *dorg*, who in attempting to be landed in the boat by one of the officers, from the ship, lost her equilibrium, and with her arms about the officer's neck, who was trying to disengage himself, both commenced a series of gymnastic leaps, resulting in an immersion to the depth of some twenty feet in a cold salt water bath. They rose to the surface amid roars of laughter, and after some well directed efforts with boat hooks, etc., both were extricated.

Crescent City was settled about two years since, and contains some five hundred inhabitants. It is the depot for trade to the mines, which are located some seventy-five miles in the interior. The place has one Church, a Theatre, a Hose Company, two Express Offices, and many handsome Billiard Saloons, and I saw in two or three places "The Spirit of the Times" on file.

We next stopped at "Port Oxford." At this point there has been a Military Post, under the charge, at present, of Lieut. R. M. FEELY of the *4th Infantry*, but the cessation of the Indian hostilities with Rogue River Valley has led to the breaking up of the station. There are some one hundred residents here, and business is quite limited. The climate at this season of the year is mild and lovely. On the morning of the 25th, our steamer arrived at "Astoria," made "classic ground" by the immortal pen of "Geoffry Crayon, Gent," and it carried me back to the days when I first revelled in the beauties of the "Sketch-Book," the "Legend of Sleepy Hollow," "Rip Van Winkle," and the book which bears its name! This town is situated about twelve miles from the mouth of the Columbia river, and will, I think, eventually be the sea-port town of Oregon. It is now the port of entry for this Territory, and the Collector General, John Adair (no relation to Robin!) is one of the oldest inhabitants, having resided here some ten or twelve years. Lying a short distance above the town, upon a sunken rock, I saw the wreck of the good old ship "Silvie de Grasse," formerly of the Havre line of Packets, owned by "*Bolton, Fox and Livingston*," and singular enough, one of our passengers had made a voyage in her to France seventeen years ago! and there she lay (after buffeting for a quarter of a century the storms of old ocean) stripped of her glory, a shapeless mass of timber; and where once her streamers fluttered the sea-gull roosts, and the waters of the Oregon wail their requiem.

LXXVIII.

THE COLUMBIA RIVER.

THE Columbia river is really one of the most beautiful I have ever seen. I have written from the Bosphorus, the Rhine, the Rhone, and the old Hudson, yet must I proclaim from this distant region, the majesty, greatness, sublimity and beauty of this the finest of them all! As our stately steamer moved gracefully through its placid waters, in the far distance might be seen looming up the snow-capped and gigantic mountains of "Hood," "St. Helens," "Jefferson" and "Ranier," forming a superb contrast to the matchless and variegated colors of the hill sides and plains. The banks for most of the distance are very steep, and covered from their base to the top with tall and stately fir trees.

The waters of the river are filled with fish of various kinds, among which are great quantities of salmon; some weighing seventy-five pounds each. Located upon the banks of the river, about eighty miles from Astoria, is situated the pretty little town of St. Helens, at which place we stopped for supplies. There are here about two hundred inhabitants, and it is at this point that the Pacific

Mail Steamship Company have erected a splendid stone house and wharf, at the expense of over $35,000, for the accommodation of ships and steamers, in receiving and discharging freight and coal. At "Vancouver's" we next stopped. This is without doubt the finest location for a city or town, of any I have visited, and the depôt for the U. S. Troops for the Territories of Oregon and Washington; and the 9th Infantry are at present stationed there. Most of the officers of this Regiment have their wives and families with them. I had the pleasure of shaking hands with Captain Wallen, Captain Ingalls, Lieutenant Hodges, and many others. The officers of this garrison are noted for their attentions and hospitalities to strangers. The parade ground covers some twenty acres, and is elevated fifty feet above the river, commanding one of the finest views of the surrounding country. From this point we proceed to "Portland," situated on the *Willamette* river, from which city I am now writing. The city contains about two thousand inhabitants, is prettily built, and there are some four or five churches; three weekly newspapers flourish here, and there are many schools, and one chartered Academy; there are also thirty-six mercantile establishments, a large foundry, where all sorts of machinery are cast, and indeed all kinds of manufactories abound here, and their owners making money. There are six river steamboats now running from this city to various points on the Columbia and Willamette rivers, and two new ones building.—A telegraph line extends from this city to Coorallis, a distance of one hundred and fifty miles, and the intention is to connect it with the Pacific Telegraph Line to California, thereby forming a quick communication between this and San Francisco. I can hardly believe I am writing you from "the continuous woods where rolls the Oregon," "and hears no sound, save his own dashing!" which William Cullen Bryant, in his *Thanatopsis*, writes about —yet so it is—and I feel I am further off than I ever was before, from the dear old City of New York—yet something whispers in my ear that there shall be more "cakes and ale," and a pleasant shaking of hands, ere yet the "silver cord is loosened, or *my* pitcher broken at the fountain!"

LXXIX.

ASTORIA.

ASTORIA lies just within the bar at the mouth of the Columbia river. The location of the city is advantageously made, but hitherto Portland has held pre-eminence as the commercial emporium of Oregon. It has been gradually manifest, however, that the navigation of the Columbia from its mouth to Portland, by vessels of the larger class, would not continue to prove profitable, and the greater advantages for sea-going ships and steamers which Astoria presents, must soon give a considerable impetus to its growth and bring into recognition a new and important commercial port on the Pacific coast of the United States. Already merchandise finds its way to Astoria from Victoria and other points in British Columbia, to be transhipped thence to San Francisco. The navigation of Puget Sound and the Columbia river and its tributaries, is more economically accomplished by a smaller class of vessels than those which are employed between San Francisco and the North Coast. Astoria thus promises to become the chief *entrepôt* for the trade of Oregon and Washington Territory, and may soon prove a formidable rival of Victoria, as the warehousing and distributing point for a large portion of the English colonial settlements in the North. We have yet seen no notice of the dawning future of Astoria. That it is a bright and prosperous career which awaits that hitherto rather overlooked and neglected little city, we do not doubt, and herewith offer our congratulations upon her new birth into commercial consequence as one of the ports of the Pacific.

At this flourishing little town I gave an entertainment, in the course of which I introduced, as one of the "Readings," Bryant's "THANATOPSIS."

I prefaced the reading with the following introductory remarks:

The Poem I am about to read you is looked upon as the masterpiece of the American poet, William Cullen Bryant, and it was in relation to this gem (as I am informed by my friend Mr. Fitz Greene Halleck) that the author of the Pleasures of Hope—the poet Campbell—remarked that had he been its composer, he would have written no more, as he deemed this one piece sufficient to immortalize any one.

I fancy when Mr. Bryant wrote this, nearly forty years ago, he little dreamed that it would ever be recited in so distant a region as Oregon—the name he mentions in the poem—then looked upon as one of the remotest portions of the globe. But now, how great the change!

Civilization, and the indomitable will, energy, and enterprise of the American people, have raised cities, where, but a few years since, naught was heard but the war-whoop of the Indian, and the wilderness has indeed been made to bloom and blossom as the rose.

It was my desire and (if possible) intention to read this poem on the *very spot*, Astoria, where first was heard the echo of the axe of the woodman, breaking the solemn stillness of the hitherto desert wilds and forests of the great Pacific shores—and my wish is now accomplished.

LXXX.

A RUNNING TRIP FROM PORTLAND TO CORVALLES—ITS PERILS.

Monday, August 11.—I left for Oregon City at half-past two, on steamer Jenny Clark. Day very hot—three passengers—boat couldn't get up to city in consequence of "low water." I therefore had to get out and walk about half a mile over some rough stones to reach a flat-boat, in which we were rowed to the town. Oregon City deadly lively—made some calls—next day bought a horse for $200, and started in company with Dr. McI—— for Salem, distant forty miles.

Day lovely, and ride most pleasant—scenery varied—prairie, forest, hill, dale, and valley. Stopped at a farmer's to take a bite and feed horses; farmer and family very primitive and very peculiar. Commenced by eating two apples, then a piece of very greasy pork, some bread—from a very original bakery—dipped in molasses, and some good water—asked for the bill, and found it was "six bits"—cheap and nasty.

Renewed our journey, horse rather rickety—stumbled often and shied—getting very hot and tired—horse shied again—belly-girth broke, bringing me to the ground, with one leg dangling in the stirrup—covered with dust, perspiration, and fright. The mule upon which my melodeon was strapped, ran off—my agony of mind great—assisted on my *rosinante* by Dr. McI——, and I, by the united aid of "main and tail," managed to keep my seat. Donkey out of sight with box of music—rode faster and faster—caught sight of donkey in a turnip field "grazing," with box of music hanging by a cord—strapped it on again, and proceeded on our journey—arrived at SALEM at half-past four. This is the capital of the State, and, like Washington, a city of magnificent distances—succeeded in obtaining a piano, and the Court-House for a concert. Wednesday—concert came off—people pleased—room lighted with six tallow candles—puff of wind came and blew 'em all out—total darkness—eclipsed anything I had ever *seen* before—roars of laughter—I was in the middle of singing "The Light of Other Days"—people took the joke—I didn't think much of it.

Started next day for ALBANY, on my horse—distance twenty-five miles—kept losing my way, and finding it again—scenery superb—begin to feel myself a pretty good horseman.

Arrived at Albany about two o'clock—found a "city" composed of about seventy-five inhabitants—saw two men cross the street—saw an ox-team, a tin shop, a school-house half a mile from any habitation, and a "hotel" with nobody in it—saw in the bar-room an old hat, a bridle, half a newspaper, and a horse collar—knocked, and nobody came—knocked louder, and the result the same. Went in dining-room, nobody there—saw two girls washing dishes in a wretched looking place—asked 'em if I could have my horse taken care of?—she said, "didn't know"—asked if anybody ever lived there, and if this wasn't a hotel?—she said, "guessed it was, but the landlord was sick, and there was nobody in"—asked her if she wasn't "somebody?"—said she "guessed not"—asked if I could have something to eat?—said she'd see. I sat down most despondingly—gal set the table, brought me a plate o' ginger cakes, a bit of rank butter, and a piece of meat on a skewer, that looked like a dried rat and tasted like nothing at all.

Horse stood outside and neighed hard—asked for bill, and found it, as usual, "six bits."

Met a man in a carpenter's shop (one of the leading citizens) who introduced me to a "Doctor," who (another of the first families) told me that he would like me to stop and give a concert, but he did not think he could "scare up" more than fifteen or twenty persons. Thought I wouldn't "scare 'em"—thanked the carpenter and tinman, who seemed to compose the town, for their kindness and attention, and after trying to imagine a glass of root beer was a draught of Burton ale, I left. Passed the jail with one man in it. I was informed that a man was taken up at Corvalles (of which flourishing city more anon) and sent to Albany for trial, I think for stealing a sheep. The authorities managed to get him inside the jail door, when he (the prisoner) immediately let out two or three confined there, knocked down and locked up half a dozen citizens, and "cut."

Corvalles was reached at about five o'clock. Met Dr. McI. and H. G., who are putting up a telegraph to run between this point and Portland. Found the town all life and bustle; lots of good fellows, who welcomed me right heartily.

Town situated on a magnificent plain, flanked by hills and forests and beautiful trees. Healthful breezes from the mountains and the sea prevail all the time.

Hotel life in this country is perfectly awful. It's no use—I can't eat "when the bell rings." They breakfast in the middle of the night, dine when they ought to be breakfasting, and take supper when they should be dining; and the "feed" is most distasteful—all noise, dirt, grease, mess, slop, confusion, and disorder; chunks of meat of all kinds, and no flavor, placed in plates, and "sot" on the table; and before you have had time to look at your meat, a piece of a very flat pie, with a doughy crust, and dried fruit inside, is placed under your nose, or on the same plate with your meat. Men pick their teeth with forks and jack knives, gobble down gallons of water, and "slide." This is the style in all the country hotels in Oregon.

Friday.—Concert at Court House. Mrs. C——, a most delightful woman, very kindly loaned me her piano. Eight men carried it on their shoulders; four keys would not speak, and the pedal was quite out of sorts—managed to get along. House was quite full—so was the moon. Went to the tavern, and tried to sleep; rooms look like bathing establishments; walls of paper muslin and thin plank; hear all sorts of noises and every variety of snore; heard a report in the middle of the night like a subdued gun—smelt powder—a little scared about the Indians; put my head under the red blanket (no sheet). A great big bat flew in at the window, and I bawled out—thought it was a small negro—probably I was dreaming—awoke—found no place to wash, so had to remain dirty; found a teaspoonful of water in a tin cup—dipped my handkerchief in it, and imagined I had taken a bath.

Shook hands with half the town, and left this really

pleasant place, where I was treated with much kindness and attention, in company with Commissary-General C—— and Dr. Harry G——, together with a bottle of rooster-tail to sustain us on our return trip to Oregon city.

Passing through Salem and Albany, and when within three or four miles of Salem, feared my *caballo* was giving out; began to stumble, at last fell down, throwing me into the air several feet high—horse on the top of me; he began to nibble the grass—I to take a "snifter;" doctor made me a *sling*—thought there was no *'arm* in that!!!—rest of the journey I sat very gingerly upon my "hoss."

Arrived at Salem, where I rested at the quiet and hospitable ranch of Mr. C. G., formerly of Washington city. Greatly indebted to him, also to Mr. and Mrs. G——, for the use of their piano, and many others for acts of courtesy.

Left on Sunday morning for Oregon city—day bright and pleasant. Met General McC——, formerly a neighbor of mine in Sacramento—lunched together.

General invited me to his house—charming family—slept and breakfasted there—got on horse—glad (horse was) to get back after having carried me *three hundred miles!*

Left next day for Portland. Saw James O'Niel, Esq.—kind, genial, and delightful—takes me around. Went to Fort Vancouver; stopped at Col. Thompson Morris's quarters—most kindly received by the officers, one and all. Met Capt. Wallen, Capt. Ingalls, Major Alvord, Lieuts. Hodges, Wicker, Withers, and Olven; as also Mrs. Wallen, Mrs. Anger, Mrs. D. Potts, and others. Society here most delightful. Superb band plays on the parade ground night and morning.

Here I also met the Rev. Dr. McCarty, celebrated in the Mexican War as the "fighting priest," and who was at that time chaplain in the army.

On a very rainy day at Buena Vista, he was heard to say, "Gentlemen, *if you must fight,* it will be necessary *to keep your powder dry!*"

Saw a splendid breed of pointers at Capt. Ingalls'. The other day the Captain killed and bagged sixty-five ducks in three hours!

Gave a Concert in Company G.'s quarters. Thank Corporal Fox and Sergeant Fritz for their services.

Went to head-quarters of the Hudson Bay Company. Saw Chief Factor Graham; very civil and courteous in showing me around. Gov. Dougal McTavish not in. Saw immense warerooms, filled with all sorts of merchandise, from a toothpick to a bale of cotton.

Went to the Indian Reservation—saw some splendid "squaws;" went in steamer Senorita to Portland, where I met my old friend Frank Panton, of New York; left again in steamer Columbia for San Francisco. Thus endeth my trip to Oregon.

On the morning of my departure, the *True Californian* contained the annexed graceful farewells:

"DEPARTURE OF STEPHEN C. MASSETT FOR AUSTRALIA.

"We publish below a very graceful poem, by Frank Soule, addressed to the above mentioned gentleman on his contemplated visit to Australia. We have been acquainted with the veritable Jeems Pipes, of Pipesville, for a long time; and since we have known him, we have learned to admire him as one of the most gifted men in California. He is one of that band of pioneers who very early immigrated to this state, and sought to tame its wild spirits by the cultivation of music, wit, and poetry.

"Some of Massett's songs have taken a permanent place in the temple of the Muses, and many of his sketches will last as long as the memory of the early incidents of California life. He who has never listened to the adventures of the Cockney gentleman, who got bitten at Hock Farm by a *dog*, and in San Francisco by a *Bank*, has hitherto lived in vain; and none who ever heard the sweet notes of 'When the Moon on the Lake is beaming,' as they have died upon the lips of beauty, can ever forget them.

"Farewell, inimitable Jeems; and when across the broad Pacific, if the *cacoethes scribendi* should ever seize upon you, remember that the columns of the *True Californian* are always open to the lucubrations of 'Jeems Pipes of Pipesville.'"

LINES TO STEPHEN C. MASSETT.

ON HIS DEPARTURE FOR AUSTRALIA.

You're going far away, Steve,
O'er waters deep and blue,
The winds are strong, the voyage long
That you must buffet through;
But when the clouds are heaviest,
And breezes pipe most shrill,
Remember there are loving hearts
That think upon you still.

There's treasure in that land, Steve,
Beyond the Ocean old;
There may you float, and change each note
Of music into gold.
And warm hearts in that southern clime,
And true hearts will you find,
But none more faithful than a few
Which you will leave behind.

We'll think of other times, Steve,
And pleasures we have seen,
Though wind and wave around us rave,
And oceans spread between.
For though we are antipodes
The earth's full width apart,
There's but one language for the soul,
One climate for the heart.

So whether on the wave, Steve,
Or in the music hall,
My toast shall be success to thee
Where'er thy feet may fall.
Bright nuggets for thy stories, Steve,
And dust and lumps untold,
And every ballad bar you sing
Become a bar of gold.

FRANK SOULE.

San Francisco, Sept. 15, 1856.

LXXXI.

THE OTHER LAND OF GOLD.

ON Monday the 8th of October, 1856, I took passage in the French barque "Fœderis Arca," Captain Cassimir Heauvenu, bound for Melbourne, Victoria.

Now upon the setting out of these, my Australian reminiscences, I wish to correct a little geographical error, that obtains, both in California and in this country, in relation to the localities of the different cities, and the colonies to which they owe their allegiance.

There are four distinct colonies, or states, as we call them, viz. New South Wales, South Australia, Tasmania, or (as it was recently called) Van Diemen's Land, and Victoria. Now, Sidney, the oldest city in Australia, is the capital of New South Wales, Melbourne the capital of Victoria, Hobart Town, the capital of Tasmania, and Adelaide that of South Australia; having enlightened the reader upon this head, I drop until further notice my researches geographical, as my knowledge of that illustrious science is about on a par with my attainments arithmetical.

By this time the reader will have perceived that I have been pretty well used to the sea, and never having been troubled with sea-sickness, looked upon a long voyage with about as much indifference as going up the Hudson river to Albany.

This journey, then, with the exception of *one* other, about which I shall have to say something presently, was one of the most tedious I had yet made.

Of the passengers, there was hardly one with whom I could hold any communion, and the captain, officers, and crew all French, hardly speaking a word of English.

The vessel was small, badly manned, and wretchedly provided. Over the cabin-passengers, of which there were about twenty, composed of mechanics and their wives, and returning emigrants, I cast my eye in vain, after being at sea several days, for a genial mate; the one hundred and fifty in the steerage resembled more the third class passengers of an emigrant ship, and the appearance of things altogether was to me most dispiriting and uncomfortable.

I am not going to bore you, my dear reader, at this time, or any other, with descriptions of a sea voyage, they are generally most monotonous affairs, and particularly uninteresting at the time of their occurrence, or to be afterwards referred to, but an incident of so strange and exciting a nature took place on this trip that I shall not hesitate briefly to endeavor to describe the scene.

LXXXII.

AN EXCITING OCCURRENCE AT SAVAGE ISLAND IN THE SOUTH PACIFIC OCEAN.

WE had been at sea about four weeks, and were enjoying the most delicious tropical weather, such sunsets, such delicious moonlight nights, such steady and invigorating breezes, when all of a sudden, we were becalmed, and almost within hailing distance of an island, known on the French chart as "Danger," on the English as "Savage." In the chart of the French skipper he was warned not to approach too near the island, for the natives were not only most treacherous, but esteemed to be the most savage of all the group of islands that dot the waters of the South Pacific.

At early dawn I noticed our captain apparently in a very nervous state walking the upper deck, looking every now and then very uneasily through his glass, and talking earnestly with the mate.

In the distance land was plainly to be seen, and numbers of black objects moving upon the water. In due time it was discovered that they were canoes filled with natives; nearer, nearer, nearer they approached, when in due time a perfect swarm surrounded our vessel.

When I came on deck I counted one hundred and twenty of them.

Such a sight I never before witnessed. In the first

place the natives were the handsomest specimens of dark humanity I had ever seen. Superb figures, very handsome faces, with glossy black curly hair, entirely naked, save and excepting an apron of seaweed and long grass extending from the waist to the knee.

The first boatload had managed to scramble upon deck, gaining which the foremost seemed instinctively to find out the captain, and instantly prostrating himself upon the deck, kissed both of his feet; the rest, some twenty or more, were busying themselves by jabbering with the passengers, laying hold of their garments, and seeming particularly struck with the bright red of the flannel shirts, and the figured cotton dresses of some of the women. All this time the boats or canoes increasing in fearful numbers were surrounding the ship, and the noise and hubbub of the savages, the cackling of geese, the cackling of cocks and hens, and the squealing of pigs, added greatly to the general excitement.

The captain, with sword in one hand and pistol in another, the mate being similarly armed, by signs and gestures refused to allow any more to come on board, and endeavored—after a great deal of trading had taken place between the natives and the passengers—to clear the ship of the natives. This seemed to be an impossibility. Now, it appears, that among the crew there was a New Zealander, a native of one of the group of islands near Auckland, who had been very busy with one of the cannibals—there being quite a similarity in their dialects, and we thereby were enabled to obtain some information relative to the intentions of our formidable visitors—now every moment increasing in number by the hundreds, nay, thousands!

A dead calm prevailed. Apart from the evident and increasing anxiety of the captain, some most laughable and amusing scenes were occurring upon deck—a native with a squeaking young porker in one hand, and a string of cackling geese in the other, would lay hold of, and even pull up, the dress of one of the affrighted steerage passengers, and shaking the young swine in her face, intimate by his gestures that an exchange would be accepted; remnants of carpeting, old petticoats, and flannels, were eagerly bartered away for all descriptions of live stock and "yams," and everything so far had gone on peaceably enough.

But a storm was brewing.

I had managed to make out—though somewhat unintelligibly—that but *one* vessel had ever before been so near this island, that but *one* white person resided, and that he was a Catholic priest, that the natives were extremely averse to the whites, and were excessively treacherous.

We had been at sea some forty days, and the tediousness of the voyage was great, and consequently the chance of a run on shore, and a sniff of the land, was most enticing. The beautiful island with its countless cocoanut and banyan trees looked most inviting, and the aroma from the spicy groves and wild foliage of the trees was quite too much for my olfactories, and wooed me by its grateful incense to pay a visit to the solitary and priestly occupant, and my respects to the inhabitants generally.

Obtaining the captain's consent, he first charging me to return as speedily as possible, I left the vessel with the second mate, three of the crew, and the New Zealander.

I had provided myself with a very rusty formidable looking (unloaded, of course) French horse pistol, and an old cutlass, had rolled up a bundle of old clothes, flannels, &c., and strange to say, I had with me—thinking it might be agreeable to the isolated stranger—a file of "New York Heralds," and of the "Spirit of the Times."

Half an hour's pulling brought us to the beach, and the sight, upon gaining terra firma, I shall never forget. The shore for miles seemed literally covered with human beings; huts in countless numbers, and of all sizes and shapes, poured forth their teeming inmates, and in the midst of this dense throng, stood forth, in the habiliments of the Holy Church, the commanding figure and pleasant face of "Father Glencairn"—for that was the missionary's name. For over seventeen years had he been a resident of this island, and from the time of his arrival to the day of the landing of our boat's crew he had not set his eye upon a white man. The reader can imagine the interesting nature of our interview.

All this time the natives appeared perfectly quiet and docile, and I was not only struck with the handsome appearance and superb figures of the men, but perfectly captivated with the almost ravishing beauty of the women, of a dark brown complexion, with long waving and raven black hair falling to the waist in profusion, over superbly rounded and voluptuously shaped shoulders, the waist girdled most tastefully with a sort of trellis-work of green leaves, which interwoven with some aromatic herbs, sent forth the most delicate and grateful odors, while the perfect symmetry of the limbs, the smallness and beauty of the feet, completed not only a model of a figure, but such a one as I had never before in all my wanderings gazed upon.

The island was most romantically situated, and seemingly completely covered with cocoanut and orange trees, while each of the curiously constructed huts or "grass houses" was covered with grape vines, loaded with bunches of this luscious fruit.

A nod from Father Glencairn, and we proceeded with one of the chiefs to his abode, and "chapel."

It was a building, if it can be dignified by that name, of "adobe," a sort of baked mud, and the largest on the island. Inside was an altarpiece very neatly arranged, resting upon which was a large wooden crucifix. Some wild flowers and a few ornaments completed the furniture of the apartment.

Myself and the priest were chatting very pleasantly, he having greatly interested me by the recital of many startling and curious facts connected with his seventeen years' exile, when he remarked to me that the handsome "chief" had suddenly disappeared, adding, that he didn't like the looks of it; that though apparently he seemed safe enough, and well liked by them, they were treacherous to a degree, hating the whites, and as savage as demons!

Upon my noticing the shouting, hooting, and hallooing of the natives outside, and at the same time the agitated countenance of Father Glencairn, I confess I felt a little "shakey," and regretted ever leaving our poor ship!

At the same time I felt I had exceeded, by several hours, the time the captain had told me to be absent; that I was at least a couple of miles from the shore; and that if a breeze sprang up—such was the fright of the captain of being seized by the savages—that he was certain to put to sea.

I watched with the most painful anxiety the countenance of the priest. We were not long in doubt as to their intentions. Beseeching me to remain perfectly quiet, and not to exhibit the slightest trepidation, he told me to hold my old horse-pistol in my hand (I had informed him that it was unloaded), and to stand by the altar while we would "face the music."

With a yell, that seems to be still ringing in my ears, they rushed in, but at the lifted hand, and calm and dignified demeanor of the priest, they stood seemingly abashed; in that terrible interval I seemed to have passed a whole lifetime. Escape seemed impossible, resistance useless, and I felt almost certain that the ship had departed.

The sight of those magnificent-looking savages, with their handsome faces and superbly proportioned limbs, almost bursting with frenzied excitement, and carrying in their hands their wonderfully carved instruments of warfare, can never be erased from my memory.

There they stood, while the priest briefly translated to me their intentions, still charging me to remain where I was, and to try and appear perfectly indifferent.

He also informed me that they told him the ship had been taken by them, and that it was useless for me to think of leaving; he adding, to comfort me, that he didn't believe it.

Six of the chiefs approached nearer to me, each having in his hand a lance of polished cedar-wood, when suddenly the priest rushed in front of them to the altar, and seizing the crucifix, reverently lifted it on high, and falling on his knees, directed me to follow his example.

At this exciting moment—so seemingly were they under subjection—their faces not only assumed their natural expression, but with bowed heads they slowly one by one left the apartment; and of the hundreds of uproarious voices that a few moments before were shouting for the sacrifice, none were raised above a whisper.

I certainly breathed freer, but the danger, my kind friend said, was not yet over. We must hasten to the beach, for it was near sunset; we had some distance to go. I had not seen or heard of our boat's crew for hours; and though for the moment the natives seemed pacified, they were not to be trusted, and there was no time for trifling.

Upon coming in sight of the ocean, and seeing the ship lying quietly where in the morning I had left her, I will not attempt to describe my sensations of joy. Our boat and the crew were all safe at the landing; a very light breeze had just sprung up, and the yo-hoing of the seamen, so grateful to our ears, warned us quickly to be on board.

I hesitated when the moment came for me to bid adieu to my kind friend and preserver; and as he pressed his hand in mine, and gave me the parting benediction of his holy church, and I felt that in this round world of ours we should not meet again, I found it difficult to repress my emotion.

I could not resist the temptation, at parting with him, of repeating to him a verse from Robert Burns, that struck me as strangely appropriate; and though the poet inscribed his verses to one whose head was circled in the jewelled coronet of an earldom, it seemed to me that a halo of a richer and more heavenly lustre rested on the head of the reverend father I was leaving now for ever:—

"The bridegroom may forget the bride
Was made his wedded wife yestreen;
The monarch may forget the crown,
That on his head an hour has been;
The mother may forget the child
That smiles so sweetly on her knee,
But I'll remember thee, *Glencairn*,
And all that thou hast done for me!"

LXXXIII.

MELBOURNE.

WEDNESDAY, Dec. 10, at half-past two, sighted the Melbourne Heads. At three took pilot on board—blowing a perfect gale of wind; anchored in Hobson's Bay about six, and shortly afterwards landed at Williamstown, distant from the city of Melbourne about eight miles.

One hour more, and I, by the aid of a carefully constructed rail car, had reached the town, and was comfortably quartered in a very cozy room at the Prince of Wales Hotel.

Melbourne is decidedly a handsome city.

I was struck with the beauty and the solidity of the buildings, the wide, well laid out, and carefully paved streets, and the life, bustle, and activity of everything and everybody.

Melbourne, the capital of Victoria, stands on what they call the "Yarra Yarra," and is distant from Sydney about six hundred miles. The city is built on rising ground, in a fertile and beautiful valley, extending for some miles along the banks of the river—the latter yielding a goodly supply of fresh water to the inhabitants.

The population, I was informed, was 100,000.

There are some very elegant public buildings, very creditable to the community which has sprung up with such startling rapidity.

One of the most notable structures is the Queen's Bridge, spanning the before mentioned Yarra Yarra river, by a single arch of over 150 feet.

This beautiful structure cost over $75,000.

St. Peter's and St. James's are the most costly and conspicuous of the churches; and the Roman Catholics have a very superb cathedral called St. Francis Xavier.

Independents, Baptists, Wesleyans, Presbyterians, Jews, and Quakers, have their respective places of worship.

There are three or four theatres, the Theatre Royal being the largest.

The city is built of brick and stone. The handsome granite fronts of many of the houses would be considered an ornament in London or Paris. The appearance of the city from the river is most striking; the extreme ends rise over two picturesque eminences, on the verge of a beautiful park. The general air of the place (with the single exception of Sydney) is more thoroughly English than any other town I have visited in Australia; and the superbly laid out grounds and beautiful scenery in the suburbs have all the quiet, subdued interest of an old English domain.

The three leading journals here are the "Argus," "Herald," and "Age." A "Punch" also flourishes, very cleverly edited. Of the weeklies, at the time of my visit, the "Note Book" was the most important.

The government of Melbourne is vested in a mayor, four aldermen, and twelve (so-called) town councillors.

The city is also the seat of a bishopric.

I had brought with me from California letters from my old associates of the press in San Francisco to the Melbourne editors, and it gives me much pleasure, at this great distance, to record the kind and genial manner with which I was received; and also, if not too late, to thank them and the public generally throughout the Colonies for their generous reception of me.

The Melbourne "Argus" bears the same resemblance in that community to the "Times" in London; and it seems to be a pretty well understood fact, that by its censure or praise the fate of a public performer is sealed.

The reader will presently better appreciate this remark.

Among those who greeted me on my arrival, were two Californians, Frank B——, of San Francisco, and my old banking friend Merrill, of "Hensley & Merrill" memory, Sacramento.

We were joined by George Loder (who was, at this time, conductor of Madame Anna Bishop's concerts), and had a "good time" generally.

I found, however, that "Melbourne" was no place in which to be idle. Expenses were frightful, and, as I was not *altogether* on a tour of pleasure, I proceeded as quickly as possible to business.

When my friend Bennett (who was most serviceable to me in arranging the plans of my "first appearance") saw the "programme" I had selected, and that some reminiscences of "California life" were to be given, he desired me to send him *twelve guineas' worth* of tickets! This, I thought, was as good a start as it was generous.

The "posters" were upon the walls, the shops and houses were strewed with programmes—the papers properly attended to—the "Hall" taken—the "Erard" (such a beauty) selected—the ticket "taker" and "seller" secured—the "free list" duly cared for—and the fatal moment of my "first appearance" before a colonial auditory had arrived.

Accordingly, on Monday evening, December 22, 1856, the brightly lighted hall of the "Mechanics' Institute" was filled to overflowing with (of course) a fashionable, and (to me) new and strange audience, although it *slightly* rained.

I believe it is proverbial that the Americans are infinitely more cordial and generous in their welcome to a stranger, I mean, of course, a public performer, on his "first appearance," than my countrymen are; but, on the other hand, the English are less fickle and more lasting in their attachment, providing, of course, a favorable impression is made.

As a gentleman said to me in London: "Once make a 'hit' here, and your fortune is made." But the great difficulty is to make the "hit," for out of the hosts of entertainers that, for the last ten years, have sought to win the good favor of John Bull, how few are they who have been pecuniarily successful. In single-handed, or Monologue Entertainments, I suppose the late Mr. Albert Smith and Mr. Henry Russell take the foremost rank.

But to return to the "Mechanics' Institute."

The audience greeted me kindly, though cautiously—laughing at the funny parts, and crying at the serious. But it was not until, for the first time, I had given my version of "The Charge of the Light Brigade" that I felt I had made a hit. The audience rose and cheered, the women waved their handkerchiefs, and I retired behind the little red screen, exhausted, excited, and thankful.

Thus endeth my first night in Australia.

The next day *all* the papers came out in the most laudatory manner. The much dreaded "Argus" spoke as follows:

Mr. Stephen Massett gave an entertainment last night at the Mechanics' Institute, and the attendance was more numerous, and comprised a larger number of the *élite* of Melbourne society than we have seen assembled within those walls upon any similar occasion for some time past. A more clever, versatile, and amusing mimic, vocalist, and elocutionist has not yet visited these colonies. Mr. Massett sings and reads with equal taste and feeling; his comic readings are really comic; and he can be pathetic without verging upon the limits of bathos. He succeeded in exciting and retaining the attention of the audience for two hours, and the manifestations were frequent and hearty. His comic readings from "The Lady of Lyons," his description of a novice's first appearance upon the stage in the character of *Young Norval*, were the most successful of the humorous portions of the entertainment; and Tennyson's "Charge of the Light Brigade," and the well-known ballad, "The Lament of the Irish Emigrant," obtained the greater share of the commendation bestowed upon the professedly serious items of the programme. Altogether the entertainment was as agreeable as it was unexceptionable, and can scarcely fail to become very popular in the provinces.

In reference to the "Charge of the Brigade," which, I think, I was the first in 1855 to recite in public, and which is now so frequently introduced by various self-styled "professors" of elocution, the "Herald" said: "His recitation of Tennyson's 'Charge of the Light Brigade' threw the audience into a state of enthusiasm."

The "Note Book" said: "The moving elegy that Tennyson has written upon the brave men who fell in the 'Charge of the Light Brigade' at Balaklava, he chants, rather than reads, with an enthusiasm, a fire, a fervor, I might say, a frenzy, almost beyond mere histrionic display."

The "Age" remarked: "The recitation of the 'Charge' was a 'gem' in its way. He has a distinct and correct pronunciation, a judicious regard to what we may call coloring, and appropriate action."

My modesty prevents my making any more extracts—at any rate, at present—and I accordingly proceed with my adventures in and out of the "diggings."

LXXXIV.

A CHRISTMAS DINNER AT THE FRENCH CONSUL'S.

I HAD brought from M. Dillon, the French consul at San Francisco, a very pleasant letter to same functionary at Melbourne—the "Count Lionel de Moreton Chabrillan," whom I found a most delightful, courteous, and hospitable gentleman.

I was immediately invited to his house at "St. Kilda," distant some two miles from Melbourne—and received a special invitation to dine with him on Christmas Day!

It may be news to some of my readers in these Northern latitudes to know, that in the Antipodes, this celebrated day occurs in the *height of summer!*—and therefore, they will not be surprised to hear that I left my hotel in full summer regalia, on a perfect June morning, the thick foliage of the green trees, the bright sun, and the wild flowers out in all their glory, being my companions—the only drawback in my pleasant journey being the intolerable dust of the road.

Arrived at the "Chateau" of the Count, I was very cordially received. The company seated in bamboo chairs under the veranda, overlooking the beautiful gardens of the host.

In compliment to two or three Englishmen who were present, a splendid sirloin of roast-beef, with pudding to match—Yorkshire and plum—graced the banquet, and when, prior to being seated, the butler handed to each of the gentlemen a nice cool jaunty-looking white jacket—considering it was Christmas Day, I fancied the contrast somewhat singular to the 25th of December of former years.

"Punkas" were going overhead—the waiters stood behind the chairs, keeping the flies off, with fans in hand; the open windows let in the little air that was stirring, laden with the odors of the summer flowers, and luscious fruit trees! Altogether, this was the most remarkable "Christmas" I had yet passed.

. . . . . .

The walls of the city were covered with large posters of various performers.

I found that Mrs. C. N. Sinclair and Mr. Henry Sedley were playing a successful engagement—that Madam Anna Bishop was the bright particular star in the musical firmament—that Mr. McKean Buchanan was still the great American tragedian, and that the Miss Gougenheims were the "most fascinating actresses" of the day.

I shall now jot down from my diary, brief memoranda of which I have before me—such items as may interest the reader during my six months' rambling through the colonies.

January 29.—My second concert, poured with rain all day—£30 in the house—expenses £25—cleared £5—saw on the bills at the Theatre Royal, they play to-night, "All that Glitters isn't Gold."

Thought of the appositeness of the allusion to my own case.

Large fire in Great Bourke street—crowd collected on the following day looking with intense astonishment at what was called a "Salamander Safe," which came out of the furnace unscathed.

A tall raw-boned Yankee was not only "hollering" out the following extraordinary yarn in relation to his "Salamander Safes," of which he was the agent—but had a lot of slips printed, and having it now before me, present it to the reader.

"SALAMANDER SAFES!"

I sold a safe to a big firm in "Saint Louis,"—the house was burnt down with the safe in it—said safe was embedded in the ruins of the fire seven mortal days, exposed to the most intensest heat that was ever felt—a feller from New York wrote out to inquire how it performed, on being removed from the ruins—and the man replied by mail on the following day, that the evening previously to the fire, the head book-keeper had been to the market to purchase a Shanghai·cock, and had put it in the safe for safe keeping—intending fully to take it out the next day—on removing it from the fire seven days after he found the COCK FROZEN TO DEATH!

The agent managed to sell every safe he had in the colonies.

LXXXV.

RAMBLES THROUGH THE COLCNIES.

WENT to a "levee" at Government House with the Count Chabrillan, Sir Henry Barclay, and Lady Barclay, officiating—some of the scenes very funny—in the scrambling, jolting, and pushing, the *ex-asperate-ion*, and the dropping of the "H's" were quite prominent, such as, make room 'ere, make room, you're smashing my 'at, get horf my toes, will yer? I carn't get hin, which is the way? Hin 'ere, his that Sir Enry? and the likes.

January 7.—Start for Geelong, called, I believe, the "second town" in the colony, about forty-five miles from Melbourne—it seemed a place of considerable trade, a large portion of the wool of the colony is from this point shipped.

The hot winds that obtain here, are most disagreeable; I was treated to several "puffs" upon my arrival, as I was wending my way to the newspaper offices; the dust and heat intolerable.

Met Mr. Henry Coleman, who was giving his clever entertainment at the theatre called "Masks and Faces"—engaged the "Town-hall" for Monday night, paid therefor £10.

The night having duly arrived, the rain as usual came

down in torrents, the entertainment went off well, excepting the unpleasant reverberation of sound owing to the faulty architecture of the hall, and the "sparseness" of the audience—the "Advertiser" on the following day came out in a very complimentary article, stating that the audience was very select (very) including "his worship" the Mayor, many of the merchants, bankers, and professional men of the town.

The effect was very funny, in my recitation of the "Song of a Shirt."

It was something like this:

With fingers weary and worn—(echo) . . . . worn.
With eyelids heavy and red . . . . . red.
A woman sat in unwomanly rags . . . . gags.
Plying her needle and thread . . . . . dead.
Stitch, stitch, stitch . . . . ditch.
In poverty, hunger, and dirt . . . . . hurt.
And still with a voice of dolorous pitch . . stitch.
She sang the Song of a Shirt . . . . . dirt!

And so on.

As I am going occasionally to initiate my readers into some of the mysteries of my individual professional doings, not only for their amusement and information, but for my own gratification, I shall commence by stating that my expenses here were about £20, and my receipts exactly £11.

The reader will therefore perceive that I was about £9 out of pocket—so I thought I'd *ge-long* somewhere else!—Accordingly, the next day I started for Ballarat, which is, I believe, the largest mining locality in the colonies.

I left Geelong by the morning coach at five o'clock, reaching Ballarat about four in the afternoon.

The style of vehicle in which I took my seat, and which is, with one exception, invariably used to convey passengers by land in Australia, is what they call the "American Concord Coach."

This line was established by Mr. Cobb of Boston, in 1853, is now owned by Americans, and the ribbons are always in the hands of Yankee drivers. The roads were execrable, in winter almost impassable owing to the heavy rains; and intolerable in the summer from the frightful amount of heat, dust, and hot winds, the latter peculiarly indigenous to this country.

Jolted to pieces, fagged out, dusty and dirty, I arrived at my destination.

My countenance was just the reverse of that of this pleasant-looking gentleman, who was described on p. 272, but who is put in here by way of contrast to the picture the reader may have formed of me.

The town appeared to me to be composed of one street, about three miles in length, flanked on either side and as far as the eye could reach by an immense extent of country covered with innumerable tents, their white tops glittering in the sun-light, presenting a vast panorama, looking more like a large battle-field than a mining region—for to give the reader an idea of the magnitude of the diggings here, I will first mention that the population in and about Ballarat is estimated at over 100,000 souls!

The ground over which our Jehu was galloping, at the rate of twelve miles an hour, seemed composed of a white chalky substance, some two or three inches thick, the team and wind together raising such a dust, as would every now and then envelop us in a thick fog.

On either side of the street were one story frame-houses,

tents, etc., while further in the town were several large shops, and a few buildings of brick and stone.

They publish here three daily newspapers; hotels (such as they are) are very abundant. They have, I believe, one church and three theatres, rejoicing in the names of the Montezuma, Charley Napier, and Victoria.

Large transparencies were suspended from the front windows of each: One announcing that the "Great American Tragedian, Mr. McKean Buchanan, would that night appear in his celebrated character of Hamlet;" the other, that the world-renowned Pablo Fauque would perform his daring feats upon the tight-rope; and the other, that the most perfect and faultless representation of the play of the Lady of Lyons would that night be given. The Claude by a pupil of Mr. Charles Kean, and the Pauline by a relation of Mrs. Siddons.

I could not resist the temptation of visiting the last-mentioned place, and upon the application of any of my readers to me personally will give them an imitation, finding it impossible to do so on paper!

On the next day I was engaged by a man to go to a little place called Creswick Creek, he offering me £10 and my expenses.

I acquiesced; and, after he had paid me the money, got the bills and posters out, it immediately commenced to rain.

Arrived at Creswick Creek—went to the hotel, made of canvas, with a theatre complete inside of it.

I forgot to inform the reader that my melodeon accompanied me to Australia, thinking not only that it would be convenient in the "diggings," where pianos were difficult to get, but that I might *sell it* at an advance.

The "box of music" I carried to Creswick.

The house was about half full—the rain and cold intense —the roof leaking in all directions, and the gloom and desolation, not only of the surroundings, but depicted on the countenances of my auditory, were something fearful to contemplate; and when in answer to a very civilly put question to my landlord (who had engaged me as a great card) as to whether it was best to begin, he replied, in a very unpleasant manner, "Ow the L should I know," it was not calculated to put me into a very good humor.

From my bed-room to the theatre it was a pool of water, and I had to roll up my trowsers to prevent them getting wet.

The melodeon was placed in the centre of the stage, which was quite damp and unpleasant.

I had got as far as the reading of the "Song of the Shirt," about the third thing on the bill, when I found three of my audience asleep and half of them with umbrellas up. About this time I felt, as I stood there reading and trying to keep my face straight, the rain coming down drop, drop, drop, on the end of my nose. I moved further up the stage; still I felt it on the top of my head. I then, apologizing to my audience, asked their kind permission to get under cover, and finished the reading holding in one hand a large Chinese umbrella!

I was not invited to repeat the performance at Creswick Creek.

Returning to Ballarat, put up at Golden Fleece hotel; the weather intensely cold, though in the middle of summer.

On 23d of January, start for Maryboro, a mining town of considerable importance.

Maryboro a city of "tents"—heat intense (no joke meant)—dust and fleas perfectly fearful.

Put up at the Golden Hotel.

The theatre, as usual, in the big room of the hotel—cotton walls—hard benches—stifling heat, and delighted audiences.

Paid £2 for 100 small posters. Receipts about £10; expenses £20; *profits* in proportion.

January 28, at Dunolly, another "mining" locality; stopped at the GOLDEN AGE HOTEL, inside of which was the *Royal Victoria Theatre.*

The poster which announced to the distinguished citizens that a "Grand Ballad Concert and Readings" was to be given at the above establishment, looked more like a Day & Martin's blacking placard than anything else, and my audience resembled more a gathering of persons to witness an execution, than one to be delighted by any elocutionary or vocal effort.

The night before the concert, a funny incident occurred to me at the hotel, which I shall try briefly to describe.

But first it will be necessary, for the reader more fully to appreciate the joke, to be informed that, for the last eighteen years of my life, bathing in cold water has been with me a daily habit. Now when I say "bathing," I mean that my body, from head to foot, is immersed in cold water; and it is as much a necessity with me as eating and drinking.

I intend prefacing this little anecdote with a few words upon the subject of bathing.

From a young medical friend of mine, I have ascertained the fact that the pores of the skin, by which the perspiration escapes, or ought to escape, are so numerous that a grain of sand, placed on any part of the skin, covers upwards of *one hundred thousand of these fine apertures.* The effect on the system when these are clogged up by neglect of ablution, may easily be imagined.

The devotion of a few minutes only to either immersing the body in cold water, or resorting to the more easy application of the sponge, is well repaid by the healthy glow and general lightness of the system throughout the ensuing day; and when it is added, that no medicine hitherto discovered confers good health and long life with so much certainty as uniform *bathing* and regular exercise, surely, those who do not comply with these easy conditions have no right to complain of being deprived of such inestimable blessings.

Those who cannot procure the luxury of a regular bath, may, at all events, procure a large earthenware-pan, which will prove always serviceable as a foot bath. This should be filled with fresh water every morning, and after rising the bather should saturate a towel in the cold fluid, place it round the head, so as to prevent any reaction upwards, and stand, if the ablutor cannot sit, in the pan itself. With a sponge the bather may now, after removing the wet towel, enjoy a "shower-bath" in miniature, alternately soaking the sponge and squeezing it above the head for several minutes.

The body may be afterwards sponged all over, and then rubbed entirely dry with coarse towelling.

Horsehair gloves and belts, to promote activity by

rapid friction, may be used with considerable advantage, and the bather should then dress as speedily as possible.

This plan should be pursued *summer and winter*—every morning—through *every change of the* seasons—and whatever may be the temperature, the bather may almost defy "colds," "sorethroats," and "influenza," throughout the year.

So much for "bathing," now for my anecdote.

I had managed—by dint of giving half-a-crown to "Biddy" the chambermaid—to secure a bucket of water for my morning's sousing, and had retired for the night closing the door of my primitive apartment with a latch made of leather, and watching with great attention the doings of a couple of rats, one of which was nibbling at some grass that was growing underneath my wooden cot, and the other in the act of carrying off one of my socks. A tap came to the door, and "Biddy" appeared with a big iron pot full of water, stating that there were no pails, buckets, or tubs in the house, and that this was the only "thing" she could lay her hands on.

In the morning I was awakened at an early hour by a loud knocking at the door, and by any number of voices, singing out for "Biddy," "Biddy."

I listened, and heard a man's voice call out "the Iron pot's gone," "Biddy, some one's stole the potato pot."

"Lor 'a mercy," cried Biddy, "I gave it the gentleman in No. 18 to wash in"—and with that piece of information, I jumped out of bed and ducked my head in the pot, and sponging myself to my heart's content, regardless of the streams of water that completely covered the floor, and the screams of an old covey in the room underneath me, upon whose bald head the water was rushing with "Niagara" swiftness

Knock—knock—knock at the door. "If you please, sir, Biddy has given you the pot in mistake, and we've got nothing to boil the potatoes in, sir, for breakfast!"

But the row in the old gentleman's room beggars description.

Now the reader must understand, that the floor was only an inch thick, and full of gaping seams and holes, and my temporary bathing-potato-pot-tub must have been immediately over his head—for with my plunge he sprang up, hollering at the top of his voice,

"Murder, thieves, fire, water, police!" while the pool I made by my sudden dive, not only wet everything in the room, but nearly drowned the old gentleman.

The man came in and got his potato pot—the old gentleman dried himself—all the boarders enjoyed the joke, if they didn't the potatoes, and I the *pot-pour-i*, although the old cock it is supposed put a toe down against such practices.

At Dunolly, I met some very jolly and gentlemanly fellows; among those who were particularly civil, hospitable, and attentive, were Captain Virginius Murray, Mr. Farquhar, and Dr. Cordellis, whom I met at the house of Mr. John Kerr, whither I had taken shelter, during a tremendous hail and rain storm—the hail bigger than a pigeon's egg, and I having to find my way home to the "Golden Age Hotel" by the aid of a lantern.

Fortunately I did not then wear the large hat which, according to the old lady on page 185, is distinctive of Americans, or I should have been either unroofed or carried away.

LXXXVI.

HOW I GOT TO MY HOTEL.

Now I had in California seen some pretty bad and impassable roads—and streets—streets knee deep in mud, slush, and filth, but the midnight walk, aided very feebly by a shocking bad and rickety lantern, from the headquarters of Captain Virginius Murray to the palatial residence of the subscriber, baffles description.

There were (of course) no lamp-posts, no sidewalks, no roads, no lights, (excepting now and then the indistinct flickering of a farthing rushlight from the tent of an "honest miner")—no anything—all gloom, darkness, rain, and mud.

I was told to "keep to the right," "go straight ahead," and I should soon find the Hotel—and how soon I found the Hotel, the reader shall presently be informed.

I think I had proceeded about a hundred yards from the "Headquarters" of Captain V. M——, the wind and rain beating in my face, and making several ineffectual attempts to "put out the light" by rattling up against the horned window of my little lantern; my legs encased in a pair of "top boots" that reached to my middle, and would have been considered by Mr. "Vanderdecker" in the "Flying Dutchman," a first rate "property"—had become already quite used to disappearing every now and then in a large mud-hole, and I with the greatest difficulty had managed to grope my way thus far, by the aid of my dim candle, that kept giving unmistakable signs of sputtering out, like the speech of a drunken politician, and ending in total darkness, which such oratory usually produces; when suddenly I had a sensation such as I presume would be produced by the combined action of an earthquake and a volcanic eruption, and when my senses gained something like their natural condition, I found myself reduced to a somewhat globular form; having totally disappeared from the surface of this earth, my faithless light being extinguished in my lantern, as effectually as I was extinguished from society, and the view (not very distinct either) of the surrounding country generally.

After picking myself up, shaking myself, and wiping the mud from my eyes, and looking in vain for help or succor, I think I stood still for several minutes, to "take stock." To return was impossible—to proceed was about as bad, and to remain motionless was very uncomfortable.

We have all *read* of "total darkness," but I think it was never before by me, at least, so fully appreciated; but on I went—whither I knew not—and feeling at every step, the moral certainty of my again disappearing entirely from the naked eye at any moment—nor did I long remain in doubt —for first slightly relieving the monotony of my former *gymnastycal* feat, by bumping up against the stump of a big tree, the concussion being so great, I was pitched "neck and crop" into a pool of water, my favorite element, and presenting by this time an hydraulic phenomenon rarely witnessed in that or any other country.

How I got out I know not—where I was I could not then, nor have I ever since ascertained—and my arriving at my Hotel has always remained a mystery to me.

It, however, taught me a lesson—and that was—never again to trust myself out after dark in an "undiscovered country" visiting the "headquarters" of anybody, at the risk of not only deluging my "hind-quarters," but of subjecting me to a practical illustration of the poet's simile, about the traveller never returning from *that bourne!*

LXXXVII.

ON THE WING.

My visit to the diggings, and indeed through the colonies generally, was of such an ephemeral and will-o'-the-wisp character as to preclude the possibility, even if I had the intention, of entering more into detail than I have done, in reference to localities or individual occurrences. I shall endeavor to jot down, as they flash upon my memory, a few of the most prominent incidents of adventure, and some exciting scenes, slightly assisted by very meagre and desultory notes and memoranda, which, with the reader's permission, I will transcribe from a book of items made at the time.

January 28.—Last Concert at Dunolly—pouring rain—crowded house—heat fearful—gentlemen of the camp wished a repetition—the "Charge of the Brigade" created the greatest excitement. Paid £2 for the use of a piano with only two legs, no pedal, and missing keys. Rain again coming on the audience and the performer.

February 2.—Went in a dog cart (so called) to Bendigo, a celebrated mining locality. Put up at the Shamrock Hotel. The city (?) reminding me greatly of similar localities in California, with this exception—that throughout Australia I have noticed a much greater regard evinced for durability in the erection and structure of their public and private buildings; their motto evidently being, "Not for a day, but for all time."

Public entertainments here were in a very rude condition about this time; the principal and decidedly most popular being the *Drinking and Concert Saloons.*

I shall endeavor to give a brief description of what I saw at one of them.

LXXXVIII.

CONCERT SALOONS.

THE Concert Hall of the Shamrock Hotel, then, was about 75 feet long by 50 wide. At the end was a stage, or raised platform, for the performer, upon which was one of Erard's grand pianos; the floor was covered with wooden benches, with troughs in front, upon which to place the pot of ale or "harf and harf" of the occupier of the seat.

There was no pay exacted for entrance; the proprietor depending for his profits upon the amount of liquor and cigars consumed by the audience.

The receipts were immense, as were also the salaries paid

to the performers. For instance, the conductor, Mr. Lavenu, one of the most talented composers of the day, received £30, or $150 a week, while the leading lady vocalist got £50.

The scene, when the hall was full, was intensely amusing and disgusting. The jingling of glasses and clattering of pots, the dense clouds of smoke from the fumes of tobacco and cigars, and *not* of the choicest brands at that, mixed with some of the richest colonial Billingsgate that ever came from the mouth of a costermonger, rendered this resort particularly attractive to the refined, the philosophical, or intellectual listener.

But with the exception of the Theatre, open only now and then, there was no other place of amusement, no other method of passing away an evening.

The receipts were frequently £200 and £300 a night; and the consequence was, the proprietors (two Irishmen) were making, when I left, a rapid fortune.

LXXXIX.

MY CONCERT IN BENDIGO.

THE Criterion was the name of the theatre at which I "opened" at the above place, and for which they charged me £20 rent per night—*rayther* steep, I thought, for a *quiet individual's* performance.

The town was billed and programmed to any extent, and posters, black and blue and (supposed to be) re(a)d all over, covered the walls of the city and adjacent townships.

The heat was very great, almost suffocating; and the clouds threatened rain; added to which, it was the night of the first appearance of a celebrity in the female singing line at one of the saloons; and I did not feel particularly brilliant about the result of my "show."

The theatre had been originally built, at a cost of $30,000, by an American, named Mr. Henry Clarkson, of whom I have to speak hereafter, and had been opened by Madame Lola Montez, and where she played a series of brilliant engagements; but the building was out of the way, and had proved, both to owner and stockholders, a sorry speculation.

The scenery and stage appointments were fast running to decay, as were also numbers of rats, who swarmed the building upon my entrance, early in the evening, to see if the room scene was set, the piano there, and the reading desk in its proper place.

The scene-shifter and the carpenter had been taking their evening meal on the stage aforesaid, and the remains, consisting of some choice scraps of red herring and bread and cheese, were being devoured by some of the largest black rats I had ever seen.

Upon my approach they skedaddled, and I took my coat off, then a seat, to try and get cool; for the perspiration was pouring from me in streams, and I was wondering how I should possibly get through the fatigues of the evening.

A wonderful place for reflection is the inside of a theatre in the daytime; and for a few moments I gave the rein to my fancy, and "let fall the windows of my eyes" in sleep.

It is all very fine to talk about the "annihilation of space," as seen in the operations of the telegraph or the locomotive; but they shrink into insignificance, when compared with the speed of a run in Dreamland!

Whew! In less than five minutes I was sitting in the Old Park Pit of New York, listening to the strains of the opera of the Bohemian Girl,—while the poet Milton (such funny things occur in dreams) was to play Tom Tug in the Waterman.

Milton had just been encored in the "Bay of Biscay," when I was immediately transferred to a private box at Drury Lane, where Ned Davenport was playing William in Black Eyed Susan to T. P. Cooke's Hamlet.

I was just about going behind the scenes, to shake my friend Ned by the hands, and to inquire the cause of the strange amalgamation, at the same time congratulating him upon his success in introducing, for the first time, a sailor's hornpipe in the graveyard and the ghost scene—when—oh horror! I saw, underlined on the big poster, in front of Drury Lane, that I was announced to play Richard the Third to Charlotte Cushman's Mrs. Haller, at the Honolulu Theatre, Sandwich Islands, on the following night.

I had just packed up my trunk, and arrived at a hotel, situated on the back of a large whale, in the middle of the Pacific Ocean, when I was informed by the stage manager, Captain Cook, that the Rev. Mr. Spurgeon would preach in Park Lane Chapel every Sunday, until further notice, morning and evening; and that if I would adjourn to his house he would regale me with a nice slice from the cold shoulder of a departed missionary!

I was wondering whether the delicate morsel was roasted or boiled, when I was aroused from my reverie by a shaking of the arm, and seeming to fall from the top of a six-story house to the street, without hurting myself—a feat never failing to be accomplished with great success in sleep—I found myself, with the house half-filled with people, sitting in the middle of the stage, and expected to commence my performance.

There was no "backing out" now; and making my way off as quickly as possible, I inquired the reason of the man's not waking me before.

Seeing the fellow turn his back upon me, and walk away, I questioned him again, and angrily asked him why he had not fixed the stage earlier? he made no reply; but another man began talking with his fingers, and motioning me to come along with him. I now began to think that my assistants were either drunk or mad; and in my despair—for there was no time to be lost—I ran to my hotel, made a hasty toilet, and in a perfect vapor bath of perspiration returned to the theatre to go through a very heavy programme.

It was on such occasions as these that I felt the weight that rested on my shoulders; when entirely alone, and single-handed, I was expected to amuse an audience of strangers for two hours: to be serious and funny, to imitate the cracked voice of an old woman, sing a ballad decently, change my voice at least a dozen times, and screw my face up into every imaginable shape, when I felt perfectly wretched, and more like bursting out a-crying than anything else.

Upon this night, what would I not have given for the look of a well-remembered face, for the touch of a friendly hand?

I think I never felt so desolate, or so disinclined to go through with my motley programme.

Now for the fun!

I called to the man to "ring up."

He replied, by running away to the opposite side of the stage, and returning with a dirty scrap of paper in his hand, upon which was written:

"I'm deaf and dumb,
"And t'other man's gone home!"

Now I don't pretend to say I'm a model of either patience or endurance, or that I am very nervous; but at this particular moment of time, if I had spoken at all, I think I should certainly have exploded—burst, with indignation, rage, and fury.

The *uselessness* of it at once flashed upon me, and I endeavored to be calm. The poor fellow couldn't help being deaf and dumb, though certainly I deserved better treatment from the theatre folks, and I proceeded at once to do my best.

Writing, then, "*ring up*" on the wall, with a piece of chalk, I walked on, commencing my first song.

My audience was not particularly enthusiastic, though I think I succeeded in getting one or two faint laughs, at the scene from the "Lady of Lyons," and the imitation of Madame Anna Bishop; and the delight I felt when I found I had arrived at the "ten minutes intermission" period, can be easily imagined.

I *signed* to my deaf and dumb man to ring down the curtain. This done, I wrote hastily on a piece of paper:

"Go to my room and got a shirt, you'll find it on the bed."

I have told the reader that the heat upon this occasion was something fearful; for never before or since, not even in India, have I been so perfectly prostrated as I was upon this night.

The time was short, the audience impatient, and already had commenced clapping, thumping, and "hi hi"ing for the unfortunate performer; I, stripped to my smallclothes, anxiously awaiting the cooling and refreshing change of linen, when, to my disgust and horror, the man appeared with a *birch broom and a sheet*—(having translated my hurried scrawl of *room* for broom, and *shirt* for sheet!)

What I said I know not; to blow the man up was useless, for he couldn't hear; but I think I must have looked like a madman; for upon seizing hold of the sheet and broom, and throwing them from me, they went right through a forest of trees and a church steeple, and the man after them, leaving me all alone in my glory.

The first part of my programme was over, thank Heaven; and when the readers are informed that I had sung four ballads, given a comic scene of a Pauline and Claude in the Lady of Lyons, an imitation of Anna Bishop, a lengthy reading from Blackwood, the "Charge of the Light Brigade," a comic adventure in Sacramento, and read an autograph letter of Queen Victoria, they will sympathize with me in my affliction.

My ten minutes were up, and having managed to "hoist the rag" myself, on I went, and strange to say, my first recitation was

"The Song of a Shirt."

Now, if any one in the audience had the slightest idea of what had been going on behind the scenes, I should have been ruined; as it was, I proceeded with great difficulty, for not only had every vestige of my own piece of linen disappeared long since, but the incident itself, and my consciousness of the peculiar picture I presented to the audience, made it hard for me to keep a "straight face."

The second part over, and I was congratulating myself upon my speedy departure, and had just commenced my description of a "Yankee Town Meeting," with an imitation of Mr. Nathan Grunt, a grouty old chairman, when the lights of the entire establishment went out—a general scream arose from the audience—while I, in feeling my way off the stage, fell through a trap door upon a lot of *shavings*, a *barberous scrape*, that I never dreamed of getting into.

From Bendigo I went to Eagle Hawk, and at the Camp Hotel gave a Reading; about a hundred people present; tickets 5*s*.

My stage was the dining-room table. I had no piano,

and was assisted by a young gentleman who volunteered to accompany me upon an accordeon; the effect was not very delightful, either upon the audience or myself, and the consequence was, that the ballads were disposed of as quickly as possible, as was also the entertainment. Receipts and profits limited.

From Eagle Hawk to Castlemaine, another mining town, was engaged for £20, at the Assembly Room, to sing two songs, and give the Charge of the Light Brigade. This style of thing pays. Thence to a charming little spot called Taradale, where I was delighted to meet a Mr. and Mrs. Sirr, whom I had seen frequently at the French Consul's, in Melbourne. I was greeted most cordially, and at the little church on *Quinquagesima Sunday*, February 22, heard a most delightful sermon preached by the Rev. Mr. Martin, whom I had met in New York fifteen years previously.

Here also I met Mr. Hoskins, and Miss Julia Harland, both known in New York.

Kyneton was the next place, where, in the Church of England School Room, I held forth.

The room crowded; receipts over £30.

Once again in Melbourne, at my old quarters at the Mechanics' Institute, where, under the immediate patronage of His Excellency Sir Henry Barkly, Lady Barkly, and Major-General Macarthur, I gave a *Farewell Concert*, in which, by particular desire, I introduced, for the first time in Victoria, the exciting poem of the Young Gray-head.

By my Memorandum Book I find that on the 3d March I went to the Philharmonic Concert, after a good dinner with George Loder, where Madame Anna Bishop sang, and "Miska Hawsa" (any relation to Caspar?) played the violin.

4th. Passed a delightful evening with Mr. James Smith (once of Salisbury), of the "Argus."

And here, at this remote distance, should these desultory pages ever reach him, let me thank him, as well as the Press generally, throughout the Colonies, for the very great kindness and generous attentions received at their hands.

23d March. Left for Adelaide, South Australia, in steamship "White Swan."

On the 4th day arrived at the Port, and by rail to the city, and put up at a very cozy hotel, kept by a good fellow *on the Square*, named J. R. Jones.

Took White's Assembly Rooms, and gave my first Concert on Tuesday evening, March 31, 1857.

Receipts over £40, and the rain came down in torrents at that!

Adelaide is decidedly a handsome city, and has more the appearance of a quiet, well organized, regularly built English town than any that I had yet visited. The Government House, where Sir Henry and Lady Macdonald reign supreme, is a very imposing looking edifice, situated in the centre of magnificent grounds, tastefully and elegantly laid out.

The city boasts also of several very handsome churches, numbers of places of worship of various denominations, two theatres, besides several very stylish public buildings.

The harbors of South Australia are equally good with those of the adjoining colonies.

They are chiefly comprised within the large bays called Spencer's Gulf and Gulf St. Vincent.

Port Adelaide, where I landed, is an inlet from the latter, and is situated about seven miles from the city.

Near this is the roadstead, called Holdfast Bay, the

anchorage of which, I am informed, is excellent, but the winds blow here sometimes fearfully.

I must not forget to mention the kindness and hospitalities received from many in Adelaide, particularly from Dr. Taylor and his interesting family, who, during my sojourn, extended to me the most generous welcome; so much so, that I felt the greatest disinclination to say "good-by."

After giving four entertainments in Adelaide, and one at Pier Hotel, Glenelg, I started in the steamer Burra Burra, Captain Harper, once more for Melbourne.

On 11th May left for Sydney, New South Wales, in the Governor General, Captain Cottier.

On 13th, passed the spot where the California steamer, Monumental City, was lost, on board of which was my old friend Pete Strobel, of San Francisco. The place is called Tallaborga Island.

XC.

SYDNEY.

15th.—About dark arrived in Sydney, and on the following day received a visit from my old friend Col. Laurence, of whom I have before written in my "Pickersgill Reminiscences" in 1840.

Sydney is the capital of the Australian colonies, and is the largest as well as the most ancient city in the colonies; and the harbor, one of the handsomest in the world. I believe the place contains about 100,000 inhabitants.

On reaching the city from what is called the "Heads" it has a very imposing appearance. The large amount of shipping, the bright green verdure of the surrounding country, the terraced garden walks, the city stretching along the shore and on the heights in the most magnificent manner; the lower portion thereof fairly teeming with the adjuncts of commerce, the central part completely studded with churches, cathedrals, and magnificent public buildings, while the heights of the neighboring township, called Woollomolloo—what a name!—are crowned with the elegant villas and suburban retreats of the élite of Sydney society. The scene is one of remarkable beauty, not only from the picturesque appearance of the beautiful islands and inlets, the shores of which seem covered with a vegetation ever verdant, but the general effect upon the "looker-on" is most exhilarating, from the bustle, activity, and beauty that perpetually greet the eye.

It was difficult to me upon landing to believe I was really at the antipodes!

Everything was so thoroughly English.

Streets large, well paved, the bright jets of gas lighting up most brilliantly the shops of the "haberdasher" and "jeweller," whose wares astonished and dazzled the eye of the beholder, and presented as many prismatic colors to the vision as did ever Evrington's on Ludgate Hill, or Storr & Mortimer in Bond street. 'Buses passed and repassed, while "cads," with finger up, solicited a fare at sixpence a head, and "Hansoms" darted by you with meteor-like rapidity.

Piemen called out "baked taters, all 'ot," while the bright tin cans, with the little chimney of steam, looked as inviting to the hungry pedestrian as in Shoreditch or the Minories; piemen, too, with little white aprons, vended their "mutton" and "kidneys" "vith" or "vithout" gravy; while from a baker's window I read the well remembered words: "Muffins and crumpets every evening at six." It seemed that at every step something occurred to remind me of old England, roast beef "and things."

The market, a superb affair in George street, seemed as richly stocked as the Fulton or Washington in New York, or the Honey Lane in London; while if you wish a delightful stroll through well gravelled walks, verdant swards, beds of delicious flowers, go to the *Botanical Gardens*, where the floral treasures of the tropics flourish in the most entrancing luxuriousness, and breathe their fragrance in an atmosphere as balmy as in the islands of the Pacific I had so recently visited.

It seemed to me that in this superb spot all and every kind of tropical and semi-tropical rarity had been transplanted—brought from all parts of the globe—South

American and Indian exotics growing here in the greatest luxuriance.

The gardens are laid out in the most attractive manner possible; shady walks, long grassy terraces, cozy seats and lounging places, hewn out of solid rock, overshadowed by native figs and other trees of the thickest foliage.

Fountains, with every variety of jet, spurted forth their refreshing streams and sparkled in the bright sunlight, cooling the air, delighting the eye, and making the little gold and silver fish skip and jump about in the pond beneath.

Then here you have a Hyde Park, where you may see the "wealthy," if not the "noble," taking their drive regularly and with singular importance, and on this point it struck me it was difficult to tell "who's who!"

That gaudy and flashy equipage, with the liveried and powdered coachman and footman, with the armorial bearings tawdrily painted on either side, that has just dashed by you, bespattering you with mud or covering you with dust, contains, perhaps, the distinguished carcase of a man vulgarly called an old "lag," who may have left his native land for either having indulged in the pleasant pastime of "sheep-stealing," or the more desperate one of "murder." He has not only "served out" but improved his time; a new generation has sprung up; and *though he can never return to England*—mind that!—he feels now as "good as the next man," and perhaps even exchanges words with his "Excellency the Governor."

I was told that the word "Convict" must never be mentioned in Sidney, as it was difficult to say *whose corns might be trod upon.*

This appeared to be the only disagreeable element in the society of this place—I felt nervous and unpleasant in my daily intercourse with the people, having perpetually the sensation of confronting the once upon a time occupant of a cell in the Old Bailey, or a similar resting-place at the Hotel d' Horsemonger Lane.

The Jews are not merely a very wealthy but highly influential class here, and the entrée to the "upper circles" of the Israelitish population will not only be found most delightful to the stranger, but if they happen to take a fancy to you, pecuniarily advantageous, upon either a "benefit" night—or a "first" or "last" appearance.

Probably no artiste was more petted, or left Sidney with mightier proofs of the munificence of this liberal class of citizens than did Madame Anna Bishop.

And now for my opening night in the Capital.

I had taken up my residence at "Osmond's" in Pitt street, and with the assistance and friendly aid of my young friend "Ed," son of Col. L——, had taken the "MECHANICS' SCHOOL OF ARTS" for my opening night.

"Freyers" printing office in George street had issued immense "Posters" in the biggest kind of type, announcing the fact, and the Bill-stickers had faithfully stuck 'em up "all over the City," while I, with my treasurer, jumped in a carriage—(*for it was raining in torrents!*—as usual—) to convey me to the Hall in Pitt street.

My audience seemed delighted, the Hall was well filled, containing in money about thirty-six pounds, and everything went off well—the "Charge of the Light Brigade" as usual, carrying off the honors. The press the next day, without any exception, was most laudatory.

June 3.—Went to-day to the "Newtown Cemetery," a most beautiful spot for the burial of the dead, and something in the style of "Greenwood."

Conspicuous among the more attractive of the tombs is a very elegant monument erected to the renowned Harpist Bochsa, who died in this city two weeks after his arrival. Here is the Inscription:—

SACRED TO THE MEMORY

OF

NICHOLAS CHARLES BOCHSA, ESQ.,

who died 6th JANUARY, 1856.

AGED 65.

This monument is erected in sincere devotedness by his faithful friend and pupil,

ANNA BISHOP.

"Mourn him, mourn his harp-strings broken,
Never more shall float such music;
None could sweep the lyre like him!"

XCI.

A VISIT TO THE LUNATIC ASYLUM AT PARAMATTA.

LYING on my table, as I am writing this sketch, is a piece of dark brown paper, containing three little pieces of white linen, upon one of which is worked in green silk the words: "Forget me not," and upon each of the others, in the same material a "Chalice;" there is also a piece of worsted of varied colors, in the form of a tippet or collar. Upon the inside of this piece of paper are the words:

"From Miss Brady
to
Prince Albert of Saxe Coburg,
England.
Europe."

Upon the outside, I wrote at the same time the following:

Given to me by Miss Brady a lunatic, with the permission of Mrs. Statham, the Matron of the Paramatta Insane Asylum.

Thursday, *June* 11, 1857.

The scene, which will never be forgotten by me, I shall now attempt briefly to describe.

I had been invited by one of the Wardens of the Institution to visit it, and accordingly devoted an entire day to the purpose.

The Asylum itself is a magnificent structure of granite, several stories in height, containing a very large number of wards for patients, male and female, court yards of large dimensions, and grounds tastefully laid out; order and cleanliness here reign supreme, and the regulations and rules are strict, and rigidly enforced.

Upon my entrance into the Department for females, I was at first struck by the beauty of a lady seated at a desk, whom I at first took for one of the assistants, or perhaps the Matron.

I was proceeding through the room to a beautiful little garden spot just beyond, when she approached me, and laying her hand quite gently on my arm, said: "Oh! Sir; I trust I may be pardoned—but you are about returning to Europe, are you not?"

I was taken sorely by surprise, and at the same time completely dazzled by her beauty, that for the moment I was off my guard, and hesitated; when Mrs. Stratham the Matron ran to me, and quietly whispering in my ear, hurriedly said—"Humor her—it's a severe case—she's perfectly harmless—and her conversation will interest you."

In brief, she was a highly educated, young Irish lady, who from reverses had to take a situation as governess in a wealthy family in Sydney; for years—even since childhood—she had been in love with Prince Albert—and the feeling had taken so strong a hold upon her nature, that she had been for a long time a confirmed lunatic.

Asking me if I would walk with her a few steps, she said, taking from her pocket, and handing me a little package:

"Will you do me the greatest favor, upon your return to England, to go to Windsor Castle, and give this packet to Prince Albert?"

"With pleasure," I replied. "Oh! sir, if you knew how in the long cold nights of winter I have sat in my lonely cell, thinking of him—and knitting and working till my fingers bled again—at this little worsted collar for his dear neck!" and then she would kiss it, and press it to her lips—"and these," said she—"are the copies of the 'Chalice' used by me at the Holy Sacrament—tell him I pray for him night and day—and that I know we shall meet again and be happy." I asked her when she last saw him. She quickly answered—"About six months ago I went over there—and the Queen was very jealous of me, but when she found out we were engaged to be married, she was quite cordial in her manner, and received me daily at the Castle."

"This other piece of linen, ask him to wear in his waistcoat pocket—you see it has 'Forget me not' on it.

"I know you will oblige me, sir, by doing this for me, —and now"—bending her lovely face quite close to mine

—she said: "They think I'm mad—but I am not!—it's so hard to be kept in these strong stone walls! So hard to sit day after day, at that little desk, poring over the dear letters he has sent me—and waiting—O! how vainly—for the sound of his footsteps!

"But won't you use your influence at the Foreign Office in Downing street"—yes, she said Downing street!—"to get my release?—won't you"—and with streaming eyes, and burying her face in her hands, her magnificent dark hair falling over her neck and shoulders in the greatest profusion, she sat down on a bench, in front of some beautiful flowers.

I confess I was unmanned, for nothing could be apparently more earnest or sincere than her manner, nothing more terrible than her grief!

Rising in a few moments, at the approach of the matron, she said:

"I'm perfectly calm now; I don't often have these fits, but the fact of your so soon seeing the Prince, and carrying him these things, has affected me; and now, once and for ever (I give her words as nearly as I can remember), let me reassure you that I am in my right senses, and kept here against my will. Oh, madam (looking at the matron), you are very kind, but very cruel in keeping me here; but I'll go to my room and pray, it's all that's left me to do now; will you come and see my little room?" and following her, with the keeper's permission, I stepped into the apartment, kept scrupulously clean, the window open, though heavily barred, and a portrait of Prince Albert framed with evergreen and wild flowers!

I was just about bidding her farewell, with my hand upon the door, when she seized me by the arm, and with a vice-like grip pulled me inside. Her face was deathly pale, her eyes flashed fire, and with a hissing voice, subdued, though terribly in earnest, she said: "You've been deceiving me—you think I'm mad—you're like all the rest—you shant go! I'll have my revenge, and—" for a moment, I am frank to confess, I felt rather queer—nay, alarmed. It was impossible to move, and her eyes fixed on me, seemed to change every second in their fiendish expression. Luckily, I saw the handle of a bell-rope, which, with the disengaged hand, I hastily pulled. It was answered by the keeper, whip in hand, at the sight of which she relaxed her hold, and I instantly withdrew, leaving her weeping piteously.

It was, indeed, a heart-sickening exhibition.

I had fancied enough for one day of an Insane Asylum, but, on the suggestion of my guide that I should see something a little less tragic, we proceeded to the "play-ground," a large open space, where certainly some comical and laughable scenes were enacted.

A fellow immediately rushed up to me, dressed like an Indian chief; face painted, tomahawk in hand, feathers of all sizes stuck in his cap, and flourishing an old musket barrel in his hand, he said:

"Don't you know me? I'm the Emperor Napoleon! Yes, and you don't think this is St. Helena; but I tell you those —— English will feel me yet. There goes the fellow (pointing to another patient) that took me prisoner! Ha! ha! ha!" and with a whoop and a yell, he ran off.

Then came up a man dressed like a policeman, who said to me:

"I was hung about a week ago for committing murder; but I was acquitted unanimously by the jury and put in here for safe-keeping; can't you get me out?"

Some were dancing, some singing, some sitting with their faces buried in their hands, some sprawling on the ground, and so on. It was a sorry sight at the best, and I prepared to take my departure; but, recurring for a moment to the poor female first mentioned, when recently the news arrived here of the death of Prince Albert, I could not help thinking of the above strange incident; and I fancied that, perhaps, long since, she also may have found rest and relief in a visit from the great leveller, Death.

XCII.

I MEET WITH AN OLD SCHOOLFELLOW!

PASSING by the Prince of Wales Theatre, I noticed on the bills that the play of King Henry VIII. was to be performed that night—King Henry, Mr. G. H. Rogers.

Now, that morning I had been informed that a Mr. George Herbert Rogers had remarked to a friend that he thought that I was the same "Steve Massett" that was his "chum" at Troy Town Academy.

I too was satisfied that it must be the same, for the name was by no means a common one, so to the stage-door I went, and sent in my card, which was instantly acknowledged, by the doorkeeper's returning with the request that I would walk into Mr. Rogers's dressing-room.

In I went, my quondam schoolmate seated in all the regal splendor of a stage King Henry! He jumped up, and to my question, "Well, George, my dear fellow, how are you?" he seized me by the hand and shook it in a very genial though unkingly manner!

He had grown monstrously in size; was the father of a large family of children, and the pet, if not the best, actor in the colonies.

We had a jolly laugh, and (between the acts) a chat, and a little "home-brewed" arter the play.

XCIII.

I AM PATRONIZED BY HIS EXCELLENCY THE GOVERNOR AND SUITE.

It was suggested that if I could obtain the patronage of Sir William and Lady Denison, it would greatly assist, as an attraction, in filling the house.

Accordingly, presenting a note of introduction I had to one of the "A. D. C.'s," I was very kindly received, and left with the consoling information that Sir William and Lady Denison would be happy to attend.

The entertainment went off with the greatest éclat, and I cleared, by the two hours' work, *one hundred pounds!*

Bidding adieu to my esteemed friends the L.'s, not forgetting many others who had shown me much hospitality, I left the good old city of Sydney for Hobart Town, Van Diemen's land (now called Tasmania), in the steamship Tasmania, Captain Clinch, a three days' trip, for which I paid £10.

On the 17th June we passed Maria Island, a most beautiful looking spot from the sea, where Smith O'Brien and others were confined, and from which they most fortunately escaped.

June 18.—Arrived at "Hobart Town." Put up at "Todd's Hotel."

"Hobart Town" is an extremely gloomy looking place,—in fact it is a second "Sydney," though on a smaller scale—the same disagreeable "element" existing in "society," that was noticeable in Sydney; and which, to a foreigner, is so offensive.

Talking of "Society," it seemed to me that there really was only one "first class" or upper circle recognised at all in the Colonies; that was those immediately connected with the respective Governments—the Government "Officials," and the Officers of the Army and Navy.

Into this "Circle" it is difficult to get—and it struck me that *distinctions* were drawn with even a tighter rein than in aristocratic London.

I will give one or two instances. In a neighboring City during my visit, there came off at the "Assembly Rooms," what they call "a Race Ball," given by a Committee of gentlemen composing the leading members of the "Club."

The owner of the "Rooms," and the lessee thereof, a very wealthy man at that—told me himself, that much as he wished his daughter to be present, it would be impossible for him or any of his family to be admitted. No money could purchase a ticket. He was a "Tailor," and a very fashionable one at that—he was an "outsider."

Again, the proprietor of one of the Hotels—and the wealthy man—told me that he was going to take his wife—that he couldn't often afford to "treat her," but this time he was going to invest three pounds three shillings (about fifteen dollars) in a ticket; (I heard afterwards) the moment it was known who the party was, he was instantly rejected.

One more instance—the most ridiculous of all—and I have done.

A wealthy "Haberdasher," or as we call them "Dry Goods Merchants," applied for tickets for himself and family; he being at that time looked upon as the very "A. T. Stewart" of the Colony.

He even was rejected because forsooth he "broke bulk," or in other words *retailed* his merchandise.

The entrée into the best Colonial Society is open only and exclusively to three professions—Divinity, Law, and Physic.

On the 22d of June, at the "Royal Assembly Rooms," I gave my first "Ballad Concert, and Readings from the Poets."

It went off very successfully—the audience appeared pleased, and the receipts were about forty-five pounds.

XCIV.

AMUSING LETTER FROM AN "AGENT."

ONE of my "Agents," a regular out and out Yankee, whom we'll call Mr. Brick, had been getting a little "tight," anglicè "drunk,"—and as this happened more than once, I wrote him a line stating that his services were no longer required. The next day I received the following note:

S. C. MASSETT EQR.,

DEAR SIR:—Larst Monday was the fust time I got "little over the Bay," for the larst six months. The reason why I fell in with so many friends in Different Hotels whilst I was working for you Concert, that night I work harder that Day than I ever Did before to Get a house that Night.

You got me wurse by torking to me; the way you did, I sold fore (4) Tickets, which I have given you credic for them. If you want to see me you ken find me to the Shakespere Hotel. I am about starting a Cumpany here myself, providing if I can get Two persons which I want.

Yours truly,

A. BRICK.

My second entertainment was given under the "Patronage" of His Excellency the Governor, Sir Henry Edward Fox Young—Lady Young (formerly Miss Marryat), a most delightful and fascinating lady—Sir Valentine Fleming, Lady Fleming, Lady Campbell, besides many of the officers of the 12th Regiment.

I was indebted for the above to the friendly offices of the Governor's aide-camp, Captain Henry Maule; to whom I had a letter of introduction, and whose kindness and hospitality during my brief sojourn in this city I cannot easily forget. To him and his amiable wife, Lady Campbell, I offer my earnest thanks, and kindest remembrances, and yet live in the hope of greeting them again.

While at Hobart Town it was suggested that a Concert might be given at a suburban village of "Oaklands," and "Campbelltown."

Thither I went by stage.

I was indebted for the use of a very good piano to a Mrs. Whiteford, daughter of the celebrated actor, R. W. Elliston, of Drury Lane.

From Hobart Town I went per mail coach, as in the old time, to Launceston, a distance of 120 miles—fare £3.

The road, made by the convicts, was one of the finest I had ever travelled on; the weather was intensely cold, and before we arrived, the snow was falling fast. Think of this in July!

Put up at the Cornwall Hotel, attached to which was the Assembly Rooms, and for which they charged me £5 5*s.* a night.

Here I met with the old New York favorite, Mr. John Dunn, or as he was more familiarly known, "that Rascal Jack."

XCV.

STILL MOVING ON.

In a cozy little room, on the second floor of the before mentioned hotel, on a cold and frosty night, comfortably seated in a couple of old-fashioned arm-chairs, in front of a bright coal fire, were the writer of these lines, and Rascal Jack, his excellent wife and daughter Rosa sitting on the sofa reading.

The conversation was somewhat discursive, and ran into politics and the (then) present condition of the Emperor of the French.

"By the way, I see my quondam friend of other days, Mons. Henri, who was the stage manager at the theatre in Paris while I was performing there, is now a very big man—even the Count de Morney, the particular and personal friend of Louis Napoleon."

I asked him if he was quite certain as to the identity of the individual. "Quite," replied Jack Dunn; "and I only wish he'd return me the money I loaned him. It would come in very appropriately just now."

Upon questioning him further, he informed me that at the time Louis Napoleon was imprisoned in the Castle of Ham, he loaned Mons. Henri, the present Count de Morney, £15, which money was effectual in aiding Napoleon's escape.

While in Hobart Town, I was informed that the Captain of a vessel bound for the East Indies had remarked that if I had any disposition to visit those latitudes, a state room in his ship was at my service.

Now having made up my mind to visit Calcutta, I thought this was an opportunity not to be slighted. Accordingly, I conferred with my friend Captain Maule, who agreed with me on the propriety of accepting it.

And now, as I am about ringing down the curtain on my brief sojourn in the Australian Colonies, I intend letting my readers into some of the secrets of the *profits* thereof.

Imprimis: Was there ever an instance on record of a public performer, male or female, who in the announce bills, or the puffs preliminary, was not served up in something of the following style:

"His (or her) career and success was one complete triumph."—"Entertainments crowded to suffocation;"—and "winning golden opinions from all sorts of men."

Everywhere I went I was successful. Houses were crowded, if they did not contain expenses, and audiences invariably delighted, charmed, and electrified.

I had visited the four colonies, given readings in each, and upon referring to a little memorandum by my side, I find the following figures:

Gave Fifty-two Entertainments.

Total Receipts	£898	14	6
Expenses	897	0	0
Profits of the Trip . . .	£1	14	6

The reader will perceive that I have long since fully appreciated the force of the aphorism, "All that glitters is not gold."

Still, with a light heart and several thin pairs of breeches (for I was going to a hot climate), I sailed in the bark Fortune for Bombay.

XCVI.

OFF FOR INDIA!

On the 20th July, in the year of grace 1857, I sailed from Launceston, Van Diemen's Land, for the East Indies.

The reader has been informed that the Captain of the aforesaid vessel had extended an invitation to me, and being rather prepossessed in his favor by his frank and apparently open-hearted manner, I looked forward prospectively to a right jolly time.

I was the only passenger, excepting a Dr. E——, the surgeon of the ship, who had accompanied the skipper from Liverpool, in one of James Baines's emigrant ships, in the same capacity.

Now, long ere this, the reader has, I trust, found out that I am a pretty good sailor. The sensation of sea-sickness is to me unknown, and I am never so perfectly happy or content as when on the water.

It was, then, upon the third day out that I began to regret the step I had taken, and to appreciate the hornets' nest into which I had unwittingly plunged myself.

I do not mention the name of my tormentor, in the person of the aforesaid captain, nor the particulars of the hospitality extended to me, or the brutal treatment the crew received.

Dr. Johnson, I believe, likened a ship to "a prison, with the chance of being drowned."

Macaulay, in his eloquent speech on the life of Warren Hastings, says that "it is on board a vessel, where there is nothing to drive away the dull monotony of the voyage but quarrelling and love-making, that the deadliest enmities are engendered, as also the most lasting attachments."

The captain turned out to be of a most ungovernable temper, cruel, domineering, exacting, suspicious, and arbitrary; and during a sixty days' residence on the water with him fifty were passed by me seated at the same table, without exchanging a word.

Six of the crew were escaped convicts—their names and sentences were as follows:

1. King, seven years, Port Arthur—forgery.
2. James Simmonds, fifteen years, Norfolk Island—stealing silver plate.
3. Tom Johnson, eight years—mutiny.
4. Joe, five years, broaching cargo—V. D. L.
5. Wm. Johnson, five years, felony—V. D. Land.
6. Cook, three years.

A lively lot!

Had it not been for the gentlemanly first and second officers, W. Clerke and W. Harwood, and the good-natured companionship of my medical friend, Dr. E——, I know not what I should have done, and the reader will enter into my sensations of delight, when on the sixty-third day out the "Towers of Bombay" loomed up in the distance!

On Friday, the 18th September, I was once again on *terra firma*.

The sensations of pleasure and delight that I experienced on landing at the stone pier in the capital of British India, cannot be described. The feeling of emancipation and freedom from the tyrannical presence of Captain ——, a new life seemed before me, and though alone, in a city of 800,000 souls, the changes, the novelty of the scene, the delicious atmosphere, and the feeling of untrammelled independence, inspired me with hope, and filled me with pleasant anticipations.

I think it is Dickens who says "There are a few days in our lives which stand out from all others we have ever known, days on which it seems to us as if the flood of sunlight round us is gilded with so bright a glory, that even the commonest things on which it falls, glow with a beauty we never felt before, days on which the fresh breeze passing over us, and sweeping through the green leaves overhead, whispers ever to us to cast all sorrow from our hearts, for that in the great world around us, there is infinite joy, and happiness, and love;" such a day *was this*, and bright and beautiful with the blue clear sky, with the golden sunbeams, with the light laughing wind, it rises in my memory now—a day never to be forgotten.

Jumping into my "palke" or "palankeen," a conveyance borne on the shoulders of four natives, I wended my way to "Barnes's Hotel" in the Fort.

Lying at full length upon a well stuffed mattress, covered with silk or morocco leather, supported by pillows, having at the upper end a little shelf or drawer, in which to stow away any small articles, I was greatly amused at the strange sights and scenes that at every moment greeted me.

Upon my arrival at the hotel the first thing to be done was to get a "peon," or body servant, who could speak English, and accompany me in my peregrinations through the city.

XCVII.

BOMBAY.

Bombay, seen as you enter the bay from the Arabian Sea, is extremely attractive; on either side rise up magnificent mountains, which mark the western boundaries of the great continent of India. Then comes the island of Bombay with its large fortress, manned and gunned—forming the inclosure to the town.

I must confess that I was not particularly struck by the appearance of the city, as I took my first evening stroll.

The "Town Hall," a very imposing edifice of stone, is the most notable of the public buildings, and in the large room thereof, capable of holding two thousand persons, I gave my first entertainment.

There is a small theatre in an out of the way locality, but no regular concert room.

But the fact is, the heat is so great, that there are only about three months in the year at all available for public exhibitions, and then, the attraction must be somewhat novel and exciting, to insure a large audience.

Then the greater portion of the inhabitants reside at Malabar Hill, about four miles from the town, and, as they usually dine at seven o'clock, the disposition to stir out after a hearty repast, is not very great.

I was much amused in going through the bazaars, commencing at the lively esplanade where the fashionables take their evening drive, and ending in the dark forests of cocoanuts at Mazagon, where reside numbers of Europeans.

It seemed to me that no place I had as yet visited contained so motley a population. Here then, passing and repassing, were Persians, Arabs, Parsees, Chinese, Brahmins, half-naked, Armenians, Portuguese, Coolies, Hindoo clerks, Abyssinians, Jews, Moguls; and the variety of languages spoken something fearful to contemplate and listen to.

The Roman Catholic churches and chapels are very numerous here. Mosques and Hindoo temples are found in numbers, and the Parsees or Fire Worshippers have their magnificent fire temples where the sacred fire is kept up by the priests all the day long.

XCVIII.

A VISIT TO THE CAVES OF ELEPHANTA.

I HAD heard so much said of the above place, that I resolved to be one of a party to pay them a visit, and I shall proceed to give a sketch of the trip and place.

I have before spoken of the beauty of the harbor, and also of the charming marine views that are presented constantly to the eye at the entrance of the bay; studded as it is with picturesque little islands, having on one side the western Ghauts, towering in the distance, and on the other the island of Bombay itself with its dark fortress, wooded vales and hills, fishing villages, half concealed by groves of splendid cocoanuts, and rocky promontories lashed by the sea; while to give life to the scene there are the numerous and diversified shipping in the harbor, with the flags of every nation flying at the peak, and native craft of various sorts and sizes, gliding about under sail.

The island of Elephanta, containing one of the largest of those extraordinary cave temples, that I had heard so much of, is most romantically situated, and about seven miles distant from Bombay.

We reached it in about an hour and a half's sail. At first it appeared very small, being indeed nothing more than a double-peaked, rocky, woody hill, with a narrow valley winding between the peaks; and it is only about five miles in circumference; but for exquisite beauty of verdure and foliage, and for picturesqueness of form and position, the little island is indeed a gem.

It struck me as very strange, that not even a jetty for landing had been constructed, for the water is too shallow to permit a boat reaching the shore, and the only way I had of getting to land dry-footed was on the shoulders of the natives, and a comical sight we presented. One fat English woman, the wife of the skipper of a British ship, presented a most extraordinary appearance. Though the day happened to be quite sultry, she was encased in a heavy stuff woollen dress, with a fur tippet on top, and a thick shawl over that, and when mounted on the back of a sturdy native, who fairly tottered beneath the weight of this mountain of flesh, she resembled more a huge balloon, with a couple of prime legs of mutton dangling from the basket, than anything else I could think of; and her feet stowed away in a pair of heavy cloth boots almost reaching to the calf, were swinging to and fro, as if entirely disconnected from the mass of rotundity above.

Added to this she was screaming at the top of her voice, "'Enry, 'Enry—this nasty wretch is squeegeing me himproperly—I know he'll drop me hin!—to think of being drowned hin this horful bay—Oh Lor—Oh Lor—I'm fainting—I know I am!"

Upon landing she became suddenly pacified, and managed with the rest of us to get up the steep ascent, once apparently a stone staircase, leading from the beach to the great cave. This appeared to be an excavation about one hundred and fifty feet long, and the same breadth nearly, and about twenty feet high, hewn out of a mass of lofty rock.

A great big colossal three-faced and many-armed bust is carved out of the rock, at the upper end of the cave, and there are bas-reliefs of gigantic human figures in various parts, as well as numerous smaller figures of Gods and Goddesses, some with six arms, others with monkey heads, some grasping warlike instruments, some serpents, besides other monstrous devices.

Elephanta is possessed of a natural cistern, penetrating under the rock, full of deliciously pure cold water, and I found it a most delightful beverage.

The view I got from the cave's entrance is superb—the eye resting alternately upon hills luxuriously wooded, valleys, islands, verdant and lovely, lying amid the calm blue sea.

Besides the principal cavern, I noticed several smaller and seemingly unfinished caves close by; but they appeared possessed of little interest.

On the other side of the island stands the colossal figure of an elephant, to which I was informed the name of the place is generally ascribed. This rude piece of sculpture is now much dilapidated—the head lying on the gound, some feet from the body—the legs sunk in the earth.

As to the constructors of the Cave Temples of Elephanta, conjectures without number have been made. The opinion of my Hindoo guide on the subject, in answer to my query, was: "God came doanee and made the caves in one nighty."

There are not many "Worshippers" come nowadays to the caves, I was told. I noticed a few, however, and I noticed more than one of the monkey-headed deities daubed all over with red; as I found the custom with Hindoo images, and sacred emblems in India.

The sculptures in the caves have been much disfigured by the barbarous practice of carrying and chipping off bits of the works as relics, and also of cutting names and remarks on the columns, and along the sides of the cave. Here was one I made a "note of"—C. S. Governor, April, 1501, rudely but very deeply cut in the big three-faced bust.

No more of these depredations now take place, for the caves are in charge of a European sergeant, living in a bungalow close by—the only white inhabitant of the island—and he, with his two sepoys, takes good care that the visitors do no damage to the sculptures.

Upon reaching the city late in the evening, we found the residents at the Fort in a very excited state, at the receipt of some news just received from Poonah relating to the rebellion—at this time raging at the highest pitch.

MY FIRST CONCERT.

The next day having been selected for my first appearance before an Eastern audience, I did not feel particularly pleasant at the prospect—understanding that orders had been sent by the Commander of the Fort, for all Europeans to keep the closest watch, and not to leave their houses after dark.

My "programmes" of which there were some three thousand had been distributed through the City and suburbs three days before. The three daily papers had behaved very handsomely in preliminary notices, and my friends assured me that I should be greeted with a crowded auditory.

The night of the 1st of October, Thursday, witnessed my debut.

The large room in the Town Hall (the front of which presented a brilliant appearance, with variegated lights in form of flowers, and various devices) was filled to repletion —the principal portion being Europeans. The front seats occupied by wealthy Parsee merchants—prominent among them was the well known Sir Curstejee Jejeebhoy, the wealthy Parsee baronet, the only instance I believe on record of the title being borne by a native of these climes.

The heat was overpowering, and the immense size of the building, and the unpleasant reverberation thereof, made the recitations indistinct—but assisted the ballad portion of the entertainment.

The audience were (for a hot climate too !) enthusiastic in their applause, and every piece went off most satisfactorily. I think during the performance I changed my shirt three times, and used up half-a-dozen pocket-handkerchiefs; punkas were going over head—every window raised—doors wide open—yet the heat was stifling.

The papers on the following day were extremely kind and complimentary.

XCIX.

BLOWING AWAY FROM THE GUNS!

It was during my brief sojourn in Bombay, that I witnessed the fearful sight of blowing men away from the guns—and when my readers are informed that the evening of the day set apart by some of the natives for murdering the entire white population—certainly those residing in the "Fort"—was the night selected for my farewell concert—they will see how narrow was the escape!

The mutinies then existing in the upper provinces of India spread until they reached the City of Bombay, taint-ing the fidelity of the 10th and 11th Infantry Regiments, and the native Marine Battalion. Many men of both these regiments were captured at a little house near the esplanade, where they were planning to rise on the night of the 15th of October, during the native festival of the "Dewallee," and murder every man, woman, and child, in the city.

Two of these monsters were condemned, and sentenced to be blown from the cannon's mouth.

It appears then, that a Sepoy of the 10th Regiment called privately on the Deputy Commissioner of Police, and after narrating all the details of the plot in course of maturity, offered to give positive proof if the authorities would engage a room adjoining that in which the conspirators were to hold their last meeting previous to operations.

Having been introduced to the Deputy Commissioner of Police, who spoke very good English, he invited me (we first having disguised ourselves) to accompany him upon the critical mission.

In a dingy native house, in one of the lowest districts of Bombay, imagine some fifty natives, with a satanic gleam of moody satisfaction sparkling from their deep black eyes, crowded on the dirty floor of a dark room.

A deathlike silence ensues, as each one turns to a non-commissioned officer who with a quiet triumph lays before them the full and mature plan.

"Hist!" said the officer to me—"lie down—don't breathe—look through this hole!—see their hands in each other's—they are taking now the most fearful oath known to the Hindostanee."

The bright eye of the commissioner peering through that mysterious little chink in the dirty plaster, had providentially seen, heard, and found out their plan.

"Up! up!" quickly whispered he, and flying with the velocity of a deer—I following as quickly as possible—we jumped into a buggy, and rode to the Headquarters of the Governor, Lord Elphinstone.

The officer translated to His Excellency the plan as he heard it, as follows:

The native soldiery of "regulars" were to disperse in small bodies in different directions, and fire the fort, murder all the Europeans, then take possession of the

Treasury and Arsenal. The "budmashes" or vagabonds were to be rewarded by having the outside bungalows, and the English families at Malabar Hill, and other localities, left entirely to their disposal—there they would find lots of women and children to ravish and massacre!

In less time, it seems, than it takes me to write this, a mounted troop of armed men flew across the esplanade, and with a fearful sound and crash the doors were burst open, and the inmates one and all pinioned, and in one hour after, the cells of Fort St. George contained them! So quietly and dexterously was this accomplished, that nothing of it was known publicly, until the morning of the day of execution.

The afternoon of the 15th of October it will be difficult for me to forget.

I was seated about one o'clock taking "tiffin" or lunch, in company with Lieut. Timm, of the E. I. C. service, chatting with him upon the probabilities of a good or bad house for the concert of the evening, when he remarked: "I fear your chances are rather slim, old fellow, to-night—for the fact is, it's my impression that we shall all be in or near kingdom-come, by to-morrow morning!"

I asked him what he meant? He replied; "The Commander-in-chief has just telegraphed from Poonah to the Colonel of the regiment here, that the sentence is to be carried into effect upon the two ringleaders this afternoon, and at five, they are to be 'blown away.'" Adding—"I fear the natives will rise *en masse*, and murder us all!" asking me, at the same time, if I had a "Colt?"

I was too sick at the prospect to joke or I'd have replied, that I would like to run off on the back of one, if I could! So I replied, that I had never carried any fire-arms in any of my travels—and that I did not even know how to load a pistol! "Well, well," he replied; "I've got a six-barrelled one; you go on to the esplanade with me; we'll keep together—and the worst come to the worst, we'll die together."

With these reflections, and giving up all idea of "exhibiting" that night, we left the Hotel for the scene of death.

I have before spoken of the beauty of the harbor, and

the surroundings of this city, and the magnificence of its situation.

The harbor is certainly not inferior to any in the world, the beauty and splendor of its scenery are unrivalled, and indeed, many think it surpasses the far-famed bay of Naples.

In what is called the fair portion of the year, the vision is delighted amidst the fairy tracery of purple hills, and during the "monsoon" the sublimity of the tempest, and the storm careering in all the grandeur of the Torrid Zone, strikes awe into the inmost recesses of every heart.

As I gazed, the harbor looked calm and still as an inland sea, which had never felt ebb or flow of tide; flags of every nation fluttered in the orient breeze, and as the sun descended towards the horizon, the big city lay bathed in a sea of gold, and the glories of the setting luminary were painted in gorgeous crimson pictures on the western sky.

The Ghauts mountains, richly wooded to their base, showed in the gilded atmosphere their castellated summits, as if upon their tops Titans had reared their fortresses.

The nearer landscape, decked in milder beauty, exhibited the ever graceful palm; the hoary banyan tree that counts centuries as years; the stately nym, with leaves that whisper to the wind; birds with the most brilliant and glittering plumage flitted about; the cooling gentle rippling waves of the Arabian Sea, as they kissed in broken murmurs the yellow beach, and the hum of a city numbering 800,000 souls, spoke in solemn tones of the dreadful example which a mighty race was about to exhibit for the domination and the punishment of one inferior, treacherous, and cruel.

I was standing on the esplanade, and the dread hour of five was fast approaching.

Out of every gateway from the Fort, natives and Europeans were thronging to the military parade ground, while from the native town, alley, street, and lane, disgorged their thousands.

Every nation under the sun had a representative there to witness the appalling spectacle so soon to occur.

At half-past four the troops composing the garrison

moved to the ground. Of the English soldiery, there were only some 200 of H. M.'s 95th regiment, just arrived from the Cape of Good Hope; 200 seamen, American and English, had hastily landed from the ships in the harbor, armed with musket and bayonet.

There were also a four-gun battery of foot artillery, and three guns manned by the artisans of the Grand Arsenal.

The whole English force numbering only 500 men—against which were some 6000,—near them was a group of English and American captains of merchants' ships, and numbers of the civilian population. The parade formed three sides of a square.

The base was occupied by the artillery at the centre;—the right and left sides were composed of the 10th and 11th Sepoy regiments, to which the prisoners belonged.

Facing these Sepoys were placed three guns, behind which the artillerymen stood, with matches lighted—ready to meet with deadly ball, the first movement towards revolt.

Between the six cannons, three pointing obliquely to either side, were placed at right angles to the base of the square the two guns assigned for the awful vengeance or justice of the hour. Between and in the rear of them, were arranged the stern guard, and the condemned wretches whose lives were so soon to terminate.

Thanks to the courtesy of Brigadier Shoutt, commanding the garrison, and Captain William Walker, I was permitted to take my position within six feet of the right hand gun, and such a spectacle as I then witnessed will live in my memory for ever.

There was no outward excitement, such as attends ordinary public executions; no swaying to and fro of the multitude.

In all that vast assemblage of 100,000 human beings, a whisper would have broken the stillness.

The English officers rode along the lines, silent and severe of aspect. The champ of their horses' bits, the clank of their sabres seemed loud and troublesome, as they jarred the all-pervading quiet.

At five o'clock the Brigadier rode in front of the death guns—and for a moment the silence of the grave prevailed.

It was only interrupted, when a voice audible to the most distant of the listening multitude, read in tones, clear, solemn, and firm, the sentence of the Court Martial.

In the language of Hindoostan, it smote the ear and hearts of the convicts.

Thus it was rendered to me:

"The Court, having found you guilty of attending a seditious meeting in Bombay, and of having made use of highly mutinous and seditious language, evincing a traitorous disposition towards the Government, tending to promote rebellion against the state, and to subvert its authority (the above being in breach of the articles of war), sentence you 'Drill Havildar Syneed Hoseen' of the Marine Battalion, Native Infantry, and Private 'Mungall Guddrew' of No. 8 Company, 10th Regiment Native Infantry, to suffer death by being blown away from the muzzle of a cannon."

The two men were then ordered to divest themselves of their regimental jackets. This was quickly done; they were then marched between files of the European guard, each to a cannon's mouth, and there bound tightly with ropes.

The culprit "Drill Havildar" appeared composed, and assumed an attitude erect and even dignified, until he found himself in the grasp of the artillery-men.

He gazed imploringly upon the Regiment to which he had belonged—expecting, I thought, that they might rush to his rescue.

He made a last appeal!

"Oh! Sahib! captain—Sahib! pardon—dear—dear captain!"

They stood before him motionless! and that guilty breast where sanguinary resolves had arranged the midnight slaughter of defenceless men, women, and children, now heaved with the mental agony of the doomed conspirator.

While the two men were being bound, not a syllable was uttered by the assembled crowd; the suspense lengthened seconds into minutes.

All eyes were turned for an instant from the prisoners to the Native Regiments—but they moved not.

A rattling of steel along the line, gave notice that the Enfield rifle was prepared to visit mutiny with slaughter.

As the word "Prime" fell upon the ear, I noticed the 10th Native Infantry shook, as by an electric thrill.

It was now quite evident they might have feared that at the next moment the deadly rifles might be levelled against their front.

Simultaneously with the loading of the Infantry, the guns to the right and left of the criminals were pointed at the two native regiments, loaded to the muzzle with canister and grape—and there the gunners stood with signal match lighted.

From the ramparts at the Fort, four sixty-eight pounders looked threateningly upon the scène.

When the final summons was given—the handcuffs and uniform jackets removed—and the English gunners were lashing the traitors, with their backs to the cannon's mouth, it was really fearful to notice the wild despairing expression in the faces of the doomed.

There was another pause; again the silence became oppressive—thousands, and thousands of eyes, riveted their gaze upon the victims; and the heart of the strongest there stirred more quickly, when arose from Captain Bolton of the Royal Artillery, the command—

"Let all retire from the guns—except the men with the portfires."

"At the word 'Fire'—apply the match!"

When the word "Ready" was given by Captain Bolton—the gunners in a moment lighted their matches—the prisoners and the artillery-men stood immovable as statues.

The awful word "Fire" rang out clear as a clarion note—the hammers descended on the caps—the smoke rolled upwards in sluggish clouds—the cannons spoke as in tones of thunder, and the air revealed by many a ghastly witness that retribution had been terribly visited upon those who designed to revel and to dabble in the blood of massacre.

I did not linger at the place of sacrifice. Life is of motley garb—mine has presented, the reader will have by this time perceived, the giddy and the sombre in strange and often painful association.

It seems to me that Hogarth did well to represent beside the coffin of the dead harlot, the thoughtless boy, winding up his top!

I wended my way from a scene of terror, to prepare for one of business—though, as the reader will imagine, with a very sad heart!

My entertainment was advertised to "come off" this night at the Town Hall—but what with the frightful incident I have just endeavored to describe, and the common apprehension that an outbreak of the natives would immediately succeed it, I supposed my programme would attract no one—and to tell the truth when I entered my "palke" to be carried to my hotel, I fancied I resembled more Mr. Bob Acres than Sir Lucius O' Trigger! for I fear it is one of my characteristics, that I would rather continue this mortal existence, and forego posthumous fame, than to fall in the noblest battle, and live in history!

There's no disputing about tastes!

To my great surprise, however, there was a crowded house—among the number a large sprinkling of Parsees and wealthy Hindoo merchants. This too, while on the outskirts of the trembling city, many a father kept midnight vigil with belted sword, and revolver clutched, fearing the desolating storm of native revenge.

The "inhumanity," as it is called, of the above mode of dealing with this miserable class of human beings, has been so often referred to, the mode of punishment being deemed in the highest degree "barbarous," I shall simply upon this subject give one extract from a letter, handed me to read in California, prior to its being sent to England, by which the fiendish atrocities practised by these brutes will more fully appear.

The commercial letter of Messrs. Mackay and Co., dated Calcutta, 18th of June, describes some of the atrocities committed by the revolted troops in various parts of the Bengal presidency:

"Imagine the father of a family, bound hand and foot, compelled to witness the dishonor of his wife by—we are afraid to say how many of these fiendish crew; and then, when the poor creature was almost dead from the effect of their brutal assault, they cut her across the abdomen, and drew forth an unborn babe, and dashed it against the ground, and then hung the lifeless remains around the neck of the manacled and distracted father. The villains, still thinking something wanting to aggravate his feelings of horror and dismay, severed the head from the body of the mother, and bound this also around his neck. Not yet satisfied with their dreadful work, they seized the poor man's two remaining children, infants of three and four years old, killed them, cut off their heads, and strung them also around his neck, taunting him with all the obscene language the native dialect so readily furnishes, until they thought he was dying, and when, fearing they might lose the last opportunity of torturing the man, a dagger was plunged into his heart, and he died, with the heads of all those he held most dear on this earth resting lifelessly upon his breast. We have related but one instance only amongst the many that have come to our knowledge—whereas almost every act of these villains has been marked with something equally horrible."

The principal public buildings within the town of Bombay, are the Town Hall, the Docks, the Government House, two churches, the Mint, the barracks, and the Castle, containing the Arsenal.

All these are on a large and handsome scale. The private residences are ornamented with flat roofs, terraces, balustrades, and garden flats. The Governor resides at Malabar Hill, or Point, a bungalow erected upon a rock projecting into the sea at the extreme westerly point of the island.

As I have before said, the scenery in and about the Island of Bombay is enchantingly beautiful, because of the admixture of rice plains, gardens, handsome bungalows, and wooded hills, with occasional peeps of the sea shore, and the open main, or landlocked bays. Some of the little villages near the city are densely planted with cocoanut groves.

C.

A WORD AT PARTING.

THE hospitality, kind-heartedness, and generosity with which a stranger is received in India, are well known.

In returning thanks at this great distance, to those who received me so cordially (and especially to my brethren of the masonic order, here and in Calcutta, I make my most affectionate acknowledgments), I cannot resist mentioning Mr. Mawson and Mr. Pym of the Gazette, Captain Wm. Wacker, Dr. Buist, Sir Cursteje Jamsteje, Mr. George Craig of the Telegraph and Courier, among those most kind, and who did everything in their power to render my sojourn agreeable.

Having given my farewell entertainment, I bade goodbye to my friends, and sailed in the American bark Sabine, Captain Thos. H. Hendee, for Calcutta.

On the morning of November 2d, 1857, the pilot left us, and we stood out for sea. We have for passengers the supercargo, Mr. T. S. Tredick (whose father owns the ship), Major Smeaton of the Bengal army, a Mr. Briggs, and myself.

After my experiences on board the bark "Fortune," I

felt a little cautious in the selection of a ship in which to make another voyage; as this was the only vessel up for Calcutta, I had no alternative but to take passage in her, and I am happy to say, a more delightful time upon the deep blue sea I never passed. The captain, a most delightful fellow, and every inch a sailor, did everything to make our time pass agreeably, and though the most annoying succession of calms prevailed, the time passed most agreeably, and I almost regretted when on the thirtieth day we reached the Ganges, and took on board a pilot.

CI.

CALCUTTA.

I WAS perfectly charmed with the exquisite scenery on the banks of this river.

Mr. I. H. Stockqueler, in his interesting book upon British India, remarks: "It is astonishing that so little has ever been said and written about the extraordinary beauty of the banks of the Hooghly, in the environs of Calcutta. The scenery on either side of the river is charming. The mariner who has, during a long period, gazed upon nothing excepting sky and water, must fancy that Paradise has opened upon his wondering eyes. While the upper provinces of India, though boasting grander features (the Hooghly being the most sublime object in the picture we are contemplating), present, at various seasons of the year, very different aspects, Bengal is always the same. The moisture of its climate, and the nature of the soil, concur in preserving an eternal verdure, which is only to be seen during the season of the rains in the more arid districts. Even in the hottest weather, when the thermometer is up to 130°, perhaps for weeks together, and when the sun pours down so fierce a flood of light that it would seem as if its scorching influence were sufficient to dry up every blade of grass, the whole earth is covered with a rich carpet, and the moment that the sun sets, a refreshing coolness fills the air, and the eyes revel upon scenery of the richest luxuriance.

Calcutta, or, as it is sometimes called, the "City of Palaces," is looked upon as the metropolis of British India.

As I caught the first glimpse of it from a beautiful bend in the river, known as "Garden Reach," as our vessel slowly proceeded, the effect was of picturesque and matchless beauty.

About half a mile from the anchorage of the shipping, the whole splendor of the city at once bursts upon the sight.

The vast domes of the Government House, with its gates so superbly ornamented, the lofty spires of the numerous churches, numbers of public offices, magnificent private mansions, all faced with the purest white stucco, gracefully relieved by green Venetian blinds; numberless vast and handsomely built landing-places, the bishop's college, with its gothic towers, while we seemed surrounded by a perfect forest of noble masts, of every size and shape, green and luxuriantly fitted up; barges lying idly for hire, with their bright yellow rooms, altogether presented a picture of life and surpassing beauty.

Upon landing I found that between Fort William and the tower, about opposite the anchorage, there is a beautiful and well watered plain, called a *Maidaun*, somewhat similar to the esplanade in Bombay, on one side of which runs an aqueduct, and on the other side a handsome wide road, which every evening is crowded with every imaginable style of vehicles, and numbers of equestrians.

I made my way to Spence's Hotel, and having met Mr. Henry Coleman, mentioned in my Australian notes, he proceeded to advise me in reference to my opening night.

At Spence's I was furnished with a large airy room, and capital fodder (all excepting the *butter*, a thing you *carnt* get for any money in India!) for one hundred rupees (fifty dollars) a month. I had scarcely taken a seat at the table when my eye rested upon an old Californian, Aza Marvin, of the firm of Marvin and Hitchcock, the San Francisco pioneer book-store; and here I must also return him my thanks for his civilities and attentions. Flashing by me on a high mettled charger, dressed in the cool and snowy habiliments of the time, and looking handsome and bronzed with travel, was Charley S—— one of the lucky bankers of San Francisco, who was on his way to Thebes; while lying at anchor was the stately steamship "Golden Fleece," then commanded by my kinsman Captain John Vine Hall.

CII.

I MEET WITH CAPTAIN HALL AFTER AN ABSENCE OF TWENTY YEARS!

I WAS sitting quietly in my room, reading the morning paper, when I received a note from Captain Hall, requesting my immediate presence on board his steamship.

The meeting was most cordial, and questions flew thick and fast, as to my doings since as a small boy I parted from him at the London Coffee House in 1837!

He was about leaving for England, via the Cape of Good Hope, and the island of St. Helena, and though the temptation to reach England by that trip was very great, my friend offering me a passage, I had made up my mind to take the overland route; and accordingly could not avail myself of his kindness.

On the 17th December, I gave my first concert at the Masonic Hall, Calcutta, to one of the largest and decidedly most enthusiastic and aristocratic audiences, I have ever had the honor of appearing before.

Now, in these pages, I have been pretty frank and communicative with my readers, and if I had a chance to ring in a laugh at my own expense, I have done so, and as they have been informed that the result of my successful and brilliant career in the colonies of Australia was a profit of £1.10 currency, or $7.50 American coin—so shall they know the receipts of my entertainments during my brief residence in India.

In *Bombay* I gave four ballad concerts and readings, total receipts 4931 rupees. In *Calcutta* I gave one ballad concert and reading, receipts 1285 rupees. In *Howiah*, a country village on the opposite side of the Hooghly, one entertainment, receipts 450 rupees, total 6666 rupees, or £666.6—*thirty-five hundred dollars* American currency—and I think, my friends on this side of the water will agree with me that for six entertainments this is a pretty fair result.

The reader inquires about the expenses—I think £200 will cover them, so that I had about two thousand dollars clear.

And now, as I am about closing the brief account of my career in India, I wish to say a word or two in refer ence to my *first* and *last* appearance in this beautiful city.

The Masons very kindly gave me the use of their hall, and in every way were most obliging. To Messrs. Burkingyoing, the music-sellers, I am indebted for many acts of courtesy, and for the use of a very fine Erard's piano.

They sold also over four hundred tickets at two and a half dollars each, more by two hundred than they ever disposed of before for any entertainment.

The papers not only were very generous in the preliminary notices, but upon the day after the concert the *three dailies*, entirely unsolicited, and without my being personally acquainted with either of the editors, came out in the most enthusiastic manner, relating to my appearance.

CIII.

STREETS, HOTELS, ETC., ETC., ETC.

THE streets, private houses, and hotels in this city are greatly superior to those of Bombay.

The Auckland, almost as large as the Metropolitan in New York, and Spence's are the best.

The expense of living does not exceed 100 rupees or $50 a month, including bed-room and three meals a day, without wine.

The Town-Hall is a very handsome and spacious edifice, where the public meetings and dinners are given. The Courts of Justice, the Supreme Court, the Bengal Club, the Markets, the Government House, and the Racket Court, while the steeple of St. Paul's Cathedral, a really beautiful structure, reminds the looker-on of its excellent founder, the Right Reverend Bishop Wilson. Street after street is filled with stately buildings, showing the commercial importance of this city, as well as the ample means of the inhabitants and the liberal spirit which has contributed to the foundation of its many public institutions, or the tolerance of its people in religious concerns.

In the Metcalf Hall (a splendid building) is a very large public library, the Museum, and Library of the Agricultural and Asiatic Society; the Custom House, the Mint, a magnificent structure with gardens in front, Roman Catholic and Protestant churches, Hindoo Pagodas and Mahomedan Mosques, Medical Colleges, Masonic Lodges, numberless shops, filled with the richest articles of merchandise, whose gay windows and attractive show-cases dazzle the eye or tickle the fancy as if walking in Broadway or the Boulevards, all impart an importance and grandeur to this beautiful city.

Recently, in Calcutta, the electric telegraph has been introduced, and it was found most useful in the late rebellion.

Here also flourish a race-course and a cricket ground,

and the lovers of archery, rackets, and of aquatic sports have their respective "head-quarters."

And now, having taken my passage in the Peninsula and Oriental Company's steamship Candia, Captain Woodgate (a splendid fellow, by the way), for Aden, I shall say good-by to my hospitable friends in this place, and wishing them a "Merry Christmas" and a "Happy New Year," proceed upon my rambles.

CIV.

VOYAGE FROM CALCUTTA TO SUEZ.

In the first place, then, to fully appreciate the luxuriousness of travel on the "deep blue sea," you must take passage in one of the Peninsular and Oriental Company's steamships.

Large, airy state rooms, bathing rooms, wines and liquors of all kinds, *ad libitum*, obliging and attentive waiters, tables most sumptuously supplied, and the officers, from the highest to the most unimportant, gentlemanly, considerate, and obliging.

Then there is but "one class" of passengers—no "steerage," no intermediate—and, as a general rule, the time passes most delightfully.

I paid 1,050 rupees for my through ticket, or about $600. This, for a voyage of thirty days, appears rather expensive, but the trip is well worth it, and will ever remain in my memory as the most delightful of my "journeyings."

On the fourth day we arrived at Madras.

CV.

MADRAS.

We anchored in the Roads. It is very dangerous to land here. A tremendous surf rolls towards the shore with such fearful force, at certain seasons, that the greatest care has to be taken by the boatmen, or they must inevitably be swamped.

A very few hours on shore will suffice to instruct, amuse, or charm you.

The Madras houses, resting upon the sea-shore, are of white and pale yellow stucco with Venetian blinds. The total absence of all shade is extremely offensive to the eye.

We ordered dinner at one of the hotels, and started to see the sights. Went to the Hindoo school and the place where they burn the dead; returning, went into the Madras Club, where I was kindly received by the members.

Found the Golden Fleece steamship here.

Two days more brought us to the Island of Ceylon. Went on shore at Point de Galle.

After rambling about for several hours at the Island of Ceylon, picking oranges from the trees, inhaling the balmy atmosphere, my olfactories tickled by the fragrance of the spicy groves, and causing me to sing (to myself) the Missionary Hymn, we started once again for Aden.

CVI.

ADEN.

ARRIVING here at 12 A.M., in seven days.

Friday, 8th January.—I went on shore. A strange looking place, sure enough, is this! Called, I heard, the Gibraltar of Arabia!

Desolation, decay, and ruin seemed to reign supreme. Rocks barren, immense plains of sand, no sign of animated nature, and no sound save the incessant "braying of your donkey greets your ear."

The instant you land, an Arab horse or donkey is brought to you; upon one of these docile animals I was gently carried to the city (?) called Conception, some four miles off, and, with the exception of being chased by some Arabs (I having for the time lost my companions), who, doubtless, observing the shaky style of both rider and jackass, thought the capture both desirable and easy, I had a very agreeable and funny trip of it.

CVII.

SUEZ.

On the 15th January we arrived at Suez, not a very inviting locality externally. On shore everything denotes wretchedness and poverty.

The houses, built of large lumps of rock, cemented by mud or clay, mixed with water and sand; the inhabitants, looking uncomfortable and dirty, Arabs, Egyptians, and Turks; caravans of camels loading for Cairo, donkeys all ready for going, females veiled and masked, present a scene, to say the least, novel and exciting.

The hotel here was miserable, and heartily glad was I, after drawing lots for a seat in the Van to carry us partly over the desert, to find that at six we were to start.

These "Vans" are a sort of two-wheeled carriage, and carry six inside passengers—no springs, no ventilation, no room.

In the one in which I had a seat, a fat woman was my *vis-à-vis;* her weight (some 400) was too much for the concern, and down we all came.

The scene was most comical, the heat was great, the dust greater, and the delay annoying!

Some hours were consumed in repairing our conveyance, and about midnight we found ourselves in the middle of the desert, where the "snorting" of a great big steam-engine gave notice that the "cars" were in readiness to convey us the balance of our journey.

Yes! after having for a while anchored where the Israelites crossed the Red Sea, I found myself on the spot where "Joseph and his brethren" swapped coats, or where Moses and Sons (now of Houndsditch in the city of London) rested with their camels, jumping into a superb railroad car in which to make my entry into the far-famed city of Cairo! and the first view of the Pyramids of Egypt.

In 1856, Mr. George Francis Train, in his "Young America," says: "A telegraphic wire has been ordered, *a railroad is under way*, and shortly the whistling of a locomotive will startle the Bedouin from his sleep on his sandy pillow, and the rattling of a railway train across the bleached skeletons of the ass, the camel, the mule, will prove the sweetest of all sounds to those poor beasts of burden, whose labors have been so greatly lessened by the genius and the ingenuity of civilized man."

On the 16th January, 1858, I arrived in the *first train of cars*, and with lighted flambeaux was escorted to a really palatial-looking building called the British Hotel.

CVIII.

SHEPARD'S BRITISH HOTEL.

THE largest and best hotel in Egypt. The landlord has realized a fortune by his twelve or thirteen years' "keeping a hotel," and is consequently somewhat indifferent to the comforts of his guests. All is (or was) confusion, disorder, and ——— Egyptian! though from the advertisement on the back of his "card" (and which I subjoin) you would expect the comforts of the Fifth Avenue Hotel in New York, or Long's in Bond street.

THE BRITISH HOTEL.

CAIRO.

Baths. Billiards.

Within five minutes' walk of the Railroad Station.

The proprietor of this well known establishment, begs to call the attention of the Nobility, Gentry, and Travellers in general, to the recent alterations and improvements in this Hotel, which, combined with every comfort and convenience, attention *and moderate charges*, he hopes will obtain a continuance of the support he has so long enjoyed.

The wines, spirits, ales, &c., are of the first quality.

How this announcement would have astonished, and perhaps delighted the Egyptians of other days.

We found the hotel pretty full, and comfortable apartments somewhat difficult to obtain.

Took an early stroll through the city, reminding me very much of Constantinople and Smyrna, in the narrowness and dirt of the badly paved streets, and motley and grotesque appearance of the people.

Swift Arab horses, slow and sure-footed donkeys, with now and then a camel, standing in front of dirty bazaars or trotting by me, with their living freight, passed and repassed; my guide directing my attention first to the citadel mosque, where were the tombs of Mehemet Ali, called the most magnificent in Egypt. I got on the back of one of these mu-ils, and proceeded on my explorations.

CIX.

EGYPT.

My reminiscences of Egypt must necessarily be very meagre and limited, on account of the limited period of my sojourn in that mysterious land.

But managing to remain long enough to see the Pyramids, Pompey's pillar, and *threading* my way to Cleopatra's needle, besides being one of the pioneers of travel in the first train of cars that puffed and snorted its way across the desert, I feel a pleasure in devoting a page or so, worked up from stray notes made here and there in Alexandria.

It is all very well, and perhaps easy for that matter, to write learned pages about Egypt. Library shelves fairly groan with ponderous works on the subject, from which it were easy to copy; and to tell the truth, there is really something so mysterious, and almost sacred about the country, that it is difficult to resist the temptation of burnishing up one's school-boy teachings; but as my readers have long, ere this, become familiar with my "style," they will be spared the infliction of any very learned disquisitions upon the subject.

The climate here, it seemed to me, was most beautiful and inspiriting, and yet it appeared that the moon and the stars shone forth with a calm and serene beauty scarcely seen by me before, so exquisite was the scene on the night of my arrival; and then was it not worth the voyage to see the Pyramids bathed in the soft moonlight?

As I walked through some of the graveyards—of which there appeared to be numbers in Cairo—they seemed to me to be filled with the most delicious flowers; and I was informed that the Egyptians have the greatest affection for the simple and beautiful in nature—a little flower having more attraction for them than even an elaborate piece of machinery, or a sculptured work of marble. And after all, is this such poor philosophy? Isn't the heart made better by it?

> "Behold the lilies of the field! they toil not, neither do they spin; and yet I say unto you, that Solomon, in all his glory, was not arrayed like one of these."

I love flowers!—sweet is the ministry of even the humblest. We give them to the youthful bride; we lay them upon the pillow of the dead and upon their coffins, and plant them beside their graves; they are strewed in the pathway of the returning hero; and when festal days come round, they are twined into bright and fragrant garlands—and I say there is meaning, heart-meaning in their language.

I notice groups of Egyptian men and women resting by the graves of the keepers, and strewing upon and about them fresh and fragrant flowers. 'Tis a pretty fancy, at any rate, for they think the spirits of the loved and lost linger around—and perhaps they do—who can tell!

In all lands, and at all times, I think this notion—if I may so call it—has had a more or less strong hold upon the human mind. The Divine Teacher himself said of them: "Are they not all ministering spirits sent forth to minister" to us?

Perhaps some day we may better appreciate this unseen agency, and not think so disparagingly of the Easterns for it. And I think it would be a great deal better to believe in the "ghost stories" of old time nurseries, than not to believe *in incorporeal presences;* restrained by Divine revelation, it tends, I doubt not, to unmaterialize our natures.

Say what we may of Mahomedism, it seemed to me that there were some touching, nay, poetic beauties in it. It is a calm, contemplative, and almost unchanging faith, a great contrast to the Kaleidoscope-"isms" of the present age, where, in almost every street, city, town, village, and hamlet, we find places where people of all kinds of differing creeds meet, each having a different way of getting to heaven—each claiming to be the bright, particular, and only path to the heavenly life.

Another, to me, inexpressibly redeeming grace, has this same Mohammedism—*the grace of personal cleanliness!* for it seemed to me they were washing and bathing themselves all the time, and in clear running water; they have five daily ablutions, I was informed.

And now, winding up my short dissertation upon the disciples of Mahomet, I will inform the reader, that in the matter of "wives" (and I tell you I got a peep through the bars at a lot of beauties that had just arrived from the far-off Circassia)—the Mussulman is not on very short allowance; for he is permitted by his religion, four of the "second sex," as Miss Harriet Martineau styled them—and as far as his religious actions go, it is briefly this: that *prayer* takes the soul half-way to heaven—*fasting* to the door of that abode—and charity and benevolence take him in; and I think there have been worse platforms than this.

CX.

SOMETHING ABOUT THE PYRAMIDS.

It was a bright delicious morning when we started for the Pyramids; and by the way, no pen can describe the beauty of the early mornings here; the heavy dews had refreshed the earth and laid the dust—the latter the greatest annoyance in Egypt.

I had enjoyed one of Shepard's gorgeous baths, and refreshed the inner man with a breakfast fit for an Emperor; what we had before breakfast it may not be necessary to particularize.

My fat old friend, Captain M——, who is an orthodox oracle in such matters, recommended it, and we gracefully submitted to the prescription.

In all strange lands the recommendation of an old and observant resident, especially in such matters, is not to be slightly regarded; if it had been in any other place than poetic Egypt, the dose might have been called the unpoetic name of *gin-cock-tail.* At all events, it was not at all "bad to take," as the jolly party unanimously decided.

By the way, this fat friend, the old Captain, has taught the folks there a good deal about American drinks, and from what I saw, I should sav they take very kindly to them.

Although a slight digression, and in these short waifs and strays of my Egyptian recollections digressions may be pardonable, I cannot help noticing *Mrs. Walker's confectionery* establishment, for it is the rendezvous of all the American and English travellers.

A man may as well say he has not been in the Pyramids as not to "Widow Walker's."

Facing the Esbekia, one of the most delightful public walks in the two hemispheres, her shop, as the English call it, is quite an attraction.

I dined at her hospitable table one day, and a right jolly time we had of it. First of all "Stoughton and sherry," then soups, fish, flesh, fowl, fruits of every conceivable variety. With the exception of our party, there were not half-a-dozen Americans in the city; of these, two or three are missionaries, and this in a place having 400,000 population. Even the United States Consulate is held by a Greek, a most genial gentlemanlike person, by the way, doing all in his power to make Americans at home.

To continue my digression a little, I may add that very shortly numbers of Americans will be attracted to Egypt to settle.

My friend Captain M. informed me that the liberality of the present able, kind, and energetic Viceroy, particularly to Americans, is proverbial, and that many openings in business and trade in Cairo he is desirous of giving to Americans. He has taken a great fancy to them.

CXI.

ABOUT COTTON.

My informant told me that the Viceroy was bending all his energies to the proper cultivation of cotton: Egypt being a country of vast agricultural capabilities, foremost among its exportable products is the staple referred to. It is not generally known that the Egyptian cotton is of a very high grade.

In all European markets the Sea Island cotton of the United States stands first, the *next in value is the Egyptian*, the lowest is the Upland of the Southern States; the latter is hardly ever at more than half the price of either of the two former in all foreign markets.

There is no limit, he says, to the supply that Egypt can

furnish, so far as breadth of suitable land is concerned. The only difficulty is the inadequate supply of laborers.

These, it struck me, could be readily and cheaply obtained from India.

It appears that His Highness the Viceroy is quite alive to the permanent importance of this matter, and will soon furnish large supplies.

A few months before my arrival he had imported from Georgia a quantity of the Sea Island seed, and it has produced a cotton fully equal to the best Georgia.

But I had almost forgotten that we had had our breakfast prior to starting for the world-renowned Pyramids.

Let us mount our donkeys (mine began to kick immediately) and be off. Some eight or ten are before the hotel-door: one for myself, one for old Hassan, my Arab servant, a regular wag by the way, full of all manner of deviltry and fun, whom I may honor perhaps by again mentioning; another "moak" for my fat friend the Captain, and one for his servant; another for an American lady, and her attendant; making one of the merriest cavalcades that ever turned face pyramid-ward.

I must not fail to notice *the* donkey of the trip, a sort of miniature hotel, in the matter of refreshments, with a full pannier on each side.

What *was* in these panniers, or rather what was *not* in them, it would be difficult to tell.

If you wish to know them, the exclamation "Walker" will better answer the query.

A three hours' ride brought us to the base of the principal pyramid, and what a sight greeted me! I cannot find language to convey the faintest idea of the emotions it enkindled; they were not simply those of wonder but of awe. How into perfect nothingness dwindled every monument or pillar I had seen. I cannot imagine *why* these huge monuments were built. Most people, I believe, have a theory upon the subject; but it seems to me their origin as to time, circumstance, and cause, is utterly unknown.

The one I ascended was about 490 feet high. I reached the top by the aid of steps, about four feet apart; it was toilsome and somewhat dangerous, and the heat very great, but my guide took good care of me, and, gaining the top, desired me to look at our party left at the base. When lo! and behold! moving to and fro on the sand were half-a-dozen black specks, more like insects than human beings; and when my readers are informed that the *base* of this pyramid covered over twelve acres of land, standing upon a piece of ground much larger than the Park in New York, they will better, perhaps, appreciate the view I obtained upon reaching the summit.

It would be difficult for me to say, exactly, what I saw, for it appeared to me, above and below, to be one great sheet of sky and barren land; and from this dizzy altitude, as I looked on the two sister pyramids in the distance, the pointed minarets of the mosques at Cairo, I thought of those who, four thousand years ago, were standing on this same spot, and, like myself, speculating as to the origin of this stupendous pile, or the purposes for which it was erected.

Leaving the gates of Cairo, the pyramids were perpetually in sight; and as I stood on a high mountainous range, right on the edge of the desert, without any very particular thing with which to compare them, the great size of the pyramids did not so much strike me; but the nearer I reached them, the more their gigantic proportions grew upon me, until approaching the first layer of stones, I began to appreciate my own liliputian dimensions.

It took me about half an hour to get to the top. There are over 200 tiers of stone from one to four feet in height. A great part of the ascent was accomplished by me on my knees, assisted greatly by my two Arab guides.

I said just now it would be difficult for me to describe precisely what I saw, upon reaching this great altitude; but no person can stand at the top of this vast pyramid and gaze upon the dark mountains bordering the Arabian desert, upon the ancient cities of the Pharaohs, with their minarets, mosques, and domes, all glowing in the light of a burning sun, the beautiful valley of the Nile, the river of Egypt rolling at his feet, the range of pyramids and tombs extending along the edges of the desert to the ruined city of Memphis, and the eternal and boundless sands of Africa, without receiving impressions never to be effaced.

It is said that the great pyramid contains six millions of

cubic feet of stone, and that one hundred thousand men were employed twenty years in building it.

CXII.

ALEXANDRIA.

On the following day I left for Alexandria, and stopped at the Hotel d'Europe—a capital hostelry, and where I was kindly attended to; the landlord obliging, the table a capital one, and the charges moderate.

Having obtained, through the Consul, the necessary order, I went to the Pasha's palace, taking off my shoes before I crossed the threshold. Chaste and costly ornaments, floor inlaid with rosewood, pearl, and ebony; marble, highly polished and variegated; rooms fitted up with every luxury; baths of perfumed water, and bedsteads of solid silver, dazzle, bewilder, and astonish you. And really, in many respects, in and about the city, I found much to interest me.

The public square, on which the principal government buildings and hotels are situated, hardly has its superior in any city of its size in the world.

At evening it has very great attractions, especially when a gorgeous eastern full moon lights it up, and when its numerous promenaders bask in its light, listening to the capital band furnished by the Viceroy.

The environs of the town are singularly beautiful. Nowhere in the East did I see finer drives; the inhabitants seem to prize them, and the "turnouts" upon the road about sunset are of the best description; usually well built French barouches, drawn by symmetrical Arabian horses. The latter have not been over-praised, they cannot be; of the purest Arab blood, they seem admirably broken in, if broken in they can be said to be, for the Arab horse is by nature docile.

The Arabs treat their horses even more tenderly than they do their children. It is thought by many that the art which Mr. Rarey so eminently possesses is well known to the Egyptians; indeed, some think he received the idea from them.

I think Alexandria is, beyond doubt, destined speedily to become a commercial port of the first rank. The present Viceroy, it would seem, sees its importance, and is doing wonders in the premises.

The modern invention of the screw-steamer, as a means of propulsion, will materially aid him. The long and frequent calms in the Mediterranean render sailing vessels of comparatively little use, except for carrying coals and heavy goods thither, or in taking back grain; all lighter merchandise is carried by the screw-steamers.

While on this subject, and to wind up my Egyptian "notes," I may add that I was much interested in an invention which my American friend, Captain M., thinks he has made. It is that of a "*concentrated fuel.*" He reasons thus, and I think with a good deal of plausibility.

Take a ton of ordinary bituminous coal, for example, and put it under the boiler; *what becomes of this ton of coal?* A very considerable percentage, as everybody knows, escapes from the chimney in the form of smoke; another very considerable percentage is thrown overboard in the form of what they call "slag."

My friend referred to, proposes to divest the coal of these two useless elements *before* putting it on board ship; or, in other words, to "coke it" on shore. He expects to charge this coke with two important elements which are supporters of combustion; he will then reduce the mixture to a powder by proper machinery, then by powerful pressure to make it into compact, solid cubes of any desired size or weight. The experiments he has made, he assures me, are highly gratifying, and he is confident that *one ton measurement of this fuel will do the work of four tons of ordinary bituminous coal!*

The Viceroy is very desirous of creating a larger trade with the United States, and I was informed that his sympathies are most decidedly with America.

As I have before said he has had steam vessels-of-war built here; and he runs American cars on his railways.

It might be said that he could procure what he wants in the way of manufactures from England and France. But he does not like England. He has the sagacity to perceive that English influence has political as well as commercial objects in view; at least he *thinks* so; which, for all practical consequences, is the same thing. He is less jealous of the French, but as America can have no possible interest to serve beyond that which is purely commercial, he patronizes anything American.

Speaking of American manufactures, the Viceroy is just about to have under his consideration the introduction of American locomotive engines for his railway.

He also will turn his attention to American clothing for his army and navy. All these he now procures from England and France; but it is confidently believed that he can more cheaply and satisfactorily supply himself from America. An intelligent American, who has long resided there, is now in the United States, making the necessary examination; he will soon return thither, and large orders for the above will unquestionably be the result.

To dwell for a moment on the American locomotive engines. In many of the foreign countries, indeed in all where they have been tried, they are much preferred to the English. A most thorough comparative trial of them was not long since made on the Southern Railway of Chili, and the result was thus briefly summed up by the committee.

"The trial resulted in the superiority of the American Rogers' Locomotives of both classes, although the calculated power of the English engines was in each class twelve per cent. the greatest as to tractive power; and more as to fire surface and adhesion."

The time is near when American locomotives will take the place of all others in the Egyptian railways.

On the 20th of January I left Alexandria by steamship "Colombo," for Southampton; on the 25th reached Malta; on the 28th, Gibraltar.

Went on shore, made some purchases, and saw numbers of monkeys, scrambling up the rock.

Feb. 3.—Landed at Southampton, and put up at the Castle Inn—weather cold, rainy, and unpleasant.

CXIII.

SOUTHAMPTON.

ONCE again in England! After the exciting scenes I had gone through in India and elsewhere, the melancholy quiet, the gloomy and dismal appearance of everything in this sober-looking old town, was particularly noticeable.

A walk up High street, especially on a wet day, will be sure to give you the blues, and as it rains here six days out of the seven, the chances are, that you will be in that blissful state of feeling pretty much all the while.

It was in this town that I, by the advice and assistance of my agent, proposed to give my initiatory entertainment, having sent on in advance from Calcutta an advertisement to that effect.

Accordingly the walls were posted, and the papers attended to, and the Royal Victoria Rooms taken for Friday evening, Feb. 12, 1858.

I was standing in High street admiring the style of bill my printer had treated me to, when lo and behold my next door neighbors on the wall were Mr. and Mrs. Barney Williams, whom I had not seen since they left California in 1855, where by the way they played a most brilliant series of engagements, pocketing the neat little sum of $30,000 by the trip. Their talented relations, Mr. and Mrs. Florence, have been likewise wonderfully successful in England and in America, and were they to visit Australia and California, a rich reward, I think, would await them.

The rain (as usual) came down furiously, and consequently the people did not—but what with "complimentaries," distributed with a liberal hand by my indefatigable agent, H. C——, and a very decent sprinkling of paying persons—there was quite a respectable gathering of the "natives."

Now, the reader must be informed that we were both (myself and agent) sanguine, not only as to the attractiveness, but of the perfect success of at least a portion of the programme, with an English audience, the part relating to the recent *mutinies in India.* In this, as the sequel proved, we both committed an error, for the people appeared to care little about what had or had not occurred in India, or, as I thought the most likely, were entirely ignorant of there being such a country!

The "varied and interesting" entertainment (as the bills said) went off very well; the audience, though not particularly demonstrative, were appreciative and kind, and though the receipts did not warrant my engaging the Hall for several weeks, the performances elicited a handsome notice in the journals of the next day.

Taking a run over to Salisbury and Winchester, we gave a night at the Town Hall, in the latter fine old city, where I was honored by the patronage and presence of the Mayor thereof, a Mr. J. Dowling, who kept a haberdasher's shop, on the main street. I had also sent complimentary tickets to the boys of Winchester School, who honored me with their company, and seemed greatly pleased.

After visiting the magnificent old cathedral, we took the train for London, arriving there once again in my native city, on Saturday the 13th February, where, having written to my old landlady, Mrs. Scoone, for apartments, I found myself comfortably located at 30 Old Bond street.

CXIV.

LONDON ONCE AGAIN.

As the principal object of my visiting the métropolis upon the present occasion, was the introduction of my "Entertainment" and myself to the great big "public," I shall give my experience of some of the troubles, trials, and vexations, connected therewith.

First then, it is almost impossible for a *stranger*, male or female, rich or poor, to obtain a hearing—they are looked upon with suspicion and distrust. It is nothing to have received the stamp of approval from the highest in the land, in all portions of the globe,—they affect to know nothing about you in *London!*—you know! It is a fearful ordeal to pass through—but a "hit" once made here, a fortune is as certainly within your grasp as that the Sun shines in the heavens.

I came well introduced—and had been *twice* favored by being elected an honorary member of the "Garrick Club,"—had met socially the Editors of some of the leading Journals, and finally was taken in "hand" by one—whom they call "the Queen's head man," the well known Mr. John Mitchell, of the Royal Library, 33 Old Bond street—who directing his factotum—the good-hearted and erratic "John Nimmo," to superintend the "bringing of me out"—I proceeded to prepare myself to "face the music."

"Hanover Square Rooms" had been selected for the *debut*, and Monday, the 8th of March, the night of the performance.

Tickets had been most liberally scattered—not only to the Press, but had been sent by Mr. Mitchell to all the leading literary men in London.

CXV.

THE EVENT, AND WHAT OCCURRED.

As I left my lodgings in Old Bond street, about half-past seven, it (as usual) began to rain!

Upon reaching the private door of the "Rooms," the people were going in crowds, cabs and carriages lined the streets, and it was pretty evident that the place would be crowded to suffocation—and so it was! Too many tickets had been issued for the size of the room, and the noise, hubbub, and confusion were intense.

At a few minutes past eight, I went upon the platform, and commenced my "Introductory Address"—but I found it perfectly useless to proceed—as my voice was completely drowned in the storm of voices, the mingled screams of fainting women, shouting of the men, and crying of children! I stood for a minute or so, and placidly surveyed the scene—wondering the cause—and in a perfect quandary as to what to do; the noise continued—and amid cries of "order," "shame," "hisses," "put 'em out," "sit down," "we've got no seats," "humbug," "can't see," "can't hear," and the like, I walked off! fully determined on not appearing till the audience were quiet.

I waited perhaps ten minutes—when on I went—the noise still continuing—but upon my going to the piano, to sing my first song, it gradually subsided.

Now this in itself was enough to disturb and ruffle one, but as I proceeded with my motley programme—jumping from the comic to the serious—without the slightest continuity or connexion—I found out, and *felt* the mistake I had made, particularly in presenting the terrible account of the revolt in India, and the blowing away from the guns! and when my Sepoy servant—a real live native, in Indian costume, handed round the weapon to the audience, used by an English lady at Cawnpore in defending herself from the attacks of the mutineers, the effect produced was anything but pleasing—to myself or my audience. My entertainment concluded with the Charge of the Light Brigade, which was most enthusiastically received, and right glad was I when it was all over!

The papers the next day, as a general thing, were favorable, some highly complimentary—and I was strongly advised to repeat the performance, making some slight alterations in the programme; but I had accomplished my object, viz. appearing in the great metropolis before an

English audience alone and unassisted—and although in a pecuniary point of view I was not much benefited, I had gained a little experience as to the likes, dislikes, and requirements of a London audience.

As an illustration of the difficulty of making an impression, *i. e.* a favorable one, or what they call a "palpable hit" in London, and of the immense expense attending a proper introduction to a metropolitan audience, I will mention that in many instances hundreds of pounds have been sunk, houses, night after night, packed with free tickets and orders, and every conceivable plan resorted to, in order to gain the good-will of the people.

Albert Smith's first attempt as a "Lecturer" in his "Overland Mail" was a dead failure—but nothing daunted, he went at it again, and achieved success, fame, and fortune by his "Mont Blanc."

Mr. Henry Russell, perhaps, is the most remarkable instance of the success of a Monologue entertainment—he having retired some years since on a fortune of £60,000. This gentleman strongly advised me to remain in London, stating from what he had seen and heard of my first appearance, the impression I had made was favorable—that I should be patient, that I could remain profitably and permanently in London for months.

But I was restless, did not care about losing any more money, was anxious to get back to dear old New York, and make a running tour through the States, and settle quietly down.

In connexion with this matter, I shall trouble the reader with an extract from a very kind letter received by me while in London, from a gentleman of position and experience, which will be found somewhat *germane* to the subject.

PARK ROAD, REGENT'S PARK,
March 15, 1858.

STEPHEN C. MASSETT, ESQ.,

MY DEAR SIR:—Since I last addressed you, that mighty engine, the press, has pronounced on the merits of your debut at the Hanover Square Rooms. The opinions are certainly various—though some are highly complimentary, such as the "Morning Chronicle," the "Morning Advertiser," "Standard," "Lloyd's Weekly," the "Era," and even the "Times," though suggestive, and pointing out the non-adaptability of your selections to a London audience—is as a whole favorable—as it lauds your genius.

For myself, I discovered that you had not taken into account the true character, idiosyncrasies, peculiarities, and humor, of a promiscuous English audience, which is so phlegmatic and concentrative that it is a herculean task to move them, and when moved to change the current of their bent. It was in this you failed; to the discriminating yours was an intellectual treat of a high order—you demonstrated the rare genius of portraying the deepest pathos, in juxtaposition to the extravagantly grotesque. To the mercurial American, Australian, Anglo-Englishman, or Dutchman, these sudden undulations—these touches of humanity—in contrast to the graphic delineations of the incongruous—would have been like carbonic acid on wine of life—they would have relished the draught with zest; not so with cold apathetic John Bull—avoid these powerful antagonisms, and success is your own!

"Nothing could excel your various recitations. So great, indeed, was the effect produced, that several ladies were moved to tears; but to my chagrin, on the next instant you introduced a burlesque representation—though true to life, still not in taste. The mind cannot tolerate such a sudden revulsion—the antithesis is repulsive."

* * * * * *

CXVI.

MR. SHIRLEY BROOKS.

THIS gentleman, so well known and esteemed in England and in this country as a delightful writer, as well as one of the bright ornaments of the Illustrated News and of Punch, I had the pleasure of meeting upon one or two occasions, and was by him very cordially received. In a letter from him, acknowledging one I brought him from Calcutta, he thus writes—

"If there is any advice or assistance that I can give you towards promoting your object here, I need not say it is most heartily at your service.

"I have received the highest accounts of your talents, and indeed genius, and it would appear to me that an Entertainment, *written to the present requirements of London audiences*, is all that you require to secure the best possible of positions."

So much for my first and last appearance in the good old city of London.

Having taken farewell of the dear public, I turned my attention, for the few weeks I remained in England, to sight-seeing and amusements generally.

CXVII.

THE DERBY DAY.

On the 19th of May, I started with my friend H. C. for the Derby races. We went democratically, and by rail. Such a sight, in point of numbers, I had never witnessed, excepting on the Esplanade at Bombay. There were over 100,000 persons on the ground, of all sizes, ages, sexes, and degrees. From my lofty and somewhat rickety seat on the Grand Stand, that cost me a guinea, my companion pointed out to me some of the celebrities. I distinctly saw Lord Derby, standing by the head of his horse, patting him, and carefully seeing that he was properly attended to—(Toxophylite, I think the name was),—while Sir Joseph Hawley led his winning horse Beadsman, evidently satisfied that he had made *all he* could on that day! I was informed that he had won over £50,000! Dukes, lords, baronets, and knights, played at single-stick with costermongers, jugglers, pie-men, and sweeps; for all is fair on the Derby day. Thimble-riggers and "little joker" men passed the time o' day with a learned judge or a fashionable marquis; while in the snowy hand of a lady, a hām sandwich was invitingly clutched, preparatory to swallowing a glass of sparkling ale, which a distinguished member of parliament was drawing from a beer barrel on the top of a drag or four-in-hand. Patient-looking donkeys stood before huge wagons, containing miniature theatres with a stove pipe running through the roof; while a small man with a big drum, and a fat woman with a clinking triangle, on the portable step-ladder, invited the people into the show. Every imaginable style of vehicle was on the field, and all conditions of persons represented, and exchanging with each other good-natured nods. The dust kicked up on the return to town was something fearful, and the sight one to be remembered. Pell-mell went everybody and everything—dog carts, drags, broughams, gigs, cabs, hansoms, four-in-hands, spring carts of all sizes and shapes, carriages, close and open, filled with shouting men, women, and children, chased or stumbled against each other, while friendly recognitions, in the shape of a well-picked knuckle of lamb, a cold potato, or a stale loaf, with well-directed aim, from nobody knows where, caught you on the "top knot," or fell into the lap of a Belgravia beauty, unnoticed, and only laughed at; for all is fair on the Derby day.

CXIX.

THE GARRICK CLUB.

On the 17th of April, I was elected a second time an honorary member of this delightful association, and received the following note informing me of the fact:

Garrick Club, 17 April, 1859.

Sir:—I have the honor, by the direction of the Committee, to inform you that they have this day had the pleasure of electing you an honorary member of the Garrick Club.

Your most obedient servant,

S. C. Massett, Esq. Alex. Doland, *Secy.*

This is one of the pet clubs of London, and in point of comfort, completeness of its internal arrangements, luxuriousness of the living, the regularity, order and system that prevail—to say nothing of the delightful people that you meet with in close communion, and the generous welcome you receive, renders it one of the favorite places of resort for those who are fortunate enough to be elected a member.

The smoking-room is quite an institution of its kind. Over the door, in gold lettering, is a notice, something like the following:

"This room is exclusively intended for members of this club, on no pretence whatever are strangers admitted."

My good friend, Mr. Lyster O'B., had informed me, that this did not apply to me, and that I should feel myself as much a member as any one of their number; and that in this room all the fun and jollity took place.

I had the pleasure of being presented, among others, to the President thereof, Lord Tenterden, who in the warmest and most genial manner welcomed me, and from whom, since my return to America, I have received a very kind note, in which his lordship remarks:

"Should you again visit England it will give me sincere pleasure to renew our acquaintance—we propose to build a large house, and upon some future occasion will rejoice to bid you welcome to our new home, and to old friends."

Some of the most delightful hours were passed at this club. I met Thackeray once or twice, the first time in 1853, at the Fielding, immediately after his return from America, where he had given with great success his Lectures upon the Georges.

During a brief conversation with him about San Francisco, he turned to me and said, "Who is the funny man of California?"—I replied that there were a great many funny men—that I did not know exactly to whom he referred. Why, replied Mr. T., the man who wrote those astronomical burlesque sketches in the Knickerbocker Magazine. I knew then that he referred to the late Lieut. Derby. I thought the question, coming from one who is at times so cynical, something of a compliment for the late Mr. John Phœnix Squibob.

CXX.

CHARLES DICKENS'S FIRST READING IN LONDON.

On Thursday evening April 15, 1858, at St. Martin's Hall, Mr. Charles Dickens commenced for the first time in public his "Readings."

He had been advertised for some weeks beforehand, in the principal Journals of the day, and all the reserved seats had been taken.

I went with some friends at least an hour before it commenced, and had the greatest difficulty in elbowing my way into the room.

Streets fairly blocked up with carriages, men, women and children, and the greatest confusion prevailed.

Precisely at eight, preceded by Mr. Arthur Smith, Mr. Dickens stepped on the platform. It was the first time that I had seen him, and I certainly should not have recognised any resemblance to the plaster busts, with the long flowing curly hair, round and beardless chin, that were so common here twenty years ago.

Mr. Dickens was at this date about forty-six. His hair was of an iron grey color, he wore a pretty full beard, a sort of goatee; he had on a very white waistcoat, and a very large bouquet attached to the left lappel of a black dress coat. After adjusting the lamps on either side of him, and not once looking at the audience, or in the slightest degree acknowledging the storm of applause with which upon his entrance he was greeted—and opening a large book, which appeared to me to be printed on one side of the leaf, in very large type, and carrying in his hand an ivory paper knife, with which he tapped the page of his book—and first moistening his lips with the inevitable tumbler of water, he commenced to read his celebrated Christmas Carol.

Dickens, without any exception, is the finest "reader" I have ever heard; there is nothing of the stereotyped gesticulation, intonation, or attitudinizing of your professed elocutionist—there is no straining for effect—it is natural, quiet, straightforward, and from the individuality with which each character is invested, it becomes intensely interesting as the story proceeds. His voice is resonant and unctuous, and wonderfully sympathetic, and I was informed that in private he is esteemed to be one of the finest of actors.

Laughter and sobbings alternately rewarded his efforts, and when you take into consideration that there were over £400 in the house, it will be perceived that the whole affair must have been to him highly satisfactory.

Since that time, as the public is aware, Mr. Dickens has continued with the most unbounded success, his "Readings," and it is said he easily realizes £10,000 a year by this single effort.

CXXI.

THE SHAKSPEARE DINNER AT THE GARRICK CLUB.

THIS was one of the most delightful réunions I was present at in London; none but members of the Club were admitted, and I think about three hundred sat down to dinner. Mr. Charles Kean was in the chair, and made a capital speech; Dickens, I was sorry to see, left early, and did not respond, as he was expected, to the toast of "Literature and the Arts"—he had a previous engagement, it appeared, and slipped away unobserved. I had heard so much of the cleverness of his off-hand speeches, that I regretted very much his leaving. Sir Charles Taylor, in introducing, or rather calling upon Mr. Thackeray to respond, brought the author of "Pendennis" on the floor, who, first adjusting his spectacles, and placing his right arm in his ponderous waistcoat, replied somewhat peevishly at first, but at length warmed up—and drew a beautiful little sketch of an imaginary conversation that the different pictures hanging on the walls of the dining-room of the old Garrick, were having together, and wondering among themselves in their lonely apartment, what the absent members were talking about, and doing. It was excessively graphic and amusing.

This speech, and Mr. Kean's, were the principal efforts of the night.

CXXII.

HANGING AT THE OLD BAILEY.

I HAPPENED to be in London on Monday, 26th of April, 1858, the day of the execution of a young Italian, named Giovani Lani, who had been tried and convicted of the murder of a female in the Haymarket. The affair created quite a sensation at the time, and though the offence was a very aggravated one, and the prisoner himself had fully confessed his guilt, still from his extreme youth, only nineteen, and the fact of his being a foreigner, and unable to speak or understand English, he excited a good deal of sympathy.

Dining the day previous with a friend who informed me that he knew the method of obtaining two good seats for five shillings each, and that it was his intention to be present, we, on the night before, took a cab to Newgate street, and at the small tavern immediately opposite the jail, on the second floor, we secured two "chairs."

Upon some occasions, fabulous sums are paid for a good "view;" ten, fifteen, and twenty pounds, have been freely given.

I was informed that the floor above me had been taken by Lord ———, for five pounds, and that his Lordship was then up-stairs, with some boon companions, passing the night in song and merriment.

Wishing to avoid the crowd as much as possible, we were on the ground at the early hour of four, but even then the streets were filled with people, and at the door-steps of the houses were seated, men, women, and even children, some eating and drinking, having passed the night in the open air, to be in readiness for the event.

As daylight appeared, the excitement in the street below became more and more intense, and about half-past seven, one mass of human beings jammed together so tightly that ingress or egress seemed impossible, swaying to and fro like the heaving of the sea, whilst the hubbub, noise, and din of voices arising from this heterogeneous concourse of people, really resembled its roaring—as the first stroke of the big clock of old St. Sepulchre's church fell upon the ear, announcing the hour of eight, it seemed to act like an electric shock upon the multitude:—the sight beggars description: the roofs of the houses swarmed with human beings in the distance; from the railings of St. Sepulchre to the corner of Newgate, and Fleet street, it was one moving mass of humanity; and from this teemful and excited mob, there rose a yell so demoniacal and appalling that the lookers-on from the windows seemed to shrink from the hearing of it, while the clock was pealing its slow and solemn dirge—and the last note—the hour of eight—had died upon the ear, the raving, tearing, crushing, and heaving to and fro of the multitude, resembled more the ocean, when lashed by the ragings of a storm, than anything else I know of;—when suddenly the head of the culprit appeared upon the black platform, accompanied by the Sheriffs of London, the clergyman, and Calcraft, the executioner,—the yelling, tearing, and shouting ceased, and saving and excepting a few cries of "hats off"—"that's him"—and the like—all was comparatively still.

The preliminaries over—the rope was placed around his neck—the black cap put upon his head, covering his face—the rope was cut—and the body dangled in the air—then ere the spirit had fled, arose the shoutings, hootings, and yellings of a thousand voices—some crying out "'Ere's the last speech and confession of Giovani Lani, hung just now," "ony a 'a-penny"—in half an hour the crowd had dispersed, and I and my companion wended our way homeward, heartily sick, and weary of the disgusting scenes and incidents attending an execution at the "Old Bailey." As we left the Tavern, the landlord stepping up to me said: "Here's a new riddle just come out, Sir"—Vy is Calcraft, the Hexecutioner, like the Prince 'o Vales? Cos he went to Kill Lani—(Killarney!)

The following verses accompanied his "last dying speech and confession," and were sold for a halfpenny.

My victim was, which I have found,
A married woman on the town,
The Haymarket she rambled round;
  It was there I did her meet.
She had, it seems, one night a dream,
Which often caused her grief and pain;
She told it o'er, and o'er again,
She always thought she would be slain,
  Alas! it was too true.

Then I on board a ship was found,
That was to Monte Video bound,
To Greenhithe she had sailed down,
  The Sea was calm and clear,
I out of sight, thought all was right,
But oh, alas! I was deceived,
The truth I scarcely could believe,
On board when justice captured me,
  A cruel murderer base.

That barbarous cruel deed I done,
Tho' young in years my time has come,
Oh! pity your unhappy son,
  My loving parents dear,
I'm doomed to go to the grave below,
Giovanni Lani, is my name,
In sorrow, wretchedness and shame,
I do confess I am to blame,
  She never injured me.

Young men, a warning take by me,
Behold me trembling on a tree,
Think what must my feelings be,
  In vigor, youth and bloom,
A sad young man, in a foreign land,
I wish I never had been born;
To die a dreadful death of scorn,
My glass is run and now forlorn,
  I hasten to the tomb.

At the West End of London town,
Where pretty maidens ramble round,
One night I Heloise Thaubin found,
  And she looked fair and gay,
I with her did steer, to a brothel near,
That night she looked in health and bloom,
She took me to the fatal room,
Where soon I sent her to the tomb,
  'Twas there I did her slay.

I on a foreign land must die,
Look down with pity from on high,
Alas! no friend or kindred nigh,
  My wretched end to see,
Unhappy man, in a foreign land,
My days must end upon a tree,
Oh! how could I so cruel be,
A female who never injured me,
  Inhumanly I slayed.

I strangled her, you may suppose,
I robbed her of her watch and clothes,
Then from the fatal spot did go,
  Thinking that I was clear,
God's all-seeing eye, was hovering nigh,
Taken I was doomed to be,
And I from justice could not flee,
They brought me to the fatal tree,
  For I'm condemned to die.

CXXIII.

A VISIT TO DOCTORS' COMMONS, LONDON, AND TO THE SURROGATE'S OFFICE, NEW YORK. THE CONTRAST.

IMMEDIATELY in the rear of St. Paul's Church, up a very narrow court, is the celebrated place for the depository of wills.

Thither I went one morning from sheer curiosity, to look at the will of a deceased relative, who I thought might have accidentally left me a few shillings.

Entering a little green baize door, covered all over with brass nails, with an oval piece of glass let into the top panel, I encountered a bald-headed gentleman, seated on a very high three-legged stool, to whom I paid one shilling, for the privilege of looking at the aforesaid will.

Pointing dismally with a very shaky and rickety looking ink-dyed first finger, to another door, he told me to enter, and keep straight on until I came to a larger room with a number of desks in it, where I should receive further directions. This I soon found, and I will endeavor to describe what I saw—and what I did. Everything was as silent as the grave—nobody spoke above a whisper—and those who walked stepped on tiptoe from desk to desk, as though some frightful calamity had just happened. Dark, dank, dismal, and gloomy looked everybody, and everything. Shelves covered the walls of the apartment, upon which had rested for *hundreds of years* ponderous books, all duly labelled, and lettered from A to Z, and I have not the slightest doubt (though I forgot to ask for it), that the will of Adam, Cain, and Abel, or Mr. Noah, if they ever made any, could be found here.

Approaching the desk of the *clark* who had charge of the letter "C"—the one I wanted—I gave him the name, and as well as I could remember, the date of my relative's death; and when the reader is informed that I commenced to "go over the C's" at about ten o'clock in the morning, and *continued until two in the afternoon*, and was told that there were about fifty more books of the same letter and date to look through, my disgust can be imagined, and I gave it up in despair. A man, while I was standing there, actually gave the name of "Brown," which I noticed created a gentle titter among the "Noggs," one of whom, with a shrug of the shoulder, pointed in the direction of the "B's, who evidently seemed desirous of being "Busy" about other things just at that moment. Without exaggeration there were over *twenty shelves* of "B's,"—think of wading through the begrimed dusty pages of a big book covered with cobwebs, on a hot summer's day, to look for what you cannot find.

The fittings-up and furniture of this room were of the most antique description, and I should imagine had known no change for at least a century. There were the high old dark mahogany desks, with dangling brass handles and innumerable pigeon-holes, and three-legged stool to match, the top of which, scooped out and well polished by constant use and friction, was only reached by a gymnastic spring, that was particularly ludicrous upon some occasions to witness; old pewter ink-stands, with long quills, and feathers at the end, stuck in 'em, while the remaining paraphernalia might have been supposed to belong to the Bookkeeper in Noah's ark. Through the thick and heavy sashes of the window-frames, with the panes black with dust and smoke, you look into a court-yard, where there is a little scrap of verdure and a small "Fountain;" out of this window an old gentleman was gazing, with both hands stuck into his breeches pocket—very much after the order of Mr. Pickwick—when the following rather amusing incident took place. But first, I must inform the reader that all the "Noggs" in this department looked more like very gloomy and retired undertakers, than anything else I know of.

The old *clark*, above referred to, was dressed in a seedy suit of black, with very tight-fitting knee-breeches, and gaiters to match, and carried about with him as fine a pair of calves as ever twinkled behind a carriage in Belgravia; as his back was only at first visible, I could simply notice the peculiar cut of the coat, which very much resembled Mr. Toodles's—the tail descending nearly to the heel—and from one of the pockets was hanging, as if to dry, a very uncomfortable-looking handkerchief, of doubtful color; his bald head loomed up from the collar of his coat like a moon on the half shell, while sticking out from each side of his top-knot were little streaks of white hair, that—to carry out the simile—might be likened to a couple of flakes of a silver cloud in attendance on the orb of night.

The letter "H" came under this gentleman's immediate supervision; and as I noticed a man approach him, who had evidently had a drop too mnch, I thought some fun was brewing, and I accordingly remained to see the sport.

"*I wish ter-look-er Mish-er Hansom's will if splesh?*"

"Sir," said the fat old gentleman—placing the palm of his hand on the top of the stool, and the other on the desk, and giving rather a dignified spring he reached the top, securing each leg thereof with his fat calves—"what name did you say?"

"Misher Hansom's"—very emphatically asporating the "H."

Directing the applicant to about a dozen shelves, filled with immense books, with "H" stamped on each, he gloomily resumed his own occupation.

It was amusing to see the man with "a drop too much," standing very unsteadily against the railing, with trembling finger, going up and down column after column, mumbling to himself—

"*Thers-sno-Hansom-ere — died-i-year-eighteenern-nineteen dam fers an-will. Hansom's name—dam ftaint-Willm Hanson's name—(hic). I say, Mister 'sno name ere all—(hic). Wont-yer look-slf?—(hic)*—Isay"—and with this he pushed the book against the old gentleman's elbow, who, turning sharply round, said very pettishly :—

"Do you spell it with a 'Hay' or a H?" *exasperating* the last letter fearfully.

"*Vith a 'Hay,' f-course—didn't I tellr-sho-jst now!*"

Then again directing him to *look over* the first letter of the alphabet, he cast a dismal look at a series of shelves loaded with books, all marked "A," first telling the old gentleman, very disrespectfully, that he'd see him d——d first. He wabbled out of the apartment—and now for the contrast.

I had occasion to look at the will of a once resident of the city of New York, and for that purpose repaired to the office of the Surrogate.

I simply stated to the clerk the name of the deceased, when—as if it was the only will in existence—he opened a drawer, and handed it to me.

The "styles" were so opposite, that I thought a relation of the facts might amuse the reader.

CXXIV.

THE HON. MRS. NORTON.

HAVING received a very pleasant note from this delightful authoress, inviting me to call upon her, I duly presented myself at the appointed hour, at her cosy town residence in Chesterfield Street, May Fair; but let my visit be prefaced by an extract from her polite note :—

"I assure you I always regret any missed opportunities of making or renewing acquaintance with those who come from the 'far West,' where I have many well-remembered friends."

Mrs. Norton received me most kindly; and though on

the other side of fifty, is still a magnificent-looking woman, with large lustrous black eyes; dark, thick, and luxuriant hair, very slightly tinged with grey; teeth of perfect whiteness and regularity, and a voice extremely musical.

Her manners are most fascinating, and many were her inquiries of the poets of this country—of Bryant, Longfellow, Halleck, and Willis, she spoke particularly. While conversing with her, I could not help thinking of the beautiful description of this world-renowned songstress in *Willis's* poem of the "Lady Jane," and though written over twenty years ago, is still so faithful a portrait of her.

This lady will be remembered as one of the three sisters "Sheridan," who, by the unanimous voice of England, popular and aristocratic, have been indisputably pronounced the "three Graces;" they are three women of a degree of beauty seldom seen. The youngest of them, Lady Seymour, was voted by acclamation, "Queen of Beauty," for the "Eglinton Tournament." Lady Dufferin, the other sister, is the wife of Lord Dufferin, and is celebrated for her wit, as the other two for the specialities of beauty and genius.

Mr. N. P. Willis told me, that the *most beautiful woman he ever saw was Mrs. Norton.*

Here are the charming verses before referred to:—

She had a low, sweet brow, with fringéd lakes
  Of an unfathom'd darkness couch'd below;
And parted on that brow in jetty flakes
  The raven hair swept back with wavy flow,
Rounding a head of such a shape as makes
  The old Greek marble with the goddess glow.
Her nostril's breathing arch might threaten storm—
But love lay in her lips, all hush'd and warm.

And small teeth, glittering white, and cheek whose red
  Seem'd Passion, there asleep, in rosy nest:
And neck set on as if to bear a head—
  May be a lily, may be Juno's crest,—
So lightly sprang it from its snow-white bed!
  So proudly rode above the swelling breast!
And motion, effortless as stars awaking
And melting out, at eve, and morning's breaking;

And voice delicious quite, and smile that came
  Slow to the lips, as 'twere the heart smiled thro':—
These charms I've been particular to name,
  For they are, like an inventory, true,
And of themselves were stuff enough for fame;
  But she, so wondrous fair, has genius too,
And brilliantly her thread of life is spun—
In verse and beauty both, the "Undying One!"

CXXV.

LEAVE ENGLAND FOR NEW YORK.

On Saturday, 29th May, 1858, I sailed in the steamship Asia, Captain Lott, once again for New York, and arrived after a somewhat dreary and foggy passage, on the 10th June, at Jersey City.

After receiving the congratulations and kind greetings of dear and cherished friends, in this most fascinating city, after my world-rounded voyages, I set to work to prepare myself for a "First Appearance" in the Metropolis of America, in a "*Monologue Entertainment.*"

CXXVI.

A VISIT TO IDLEWILD.

Having received a very pleasant invitation from Mr. N. P. Willis, to pass a few days at his country residence on the banks of the Hudson, I wish briefly to chronicle the event, for two reasons: *First*, as a slight acknowledgment for the hospitality and kindness with which, by himself and his family, I was treated; and, *secondly*, I wish to have the pleasure of paying thus publicly a very humble tribute to his genius.

Some months since, I read in a London Journal, an extract from a Lecture delivered by a well known gentleman of the Metropolis, in which he was speaking of the relative merits of the writers of the present day.

He spoke of Mr. Willis as belonging to that class which (he thought) had *never been properly appreciated.* He did not, neither shall I, offer in this brief sketch, any particular analysis of his writings, either in prose or verse. What I wish to remark is simply this: that I have not read, neither can I conceive anything finer in the English language, than his scriptural poems; these—and they are some of his earliest efforts—have never been properly estimated, and I was going to say hardly known.

His "Raising of Lazarus," the "Leper," and the "Daughter of Nain," entitle him to occupy the highest niche in Fame's poetic temple; and as the eye runs over the word-painting of these exquisite creatures of his fancy, the picture of the scene, events, and circumstances, is as perfect as if fresh from the hand of the most distinguished limner.

In Harper's Magazine for January, 1858, is a very pleasantly written sketch, beautifully illustrated with etchings, from the pen and pencil of T. Addison Richards, the artist.

In reference to the nomenclature of this beautiful spot, Mr. Willis says: "Idlewild belonged to a very valuable farm, but it was a side of it which, from being very little more than a craggy ravine—the bed of a wayward torrent—had always been left in complete wilderness. When I first fell in love with it, and thought of making a home amidst its tangle of mountains, my first inquiry as to its price was met with the disparaging remark, that it was of little value: only an idle wild, of which nothing whatever could be made; and that description of it stuck captivatingly in my memory—'Idlewild, Idlewild' then shall be the name."

CXXVII.

"UNDERCLIFF."

THIS is the name of the summer dwelling of the genial lyric poet, General George P. Morris, who, for so many years, has been connected with Mr. Willis in the publication of the Home Journal. In the February number of the Art Journal, published in London for 1861, is an exquisite sketch of this charming spot. The writer remarks:

"It is a substantial edifice of Doric simplicity in style, perfectly embowered when the trees are in full leaf, yet commanding, through vistas, some charming views of the river and the neighboring mountains. Northward, and near it, rises Mount Taurus, with its impending cliff that suggested the name of the poet's country seat. It is the old 'Bull Hill' which, in Irving's exquisite story of 'Dolph Heylinger,' 'bellowed back the storm' whose thunders had 'crashed on the Donder Berg, and rolled up the long defile of the Highlands, each headland making a new echo.'"

A late writer has justly said of "Undercliff:"

"It is a lovely spot—beautiful in itself, beautiful in its surroundings, and inexpressibly beautiful in the home affections which hallow it, and the graceful and genial hospitality which, without pretence or ostentation, receives the guest, and with heart in the grasp of the hand, and truth in the sparkle of the eye, makes him feel that he is welcome."

No one connected with the Press of New York has been more considerate, kind-hearted, and generous to musicians, artistes, or actors, than General Morris; and the writer of these lines, who has had the pleasure of an acquaintance with him for many years, trusts he may long live to grace with his ballads the literature of his native land.

16

It is hard to find a kindlier nature than the nature this gentleman possesses.

CXXVIII.

WASHINGTON IRVING.

On Wednesday, the 11th August, 1858, I went with my friend J. T. B—— to the funeral of Judge Duer, at Trinity Church.

Washington Irving was one of the pall-bearers, and at the grave, as the mourners were standing over it and looking at the coffin, I had the pleasure of being introduced to Mr. Irving by Judge Daly, of this city.

I had just time to say that I had recently returned from England, and had brought with me, from his friend Colonel Wildman, of Newstead, a little memento of friendship, when he replied that he should be most happy, at any time, to see me at "Sunnyside."

Having been on a brief visit to Mr. Louis Gaylord Clark, then editor of the Knickerbocker Magazine, and having stated to him my desire to call upon Mr. Irving, I left his pleasant cottage at Piermont, crossing the Hudson to Tarrytown and Irvington.

The cottage is most romantically situated, amid a cluster of trees, with the magnificent old Hudson in glorious proximity, and is the very quintessence of quiet and repose.

In answer to the bell, a servant informed me that Mr. Irving was at home, and, upon taking my card, she returned with the answer that he would see me in the Library.

He very soon entered, and, extending his hand, greeted me most cordially.

I had sent him, with the picture that I had brought from Newstead Abbey, a printed sketch of my Wanderings, and he seemed quite desirous of chatting, inquiring particularly about the Sepoy rebellion, a portion of which I had the year before witnessed in India.

He had taken a great fancy to Hood's ballad "I Remember," and asked me if I had any objection to sing it to him.

Of course I readily assented, and, seeing the piano open, was about to commence when I noticed a gentleman apparently much older than himself, with very silvery locks, intently reading a newspaper. I said, "I'm afraid, sir, I shall disturb that gentleman." "Not at all, not at all," said Mr. Irving; "it's my brother Jacob, he's as deaf as a post; if you were to fire off a cannon he'd be none the wiser!" He, and his nicees, to whom I had been presented, seemed much pleased with the song, Mr. Irving remarking at its conclusion that the last verse always made him *feel like crying*, and that he regarded Hood as one of the most delightful and genial of poets.

He spoke of the delightful interviews he had with Tom Moore and Sir Walter Scott. George Frederick Cooke was his beau-ideal of an actor. In speaking of the hours he devoted to writing, he said: "I am now on my fifth volume of the Life of Washington, and I hope I shall not 'pop out' before it is finished!"

I asked him if he had ever met Byron? He replied: "No, it's very strange; but we were always playing 'hide and seek' with each other. On more than one occasion we were to have met at one of Rogers' breakfasts, but there was always a disappointment."

In speaking of Dickens, and upon my telling him how delighted I was with his "Readings," he said: "I fell in love with Dickens when he wrote the character of 'Little Nell,' and could not resist the temptation of writing to him thanking him for the pleasure he had given me. To this letter he was good enough to reply. But upon the publication of his 'American Notes' all my affection for him vanished, and I avoided calling upon him in England, and have never had the desire to read a line that he has since written."

We spoke of old Kean; he then gave me an imitation of his peculiar *whispering on the stage*, telling me that it could be heard over the whole house.

The servant having announced lunch, we proceeded to the breakfast-room, and here, alone with Mr. Irving, I had the pleasure of gratifying a long cherished wish, which was this:

As a boy I had revelled in the beauties of his "Sketch

Book," and my visit to "Stratford upon Avon" was entirely attributable to the delight experienced in reading his exploits at the "Red Lion" Inn; he winds up his sketch thither in the following exquisite sentence, which I had always longed to repeat to him in person. The time had come. I expressed to him what I have now told the reader, when he replied: "It will give me the greatest pleasure to hear it. What can it be—I have forgotten!"

I then repeated:

"How would it have cheered the spirit of the youthful bard when wandering forth in disgrace upon a doubtful world he cast back a heavy look upon his paternal home, could he have foreseen that before many years he should return to it covered with renown, that his name should become the boast and glory of his native place, that his ashes should be religiously guarded as its most precious treasure—and that its lessening spire on which his eyes were fixed in tearful contemplation, should one day become the beacon, towering amidst the gentle landscape, to light the literary pilgrim of every nation to his tomb!"

Mr. Irving held out his hand to me, and with moistened eye, said:

"It's very kind of you to remember so much of my scribbling—indeed, I had forgotten it."

In his sketch of Stratford, Mr. Irving remarked:

"I thought it something to have seen the *dust* of Shakspeare." I deem it an honor to have sat at the same table, and enjoyed two hours of pleasurable intercourse with Washington Irving.

CXXIX.

MY FIRST CONCERT AT NIBLO'S.

I HAD now completed my "Entertainment," which I had somewhat changed and remodelled, calling it, "*Song and Chit-Chat of Travels in many Lands*," and taken the Concert Room at Niblo's for Thursday evening, the 23d of September, 1858.

The result was a crowded house, the entertainment being an unequivocal success. On the following morning the journals spoke of it in the most complimentary manner.

I continued to itinerate for the next month or two in Hoboken, Brooklyn, Newark, Philadelphia, Hartford, and finally made my first appearance in the good old city of Boston.

CXXX.

HENRY W. LONGFELLOW.

WHO has not heard of the celebrated bookstore of Ticknor & Fields, in Boston? Well, it was on a pleasant afternoon in October, '58, that in the little back snuggery or "sanctum sanctorum" of the poet-publisher, James T. Fields, I had the pleasure of being presented to the author of "Evangeline." He was most cordial in his greeting, and invited me to call on him at Cambridge the following afternoon.

At the appointed hour I rang the bell of the old mansion formerly occupied by General Washington (by the way, how many places the "Father of his Country" did occupy, to be sure!), and, upon entering the Library, I found Mr. Longfellow seated.

The interview was a most delightful one. We had wandered over a good deal of the same ground in France and Italy; I had read his poems to audiences in Australia,

California, Oregon, and India, and many little incidents connected therewith were pleasing to him to hear, and doubly so for me to repeat. I had the pleasure, also, of reading to him portions of his "Miles Standish."

I was charmed and delighted with him. His voice is very musical, and his manner most fascinating; I should imagine him most genial, considerate, and kind in disposition. He very politely invited me to call upon him, upon my return, which I shall most certainly do; and now from this day ever arter I shall think of Higher-water—think of him who wrote the Poim, and how long I've wished to know him—long'd to know so good-a-fellow—long'd to see the Bard of "Standish"—Miles I've travell'd—yes, outlandish countries have I wandered o'er, wandered o'er outlandish countries—seen big bears and little monkeys—monkeys with their tails behind 'em—monkeys upon barrel organs—barrel organs without monkeys—great big Elephants and Camels—Camels on the sands of Egypt have I *rode* on, and been blown on seas so boisterous and unruly—seas so rough and Horny, truly as my pen in ink I dip, had it not been for the "Building of the Ship" that I was put in, I shouldn't a' been here to write, my delight, on meeting with to-*day* the author of "Voices of the Night."

CXXXI.

FIRST CONCERT IN BOSTON.

SATURDAY evening, November 20, 1858, I gave my first "Song and Chit-Chat of Travel," at the Mercantile Library Hall, Boston. The place was crowded to suffocation, and among the audience many of the leading literary, musical, and theatrical lions of the day. The audience were enthusiastic in their applause, and every piece, either serious or comic, appeared to give the most unbounded satisfaction. The Boston Post, on Monday morning, wound up a very lengthy and highly eulogistic article in the following words:

"It is somewhat difficult to arouse a Boston audience to

enthusiasm, particularly when the candidate for public favor is comparatively a stranger, but the effect Mr. Massett produced by his graphic and wonderful recital of Tennyson's 'Charge of the Light Brigade,' and his vivid description of his exciting adventure in British India, produced an effect almost electrical, and satisfied us that he has not only made a lasting impression here, but that his future career throughout the country will be one of complete triumph."

After this I made a pleasant and profitable trip from New York to New Orleans, proving rather more remunerative than my Australian trip.

I was gone four months. I gave thirty-seven entertainments and jingled $3,784 (cash) in my pants' pocket!

CXXXII.

OFF AGAIN TO CALIFORNIA.

HAVING a desire once again to see San Francisco, after my somewhat strange adventures, and wishing, at the same time, to look after my valuable "real estate," I determined to make a third trip to the land of gold. I therefore, on 5th October, 1859, left New York, arriving in San Francisco in twenty-two days.

Just ten years since I first "pitched my tent" on Clark's Point. The city had improved wonderfully, and I think I cannot better give the reader an idea of its rapid march and magnificence than by an extract from the eloquent oration of Colonel E. J. C. Kewen, of California, before the Society of the "Pioneers:"

To you, fellow Pioneers, a word of congratulation and I have done.

This palatial city of San Francisco, with its luxurious mansions, its granite palaces, and its costly marts of commerce, is the glorious fruitage of your adventure. The subdued waters of its bay, the extended lines of its quays, the busy hum of its thoroughfares, the exhibitions every where visible of its taste, its opulence and refinement, are the splendid creations and magnificent testimonials of your enterprise. Scourged as it has been by the devastating flame, retarded by natural obstacles, and at times inundated by swarms of lawless banditti, it has never been diverted from its onward progress, nor ceased to be the monarch wonder of the world. Like a young Titan, it has humbled the rugged wilderness, has upheaved the seated hills from their foundations, and with a conqueror's step has advanced along the pathway of progress like a prince to the throne of undisputed succession. Its harbor glistens with a forest of masts belonging to the ships of every nation, which have poured and are pouring upon our shores the accumulated riches of the East, and vaster treasures from every clime than ever freighted the galleons of Spain or the argosies of Venice.

Champollion taught the world to decipher the hieroglyphics on the obelisks, the tombs, and temples of Egypt, but a higher glory was reserved for the Pioneers of the Pacific, by whom was destined the revelation to mankind of its unavailing search of centuries—the western route to the commerce of the Indies and of the islands of the Eastern Archipelago. Coincident with the exhumation of golden treasures from the bleak summits of the Sierras, was the contribution to our shore of the riches of China and Japan, and the remote islands of the Pacific waste of waters. One other acquisition and the glory of San Francisco will have reached its zenith. When the veins and arteries of commercial life shall permeate the broad expanse that separates the Golden Gate from the Atlantic, then will its magnificent destiny proclaim it the commercial metropolis of the world, outrivalling in commerce, in arts, in science, and literature, the renown of antiquity, and the boasted pretensions of modern greatness. If this sublime consummation is defeated freedom will be deprived of its brightest hope, and a crime will be perpetrated against the social and political necessities of humanity more wicked than that which classic fable has punished with the naked rock and the gnawing vulture. Promote this glorious enterprise and the swelling splendors and far-reaching fame of this mighty continent will be imperishable monuments to the memory of the Pioneers of Freedom and Destiny.

And in connexion with the Great Pacific Railroad, which I trust I may live to see built, the following spirit-stirring lines of Mr. Frank Soulé, one of the most gifted writers of California, will be found, I think, interesting:

Hear you not the answer votive?
  See you not Progression's train?
Hear you not the locomotive
  Thundering along the plain?
List! 'tis coming near and nearer,
  Listen to its piercing scream;
Now the whirling wheels sound clearer,
  Now I hear the hissing steam.
Through the air in transport gliding—
  Heed you not those proud huzzas!
Thirty sister States are riding
  Hither on those rushing cars.
Hither, from each struggling nation,
  Weary exiles gladly roam—
Give them here a habitation,
  Liberty, and friends, and home.
O'er the deserts wide and dreary,
  Through the terrors of "the Horn,"
They are coming, brave, though weary,
  Parents of a world unborn.
See, they gather, man and master,
  Rushing to this western world,
Coming, coming, fast and faster,
Daring danger, pain, disaster,
  Seeking honor, health, and gold.
See, they come from every nation—
  See, our temple is begun;
See! the men of every station
  Meet and labor all as one.
From the cities, farms and ranches,
  From the forum's wordy strife,
Teeming from life's varied branches,
  See! the welcome path is rife.

Build a temple high and holy,
  Build a temple to the mind,
Broad and permanent, though slowly,
  Be its elements combined,

Where the mighty and the lowly
  Happiness may seek and find.
Beautiful, then, let us build it,
  Vieing Solomon's of old;
Raise its towering roof, and gild it
  With our hearts' own native gold.
Build it strongly, build it here—
  Temple of the Pioneer.

Returning once again, I arrived in New York on Christmas Eve—having been absent a little over two months. And now, my kind and considerate reader, if I have succeeded in gaining your attention thus far in my wanderings, I am truly grateful; but I am really inclined to think you will be delighted when I inform you that this somewhat strange and eventful history is drawing to a close. At any rate my peregrinations and adventures stop here. For the present, I have made New York my resting-place, and have, as the saying goes, "settled down."

I cannot close without offering my heartfelt thanks for the great kindness extended to me by the Press throughout the United States, and various portions of the Old World, in Australia and in India, during my public career. The notices and criticisms of my performances have been genial, generous, and encouraging.

I desire, also, to say a word to those who enter the field as Lecturers, Concert-Givers, or Performers.

To insure success, they must be patient and persevering; seeking for sunshine even when the storm is darkest, and aiming all the while to improve as they progress.

And now, kind reader! Farewell. You will agree with me that I have indeed been a "rolling-stone," as to the "moss" which I did or did not gather in the region of lucre, that is "neither here nor there."

I have been through many a golden district, and often supposed I would die a wealthy individual.

That ambition is not very active at present; but while I desire to win "golden opinions from all sorts of people" I cannot deny that, considering how many rainy days I encountered in the events this book describes, I am warranted in hoping for something to lay up in anticipation of that particular "rainy day" about which everybody talks, and which, I suppose, makes its appearance when our *reign* of life is about to close!

If, however, the public desire to know anything of my future peregrinations or "doings" they can be fully enlightened by addressing, post-paid, Lieutenant-Colonel Thomas H. Landon, Post-office, Harlem, New York, or at my Publisher's.

And now, reader, your hand once more, God bless you!

If in the pages, of which this is the last, I have succeeded in affording you amusement, in that result I will find one of the greatest rewards ever bestowed on your friend and well-wisher

THE AUTHOR.

THE END.

1863.

A NEW LIST OF

BOOKS

ISSUED BY

CARLETON, PUBLISHER,

(LATE RUDD & CARLETON,)

413 Broadway,

NEW YORK.

Artemus Ward, His Book.
The racy writings of this humorous author. Illustrated, $1.25.

The Old Merchants of New York.
Entertaining reminiscences of ancient mercantile New York City, by " Walter Barrett, clerk." First Series. $1.50 each.

Like and Unlike.
Novel by A. S. Roe, author of "I've been thinking," &c. $1.50.

Orpheus C. Kerr Papers.
Second series of letters by this comic military authority. $1.25.

Marian Grey.
New domestic novel, by the author of "Lena Rivers," etc. $1.50.

Lena Rivers.
A popular American novel, by Mrs. Mary J. Holmes, $1.50.

A Book about Doctors.
An entertaining volume about the medical profession. $1.50.

The Adventures of Verdant Green.
Humorous novel of English College life. Illustrated. $1.25.

The Culprit Fay.
Joseph Rodman Drake's faery poem, elegantly printed, 50 cts.

Doctor Antonio.
A charming love-tale of Italian life, by G. Ruffini, $1.50.

Lavinia.
A new love-story, by the author of " Doctor Antonio," $1.50.

Dear Experience.
An amusing Parisian novel, by author " Doctor Antonio," $1.00.

The Life of Alexander Von Humboldt.
A new and popular biography of this *savant*, including his travels and labors, with introduction by Bayard Taylor, $1.50.

Love (L'Amour.)
A remarkable volume, from the French of Michelet. $1.25.

Woman (La Femme.)
A continuation of " Love (L'Amour)," by same author, $1.25.

The Sea (La Mer.)
New work by Michelet, author " Love" and " Woman," $1.25.

The Moral History of Woman.
Companion to Michelet's " L'Amour," from the French, $1.25.

Mother Goose for Grown Folks.
Humorous and satirical rhymes for grown people, 75 cts.

The Kelly's and the O'Kelly's.
Novel by Anthony Trollope, author of " Doctor Thorne," $1.50.

The Great Tribulation.
Or, Things coming on the earth, by Rev. John Cumming, D.D., author "Apocalyptic Sketches," etc., two series, each $1.00.

The Great Preparation.
Or, Redemption draweth nigh, by Rev. John Cumming, D.D., author "The Great Tribulation," etc., two series, each $1.00.

The Great Consummation.
Sequel "Great Tribulation," Dr. Cumming, two series, $1.00.

Teach us to Pray.
A new work on The Lord's Prayer, by Dr. Cumming, $1.00.

The Slave Power.
By Jas. E. Cairnes, of Dublin University, Lond. ed. $1.25.

Game Fish of the North.
A sporting work for Northern States and Canada. Illus., $1.50.

Drifting About.
By Stephen C. Massett ("Jeemes Pipes"), illustrated, $1.25

The Flying Dutchman.
A humorous Poem by John G. Saxe, with illustrations, 50 cts.

Notes on Shakspeare.
By Jas. H. Hackett, the American Comedian (portrait), $1.50.

The Spirit of Hebrew Poetry.
By Isaac Taylor, author "History of Enthusiasm," etc., $2.00.

A Life of Hugh Miller.
Author of "Testimony of the Rocks," &c., new edition, $1.50.

A Woman's Thoughts about Women.
By Miss Dinah Mulock, author of "John Halifax," etc., $1.00.

Curiosities of Natural History.
An entertaining vol., by F. T. Buckland ; two series, each $1.25.

The Partisan Leader.
Beverley Tucker's notorious Southern Disunion novel, $1.25.

Cesar Birotteau.
First of a series of Honore de Balzac's best French novels, $1.00.

Petty Annoyances of Married Life.
The second of the series of Balzac's best French novels, $1.00.

The Alchemist.
The third of the series of the best of Balzac's novels, $1.00.

Eugenie Grandet.
The fourth of the series of Balzac's best French novels, $1.00.

The National School for the Soldier.
Elementary work for the soldier ; by Capt. Van Ness, 50 cts.

Tom Tiddler's Ground.
Charles Dickens's new Christmas Story, paper cover, 25 cts.

National Hymns.
An essay by Richard Grant White. 8vo. embellished, $1.00.

George Brimley.
Literary Essays reprinted from the British Quarterlies, $1.25.

Thomas Bailey Aldrich.
First complete collection of Poems, blue and gold binding, $1.00.

Out of His Head.
A strange and eccentric romance by T. B. Aldrich, $1.00.

The Course of True Love
Never did run smooth. A Poem by Thomas B. Aldrich, 50 cts.

Poems of a Year.
By Thomas B. Aldrich, author of "Babie Bell," &c., 75 cts.

The King's Bell.
A Mediæval Legend in verse, by R. H. Stoddard, 75 cts.

The Morgesons.
A clever novel of American Life, by Mrs. R. H. Stoddard, $1.00.

Beatrice Cenci.
An historical novel by F. D. Guerrazzi, from the Italian, $1.50.

Isabella Orsini.
An historical novel by the author of "Beatrice Cenci," $1.25.

A Popular Treatise on Deafness.
For individuals and families, by E. B. Lighthill, M.D., $1.00.

Oriental Harems and Scenery.
A gossipy work, translated from the French of Belgiojoso, $1.25.

Lola Montez.
Her lectures and autobiography, with a steel portrait, $1.25.

John Doe and Richard Roe.
A novel of New York city life, by Edward S. Gould, $1.00.

Doesticks' Letters.
The original letters of this great humorist, illustrated, $1.50.

Plu-ri-bus-tah.
A comic history of America, by "Doesticks," illus., $1.50.

The Elephant Club.
A humorous description of club-life, by "Doesticks," $1.50.

Vernon Grove.
A novel by Mrs. Caroline H. Glover, Charleston, S. C., $1.00.

The Book of Chess Literature.
A complete Encyclopædia of this subject, by D. W. Fiske, $1.50.

Tactics.
Or, Cupid in Shoulder-straps. A West Point love story, $1.00.

Sprees and Splashes.
A volume of humorous sketches, by Henry Morford, $1.00.

Around the Pyramids.
A new book of adventure and travel, by Aaron Ward, $1.25.

Garret Van Horn.
Or, The Beggar on Horseback, by John S. Sauzade, $1.25.

Alfio Balzani.
Or, The Diary of a Proscribed Sicilian, by D. Minnelli, $1.25.

China and the Chinese.
Being recent personal reminiscences, by W. L. G. Smith, $1.25.

Transition.
A Memoir of Emma Whiting, by Rev. H. S. Carpenter, $1.00.

Lulu.
A novel of Life in Washington, by M. T. Walworth, $1.25.

Lyrics and Idyls.
"Diamond Wedding," and other poems, by E. C. Stedman, 75 cts.

The Prince's Ball.
A humorous poem by Edmund C. Stedman, illustrated, 50 cts.

Gen. Nathaniel Lyon.
The life and political writings of the late patriot soldier, $1.00.

Twenty Years around the World.
Volume of travel, by John Guy Vassar, Poughkeepsie, $2.50.

Philip Thaxter.
A new novel, with scenes in California, one vol. 12mo., $1.00.

From Haytime to Hopping.
A novel by the author of "Our Farm of Four Acres," $1.00.

Fast Day Sermons.
Of 1861, the best Sermons by the prominent Divines, $1.25.

Debt and Grace.
The Doctrine of a Future Life, by Rev. C. F. Hudson, $1.25.

Fort Lafayette.
A novel, by the Hon. Benjamin Wood, of New York, $1.00.

Romance of a Poor Young Man.
A capital novel from the French of Octave Feuillet, $1.00.

Sarah Gould.
Volume of miscellaneous poems, bound in blue and gold, 75 cts.

The Monitor.
A new book of travel, by Wm. Hoffman, illustrated, $1.50.

England in Rhyme.
A pleasant method for instructing children in History, 50 cts.

Brown's Carpenter's Assistant.
A practical work on architecture, with plans, large 4to., $5.00.

Sybelle
And other miscellaneous poems, by L——, 12mo., cloth, 75 cts

Wa-Wa-Wanda.
A legend of old Orange County, New York, in verse, 75 cts.

Husband vs. Wife.
A satirical poem, by Henry Clapp, Jr., illus. by Hoppin, 60 cts.

Roumania.
Travels in Eastern Europe, by J. O. Noyes, illustrated, $1.50.

The Christmas Tree.
A volume of miscellany for the young, with illustrations, 75 cts.

The Captive Nightingale.
A charming little book for children, many illustrations, 75 cts.

Sunshine through the Clouds.
Comprising stories for juveniles, beautifully illustrated, 75 cts.

Cosmogony,
Or, the mysteries of creation, by Thomas A. Davies, $1.50.

An Answer to Hugh Miller
And other kindred geologists, by Thomas A. Davies, $1.25.

Walter Ashwood.
A novel by "Paul Siogvolk," author of "Schediasms," $1.00.

Southwold.
A new society novel by Mrs. Lillie Devereux Umsted, $1.00.

Ballads of the War.
A collection of poems for 1861, by George W. Hewes, 75 cts.

Hartley Norman.
A new and striking American novel; one large 12mo., $1.25.

The Vagabond.
Sketches on literature, art, and society, by Adam Badeau, $1.00.

Edgar Poe and His Critics.
A literary critique by Mrs. Sarah Helen Whitman, 75 cts.

The New and the Old.
Sketches in California and India, by Dr. J. W. Palmer, $1.25.

Up and Down the Irrawaddi.
Adventures in the Burman Empire, by J. W. Palmer, $1.00.

Miles Standish Illustrated.
With photographs, by J. W. Ehninger, elegant 4to., $6.00.

www.ingramcontent.com/pod-product-compliance
Lightning Source LLC
LaVergne TN
LVHW010130110826
845151LV00002B/322

* 9 7 8 1 4 2 5 5 4 0 2 7 2 *